MW01671505

® SAN ANTONIO the Saga

A VIDEO ART BY
XAVIER DE RICHEMONT

Art Video Monument History Inc.

SAN ANTONIO | THE SAGA
MAIN PLAZA CONSERVANCY

MAIN PLAZA
The Heart of the City

XAVIER de RICHEMONT
PEINTRE VIDÉO | VIDEO PAINTER

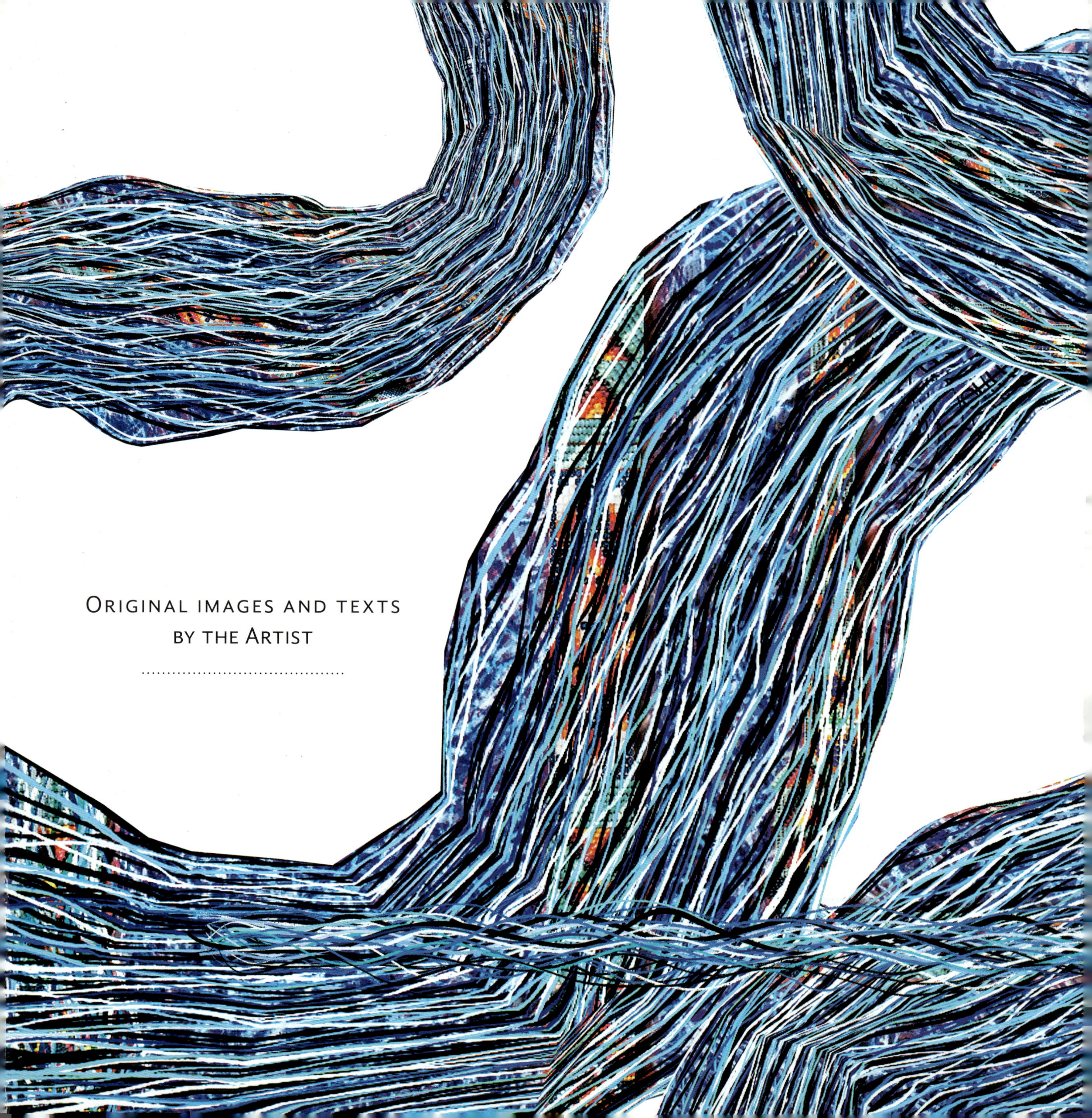

Original images and texts
by the Artist

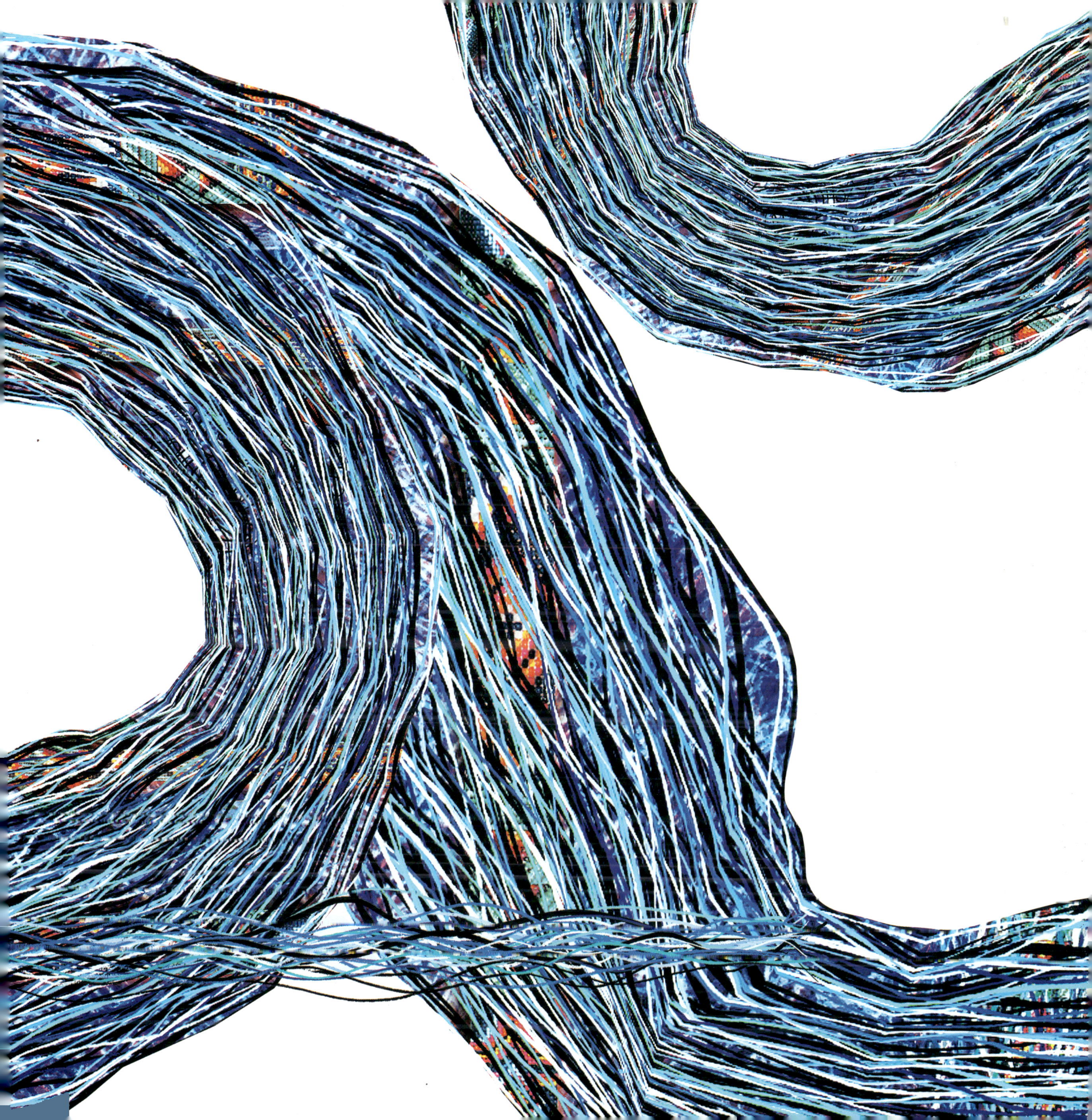

FOREWORD

San Fernando Cathedral carries the history of the City of San Antonio. As a symbol of the first years of Spanish colonization, San Fernando Cathedral with its *Main Plaza,* is located between the *Alamo* and the Spanish Governors Palace.

This historic Cathedral welcomes the video art on its façade. Respect was mutual during the creation of this artwork.

Observation of the Cathedral's architecture is very important to the design process. The façade structure induced the composition through lines, shapes and forms.

The Cathedral's identity has been the permanent link between the artist's concept by achieving images that always relate the art to the people and their history.

Long before the first Church was built, The *river* was present and was the source of living for the Indian population and also the main reason for the Spanish mission settlements.

The San Antonio river originally called "Yanaguana", meaning; *Calm waters* is constantly present in the artwork and bonds the different sequences together.

As origin of life, source of wealth and catastrophes, water remains today a major asset to the City of San Antonio.

All of San Antonio's history can be followed along the river from all directions to the City's downtown with its peculiar horseshoe design where people come to enjoy nowadays.

The project begins with the river and ends with the river. Water is constantly flowing along San Fernando's towers, irrigating the scenes throughout the entire project.

The entire nine sequences of the work are evocations of San Antonio's historical past and present alternating allegories.

All Iconography used to create the plates are taken from artist drawings and photos and from collections, archives and historical documents about San Antonio collected on site by the artist during his numerous stays in the City.

The use of these local references in creating the composition of the piece has lead to a strong appropriation of the work by *San Antonians*.

The music was re-composed by the artist as a *collage* using various ancient, modern and contemporary scores that have the same artistic intentions, as does this body of graphic work.

ENJOY! SAN ANTONIO| THE SAGA
A Video Art by Xavier de Richemont.

AN ORIGINAL VISUAL MUSICAL
AND HISTORICAL VIDEO ARTWORK
CREATED ON THE FAÇADE
OF SAN FERNANDO CATHEDRAL
BY XAVIER DE RICHEMONT
FOR MAIN PLAZA CONSERVANCY
AND THE PEOPLE OF SAN ANTONIO.

STORYBOARD CONTENTS

The video artwork consists of nine sequences in chronological order which last 24 minutes.

STORYBOARD

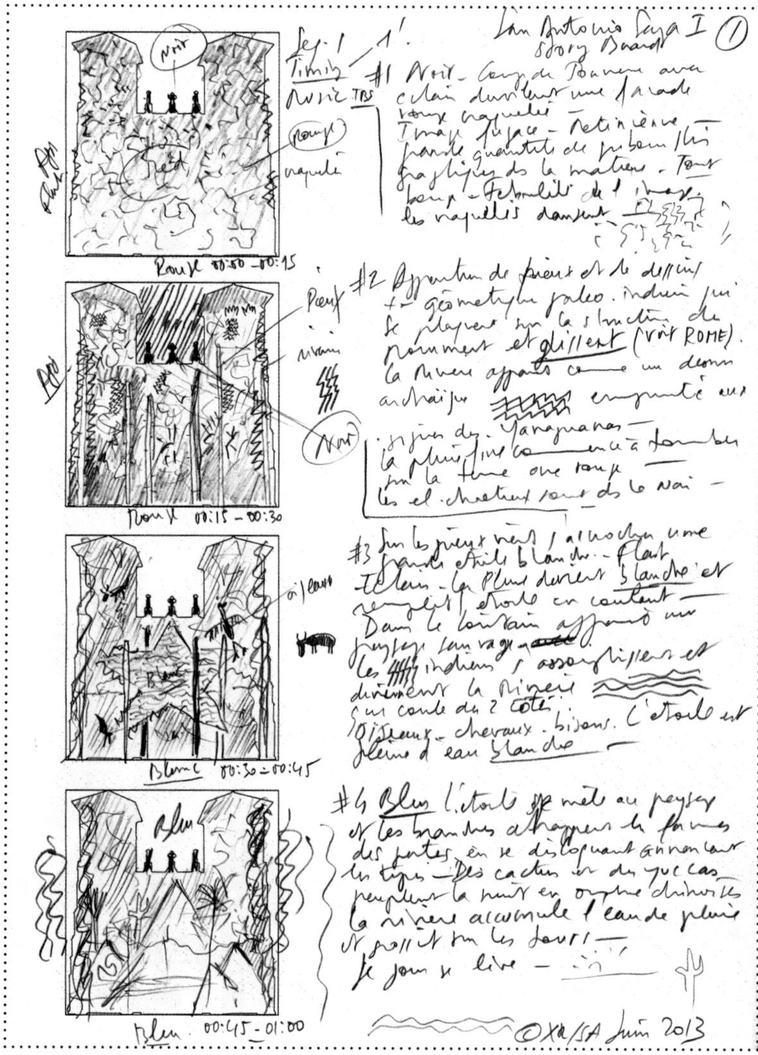

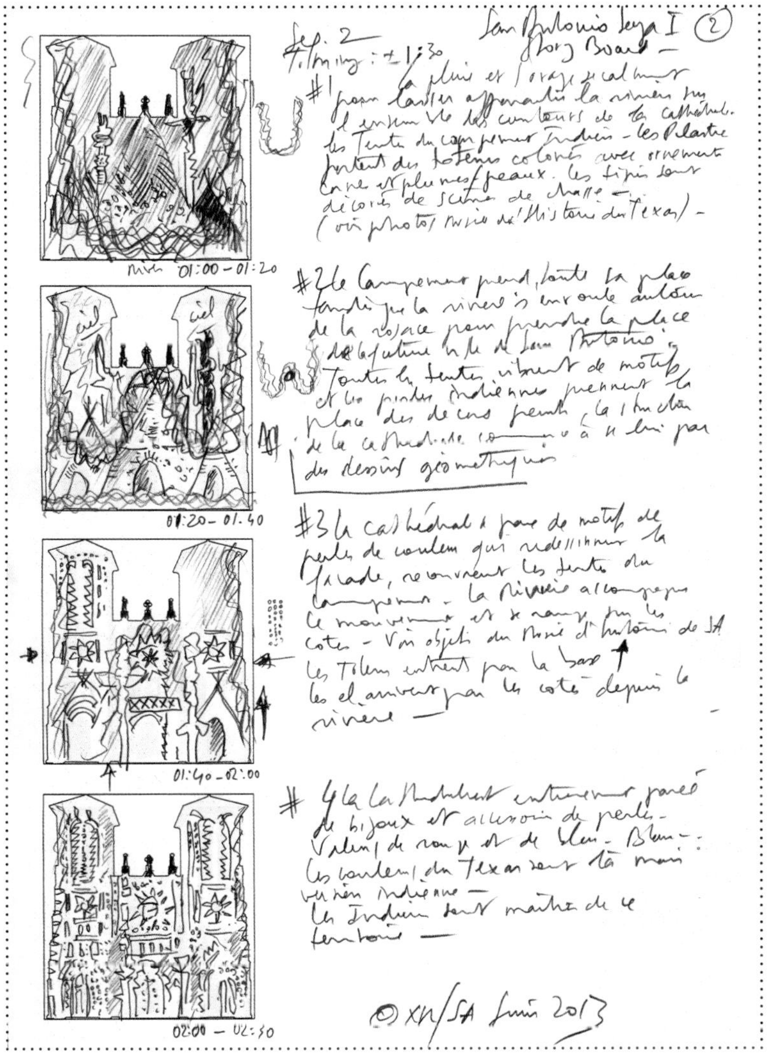
San Antonio Saga I (2)
Story Board
01:00 – 01:20
01:20 – 01:40
01:40 – 02:00
02:00 – 02:30
© XN/SA Juin 2013

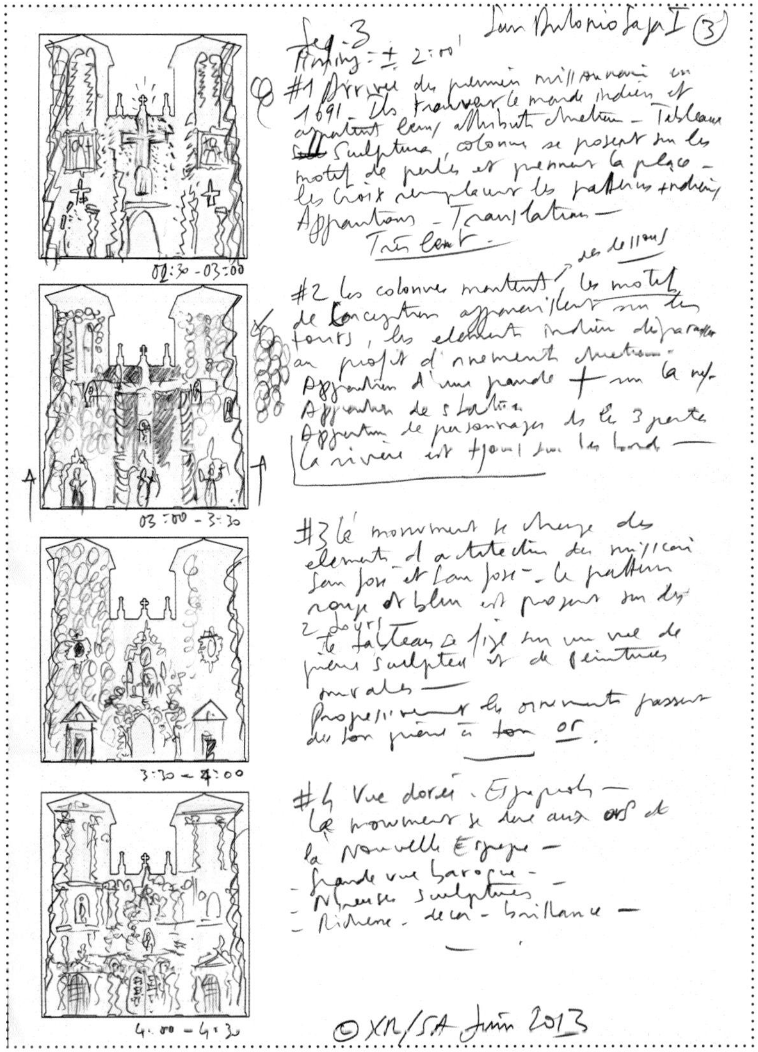
San Antonio Saga I (3)
02:30 – 03:00
03:00 – 3:30
3:30 – 4:00
4:00 – 4:30
© XN/SA Juin 2013

STORYBOARD

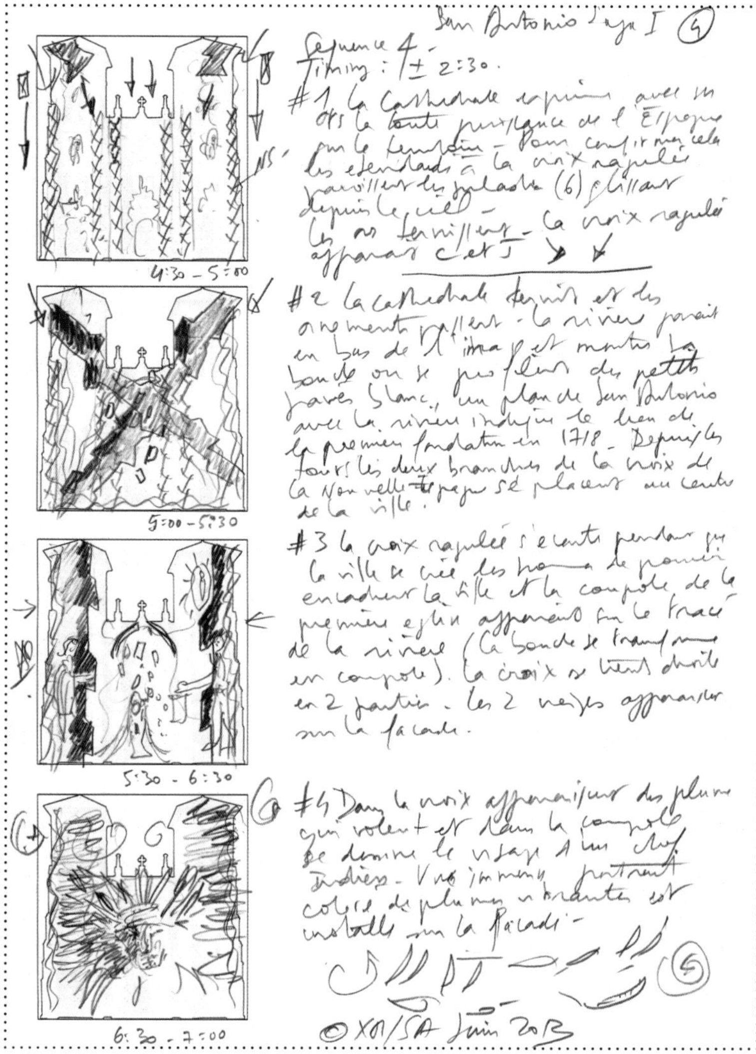

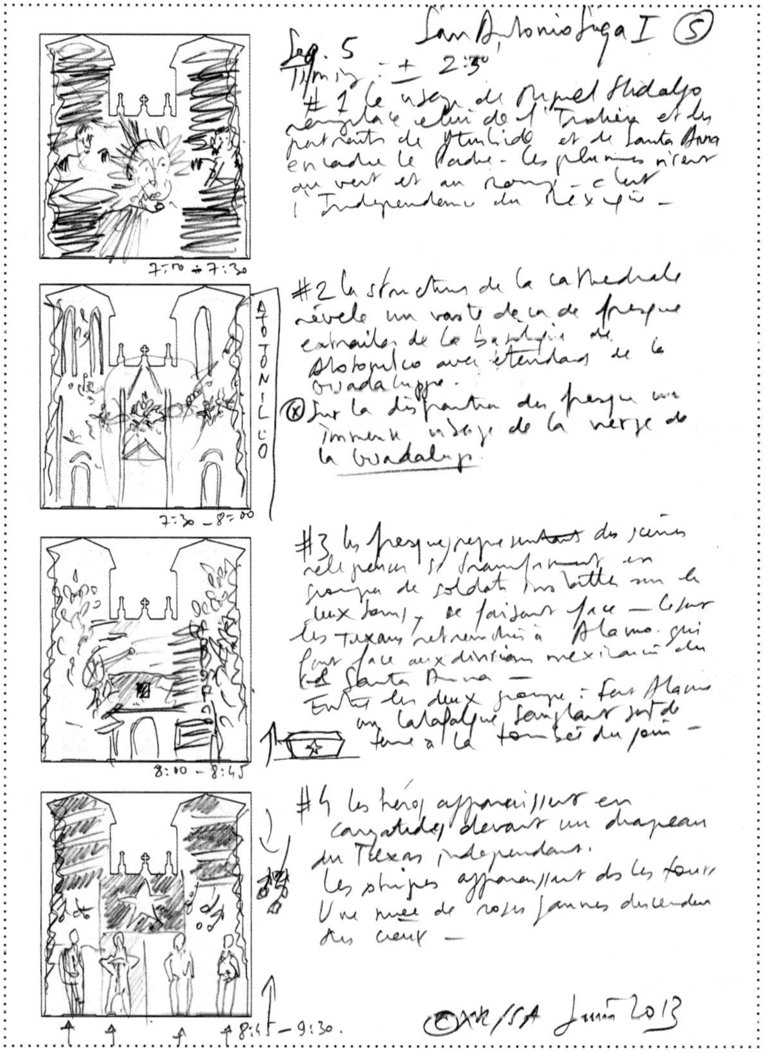
San Antonio Saga I (5)
Seq. 5
Timing = ± 2:30
7:00 – 7:30
7:30 – 8:00
8:00 – 8:45
8:45 – 9:30
©XR/SA Juin 2013

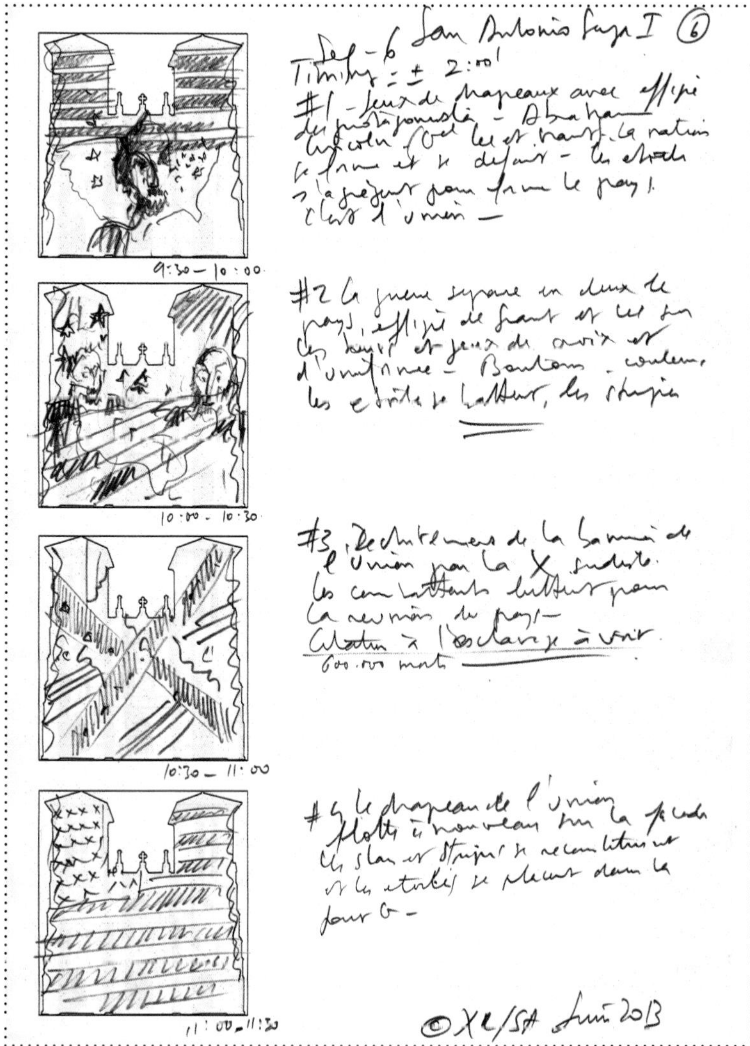
San Antonio Saga I (6)
Seq. 6
Timing = ± 2:00
9:30 – 10:00
10:00 – 10:30
10:30 – 11:00
11:00 – 11:30
©XR/SA Juin 2013

STORYBOARD

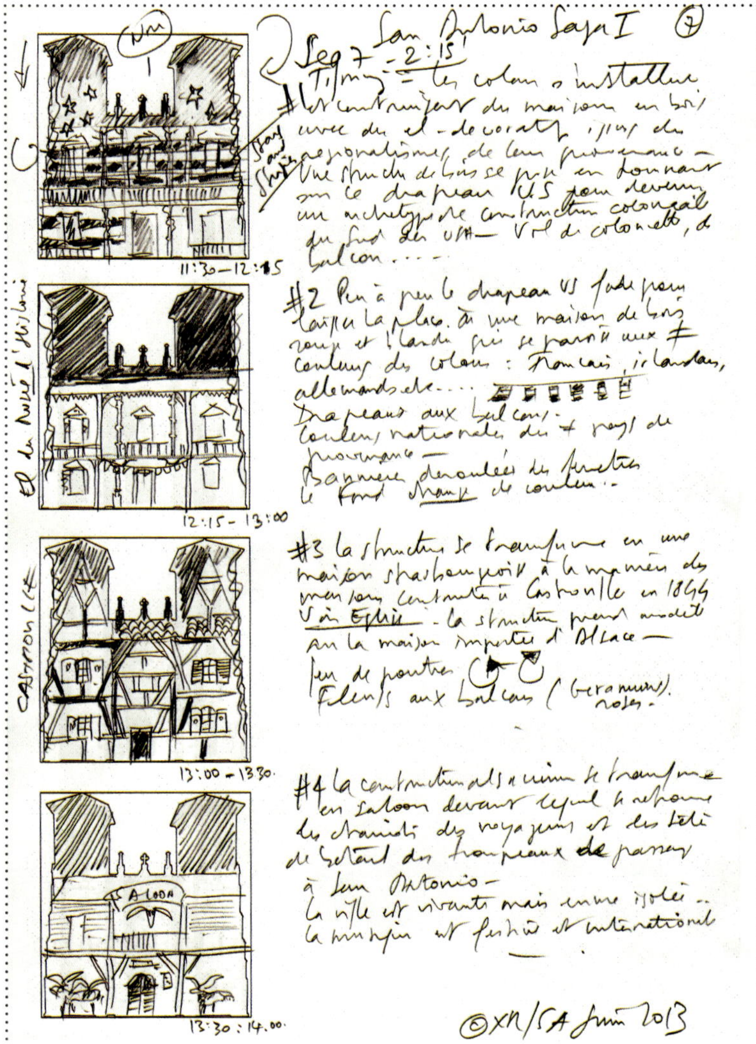
San Antonio Saga I
11:30–12:15
12:15–13:00
13:00–13:30
13:30–14.00
©XN/SA Juin 2013

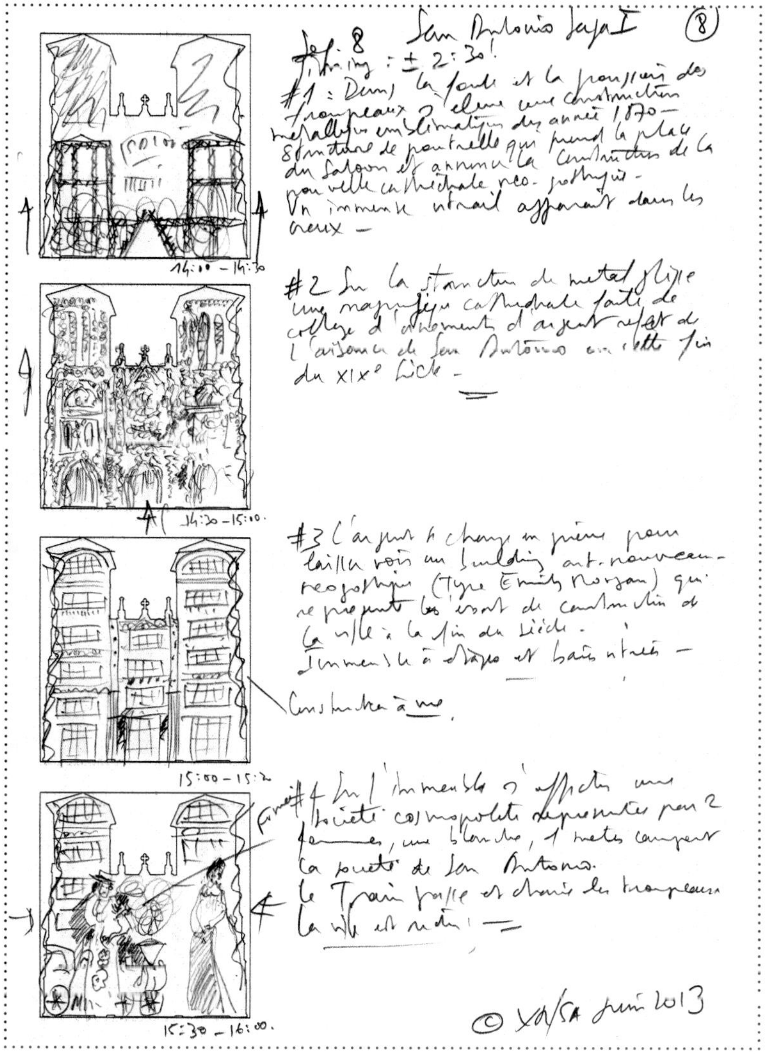
San Antonio Saga I
8
14:00 – 14:30
14:30 – 15:00
15:00 – 15:30
15:30 – 16:00
© XN/SA Juin 2013

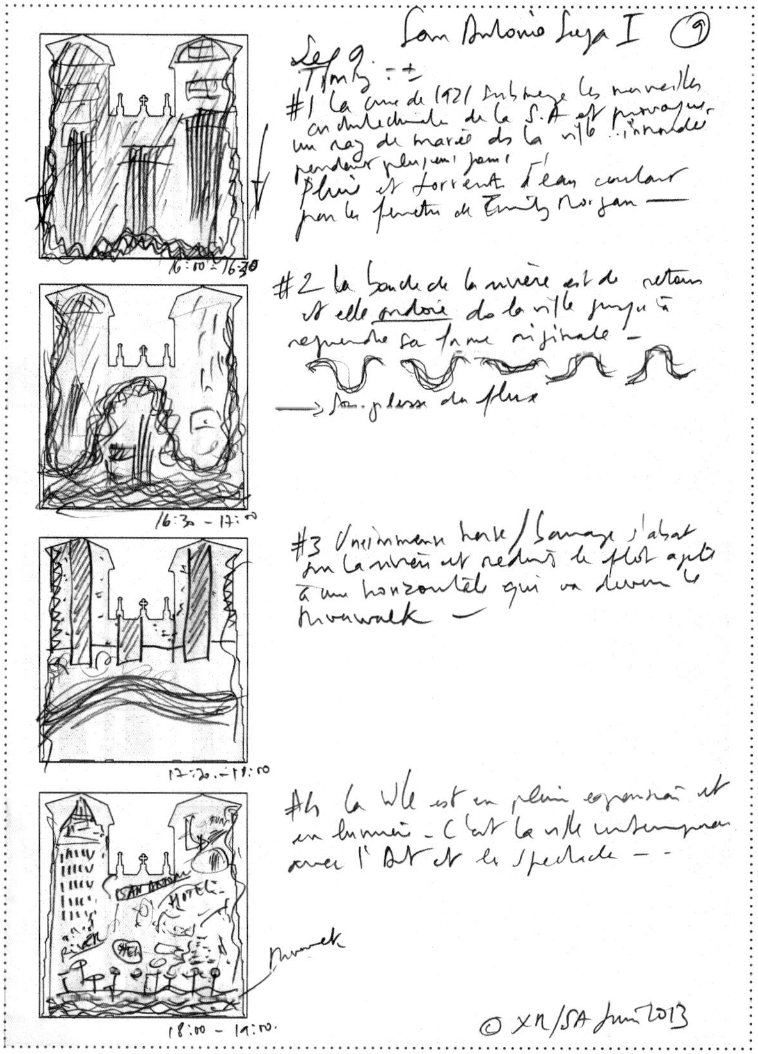
San Antonio Saga I
9
16:00 – 16:30
16:30 – 17:00
17:30 – 18:00
18:00 – 19:00
© XN/SA Juin 2013

Sequence 1

THE THREE COLORS OF TEXAS

RED

A flash of lightning highlights San Fernando's red façade.

Fugacious and moving Paleolithic Indian brilliant drawings dancing in the reddish matter.

Space is dark and primitive.

Rain starts falling.

WHITE

A second white lightning reveals a giant white Star engraved in the center of the composition. The red color turns clearer.

The rain falls heavier and heavier.

The River appears on the sides of San Fernando towers.

Guitar plays first chords.

The River bed grows.

BLUE

Rain is more intense and stamps all the composition with changing diagonals lines.

Third lightning.

Blue color replaces white Star.

Scarified white lines of indians tepees appear, red and white melt into night clear blue.

End of the night.

Animals awake and cross the land, camp appears among growing cactus, nopales and yuccas.

Commanche drums play war hymns.

It is dawn.

The day rises on "Yanaguana", *Calm waters River.*

NOTE

An allegory of Texas showing the three colors as a wild territory dominated by forces of nature. The storm reveals wild elements, the red ground, the blue sky and a white star.
The rain causes the flow of the river, the waterway grows bigger to become later the San Antonio river, place of settlement of Paleolithic Indian populations, of Indian tribes and later of Spanish missionaries.
The Paleolithic site was occupied by Native American tribes. "Yanaguana" Calm waters, *name given by the Indians to the river.*

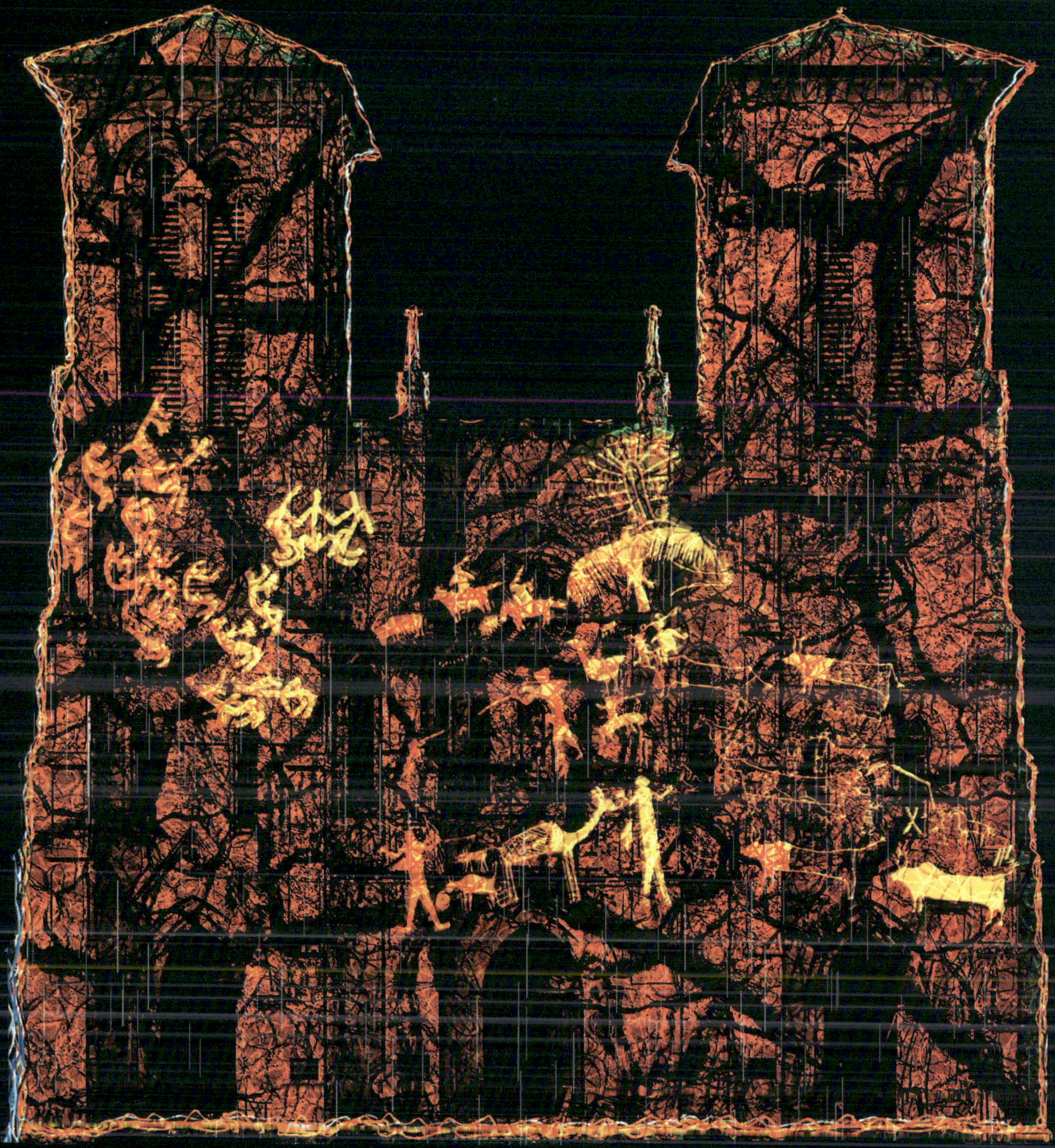

Red

Red

White

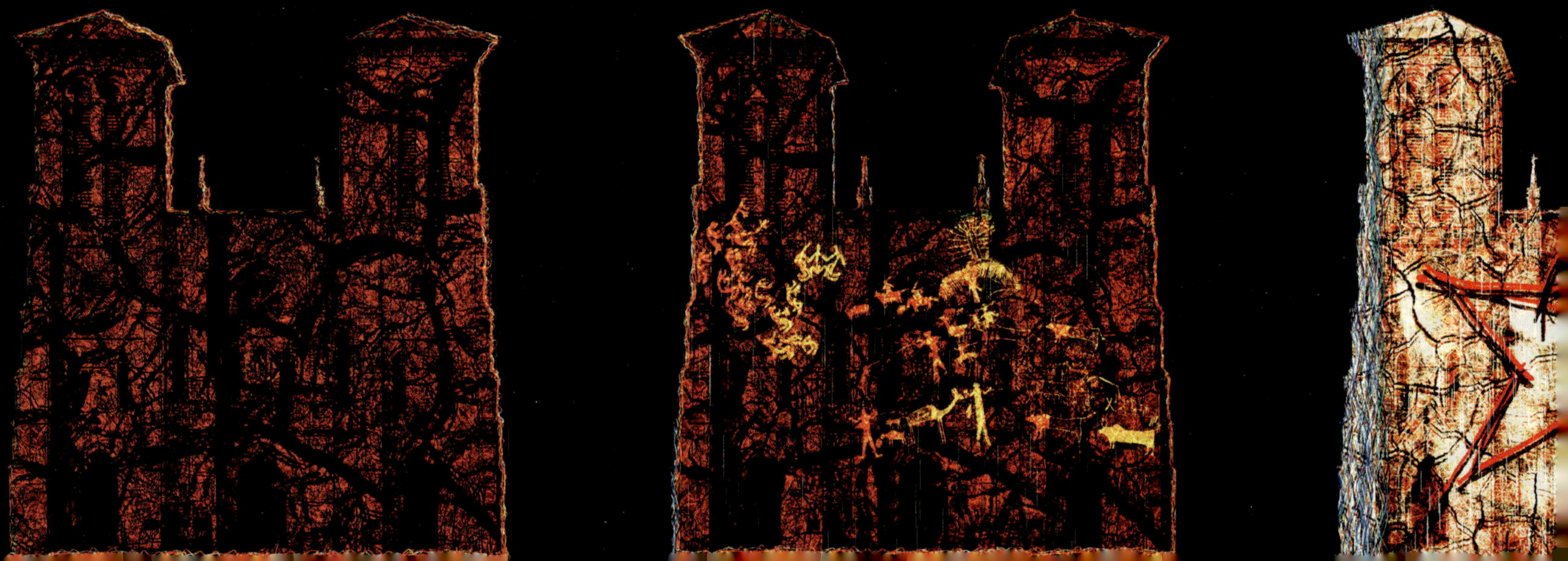

Blue

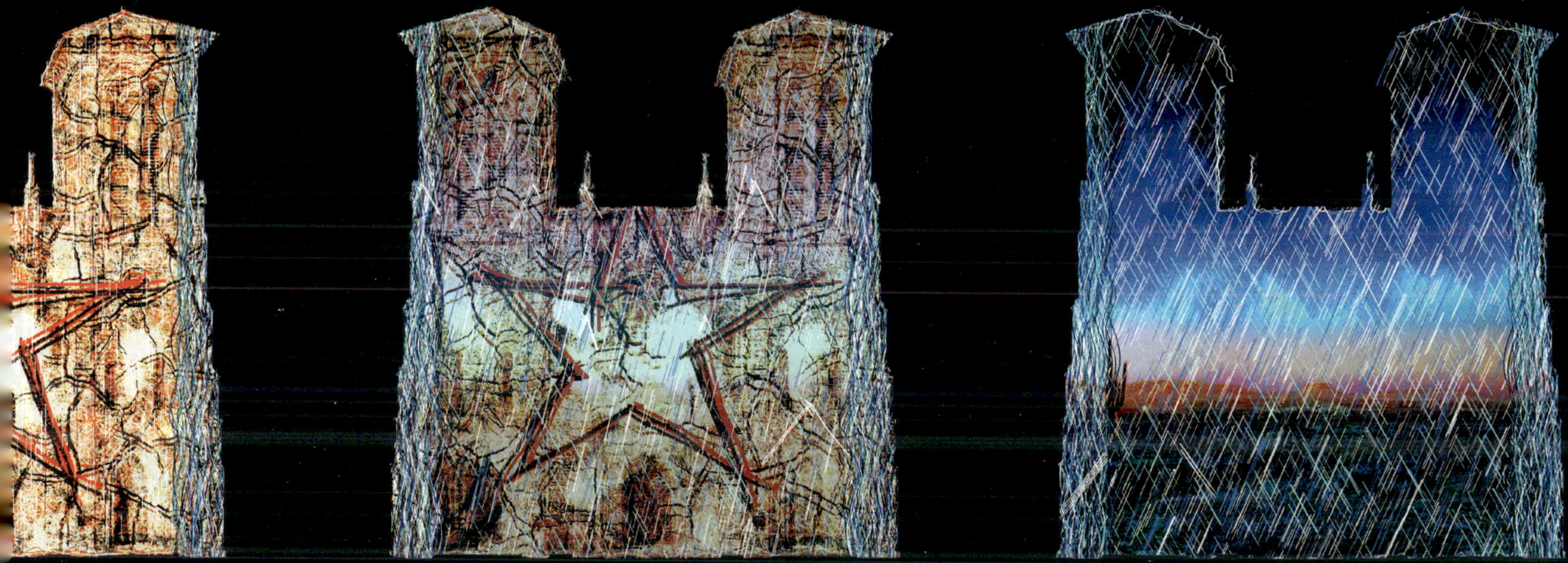

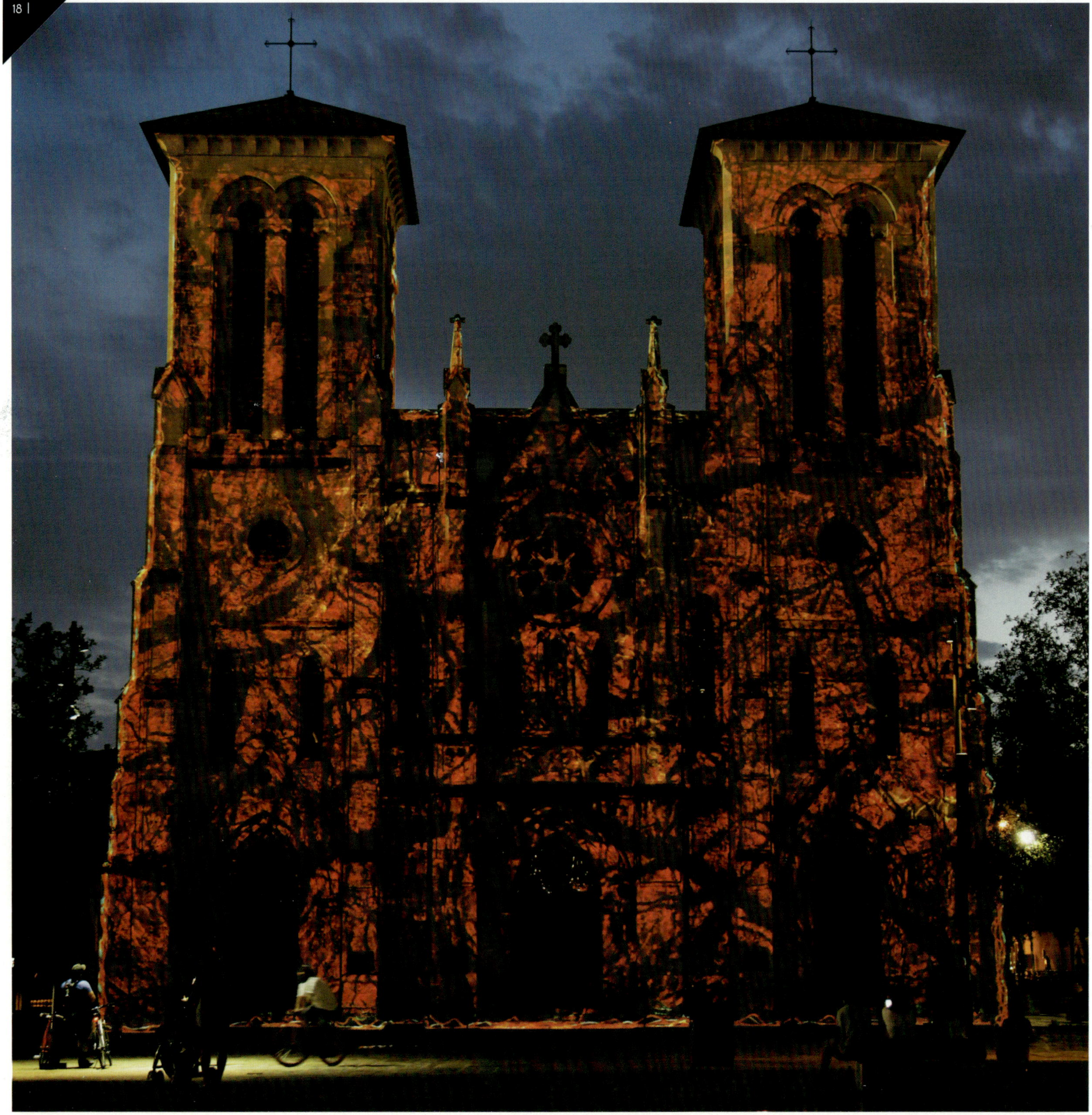

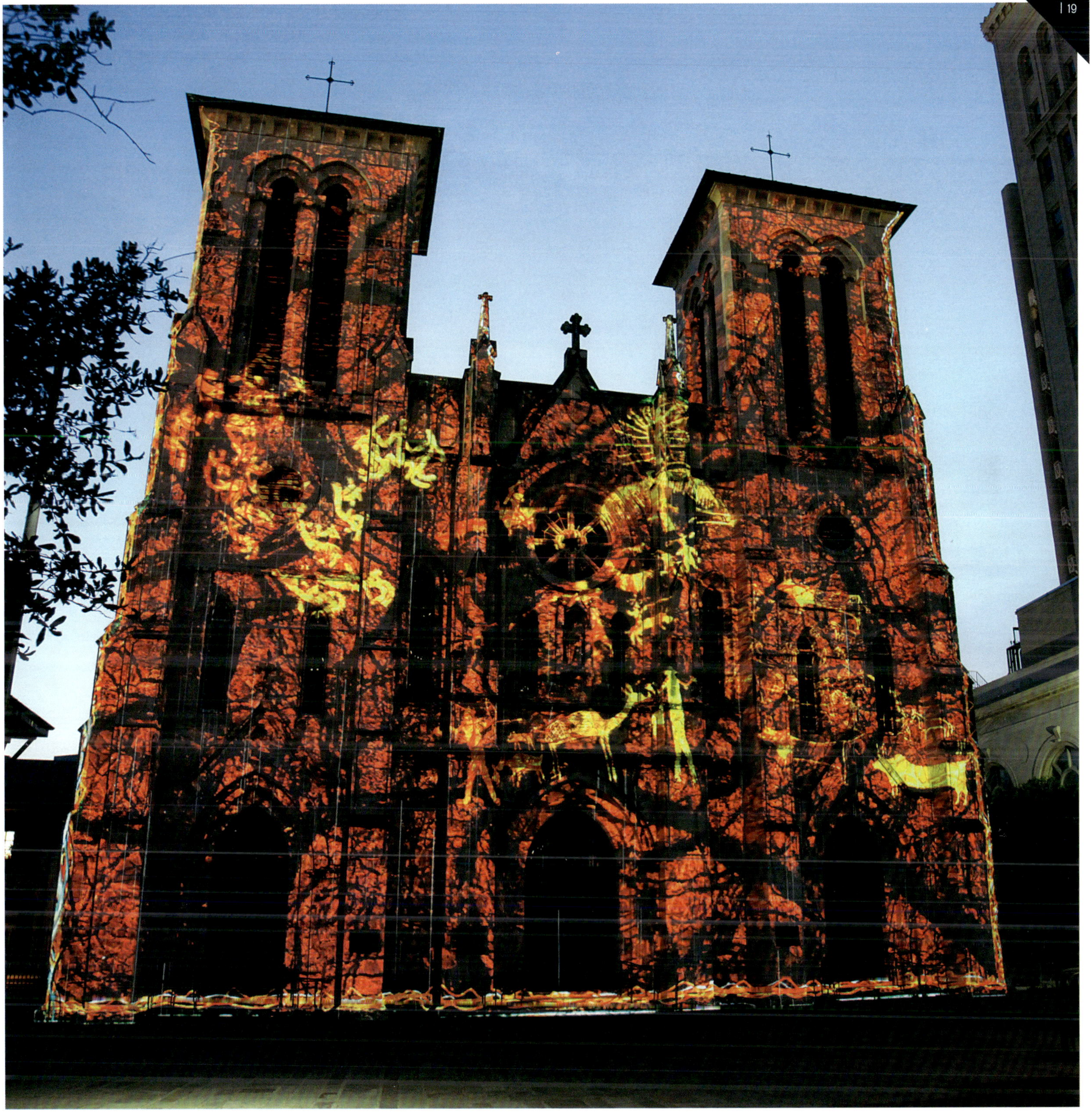

– SAN ANTONIO THE SAGA –

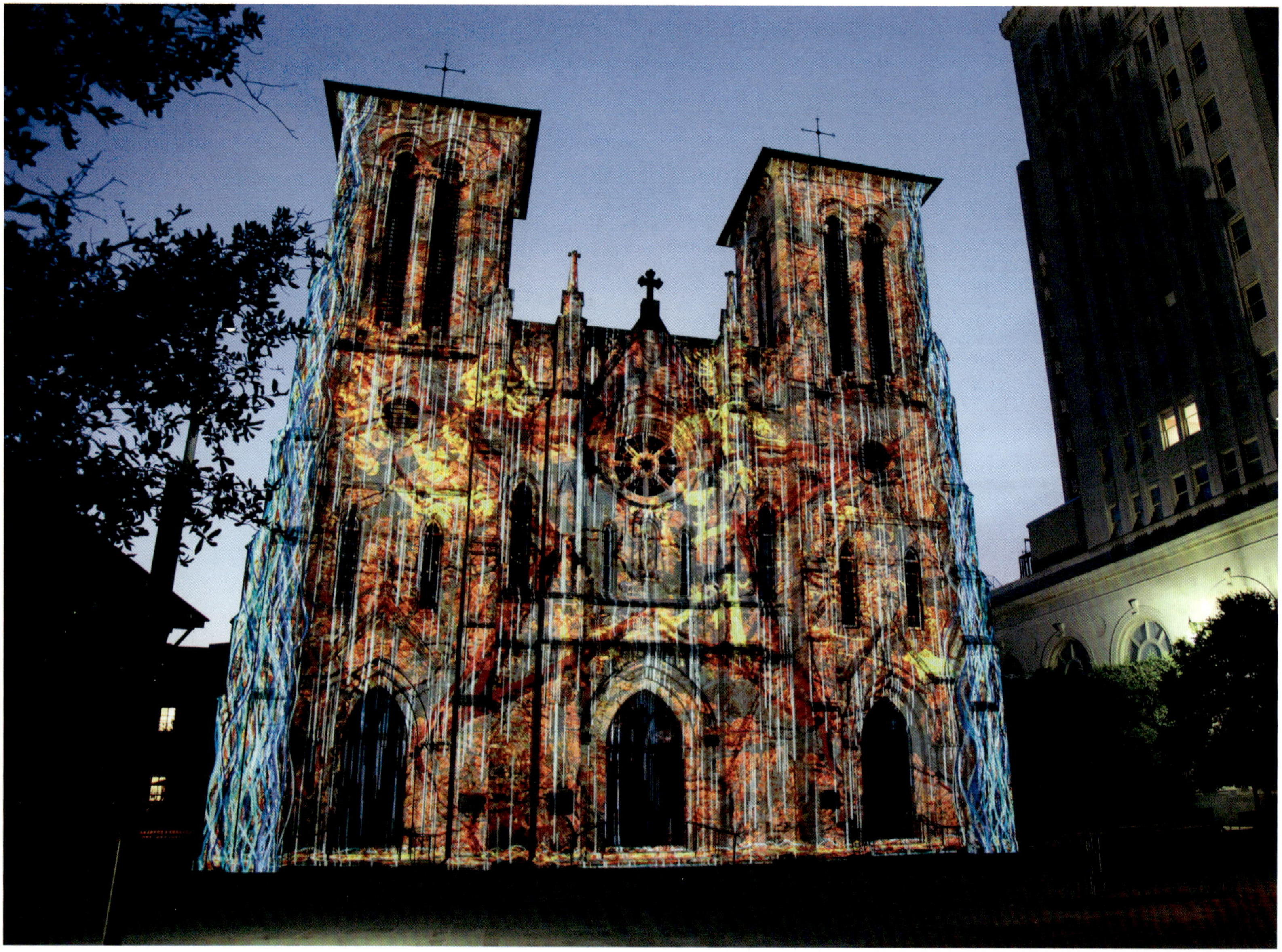

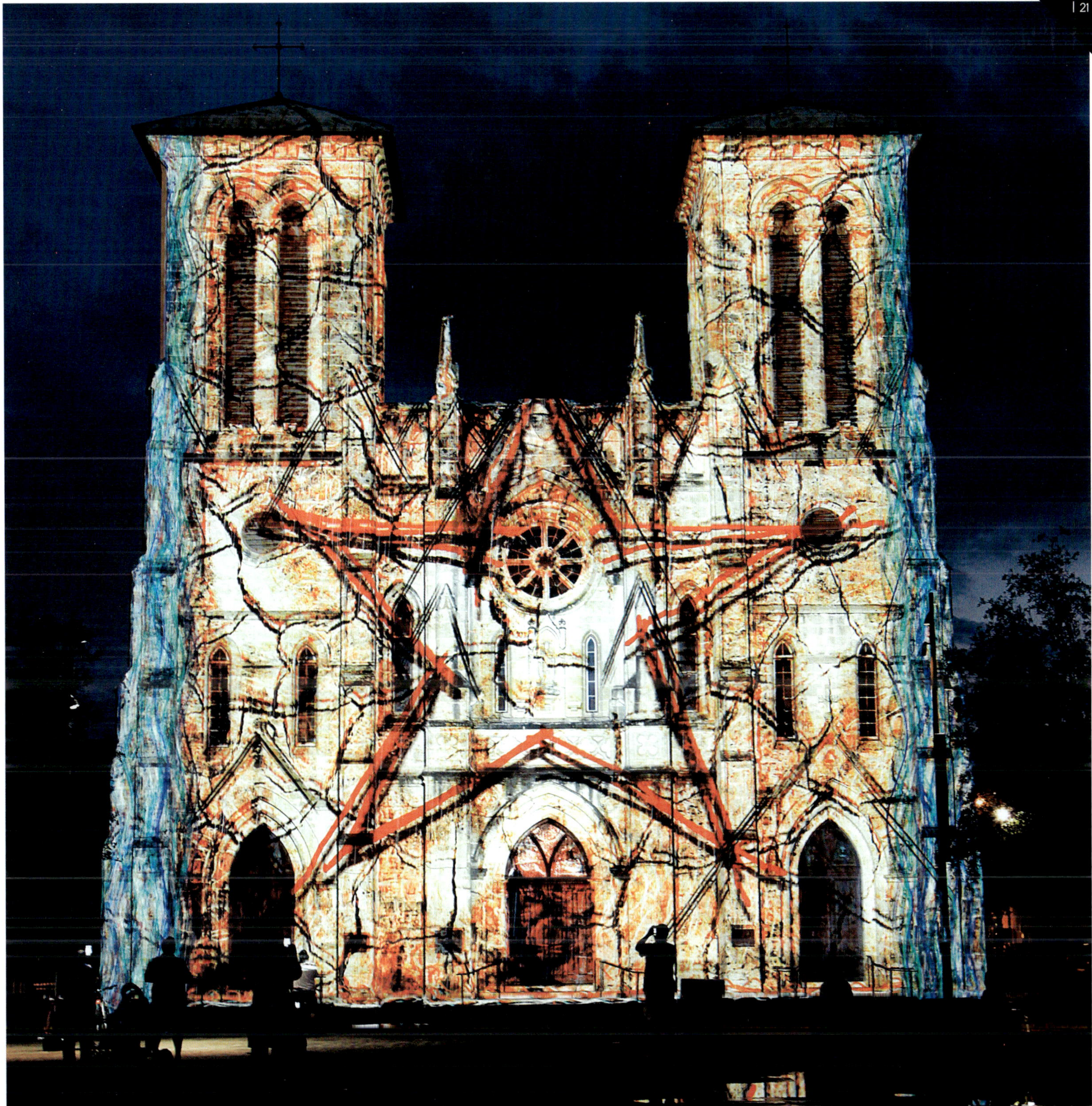

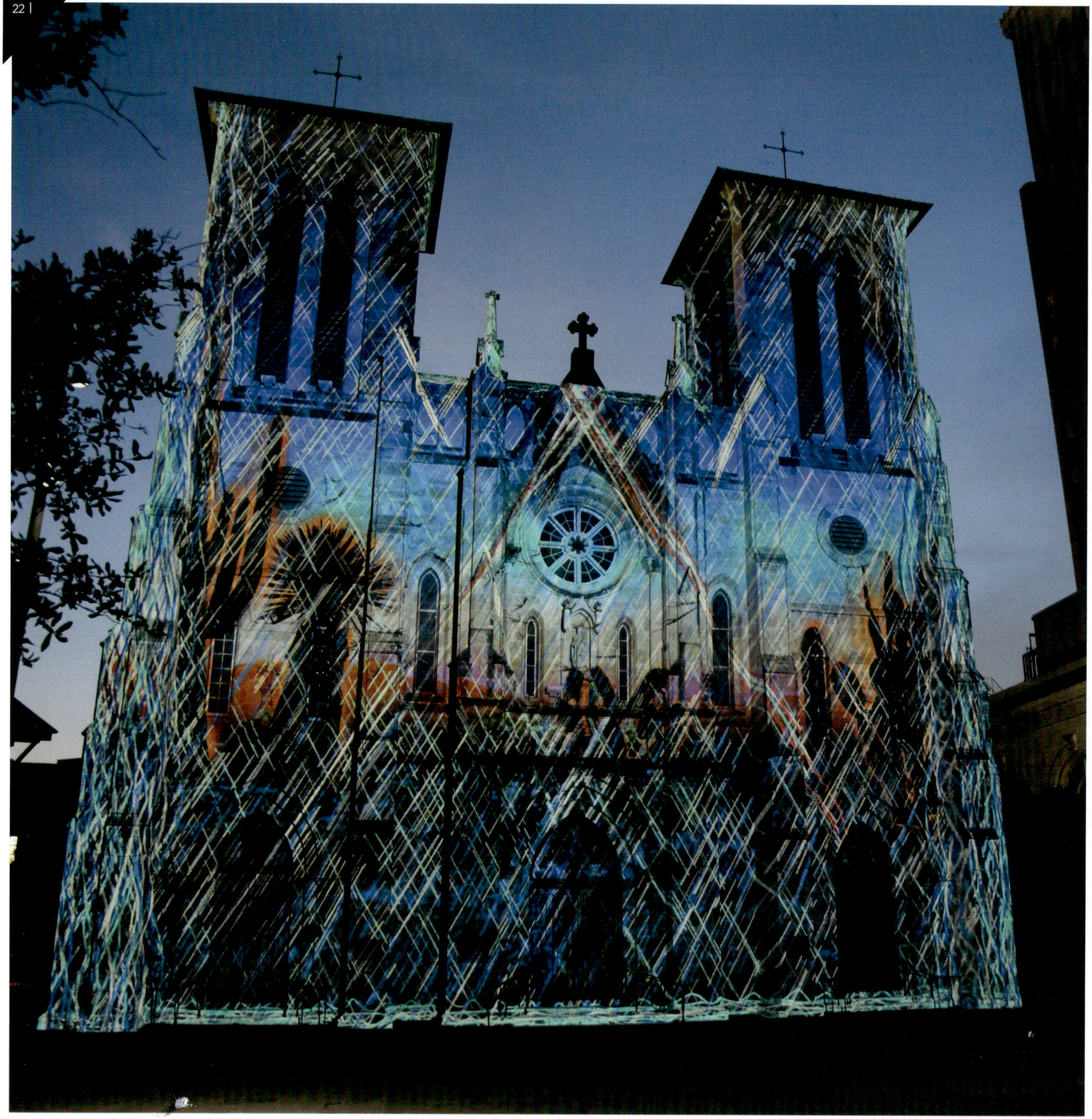

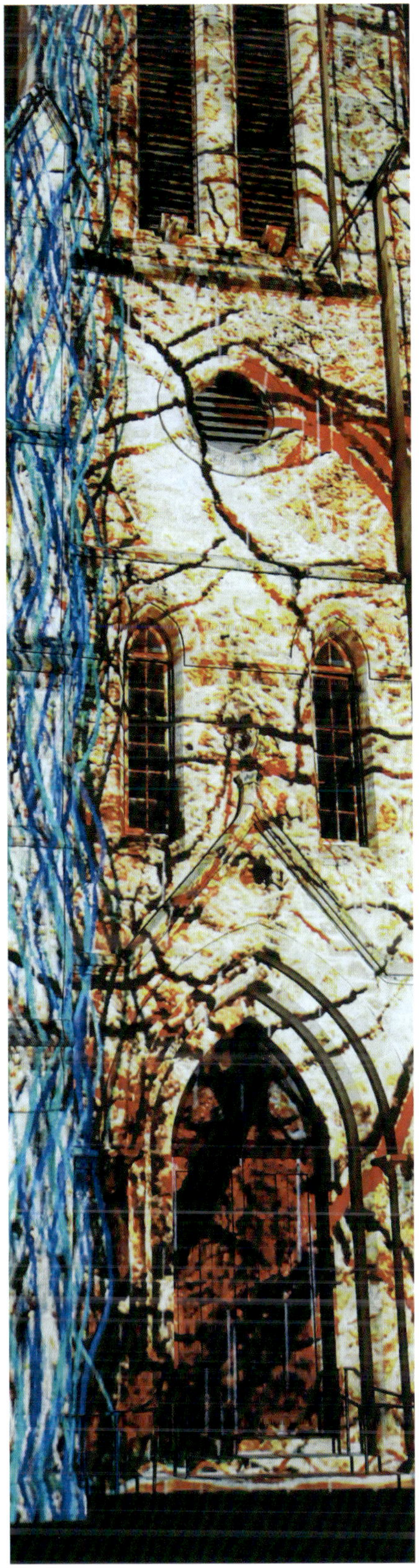

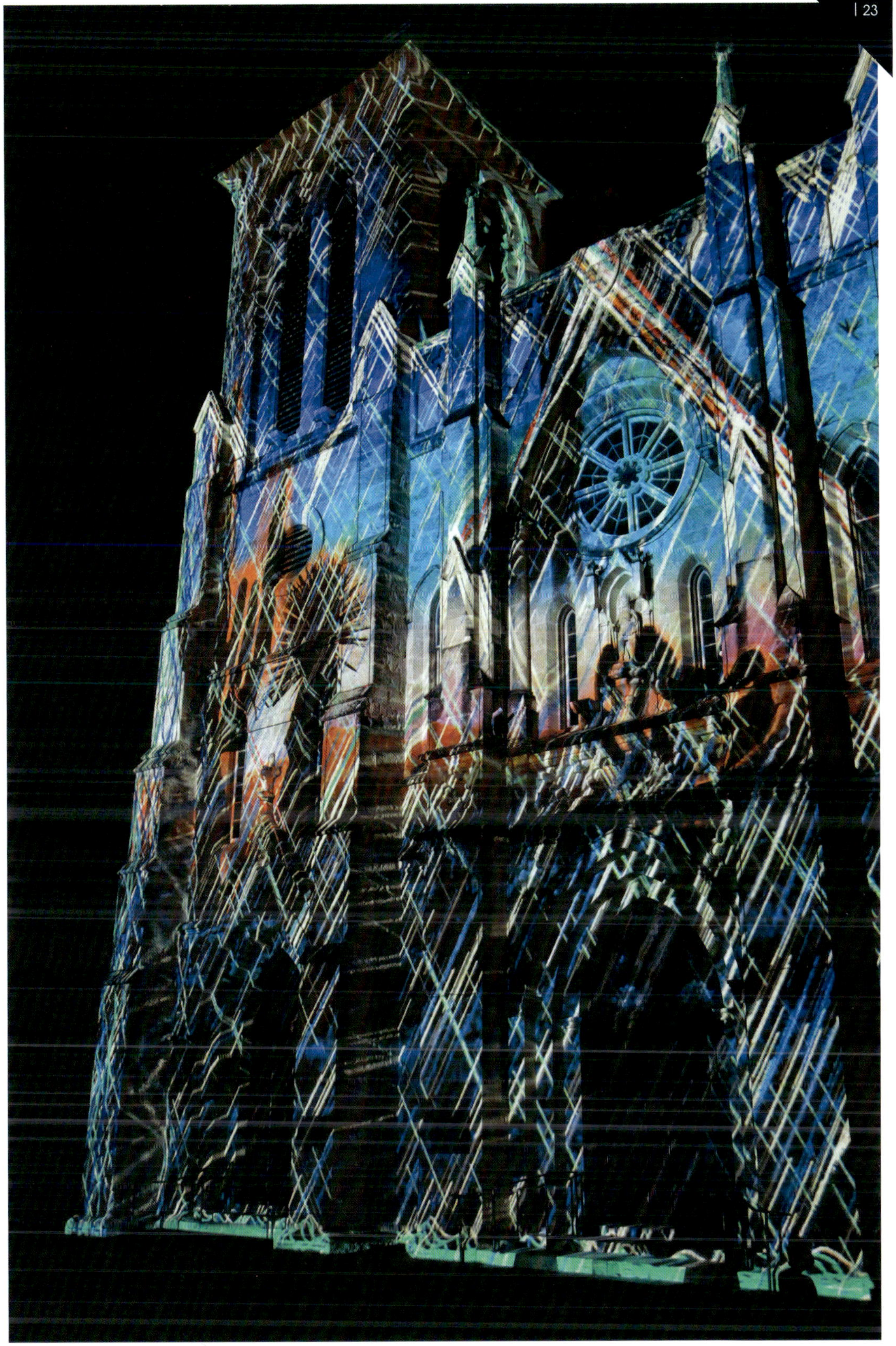

Sequence 2

LAND OF ANCESTORS

INDIAN RAIN

Rain becomes weaker, day rises, indian camp appears in hazy blue rain vibrations.

Rain creates lines designing teepee shapes that emerge on top of the Cathedral's three main doors.

Water streams on the cornices.

Appearing and disappearing triangular white shapes suggest a whole camp.

Herds of buffalo crosse the space along with pumas, deer and wild boars.

The church pilasters are alike Indian ornamented totems drawn up towards the sky.

THE RIVER

Rain stops, river rises.

On Cathedral tower sides, flows the River.

The River curves and moves as a wide sinuous movement across the face of the Cathedral, rotating down from the sky to look like San Pedro Springs and the horseshoe.

River flow plays with Cathedral's *rosette*.

INDIAN PATTERN

Camp transforms into an Indian embroidery of glass pearls and traditional fabric worn by the Cathedral as a decorative costume.

Geometrical patterns quote designs used by Apaches and Comanche in making clothes and decorative sacred objects.

Pattern gradually reveals structure of an Indian Cathedral reminding of Indian tribes who used to live in this place.

NOTE

Coahuitlecans peaceful tribes lived along the river. More warlike Comanche and Apache tribes lived in the area.
Ancient and important human presence precedes the Spanish arrival. Coahuitlecans Indians are quickly subjected and christianized.
They are the first inhabitants and the first defenders of this New Spain in progress, missions are built to host them and to defend the new Spanish establishment. Indi ans are educated and they are taught the basics of agriculture.
Spaniards use this local labour force to clear and develop the land for attracting future Spanish immigrants and colonize the area.
Attacks by hostile Indians are frequent and local natives are conviced of the cause of New Spain to defend their missions and their harvests.
One can see pearl decorated Indian objects on exhibit at the Institute of Texas Cultures in San Antonio.

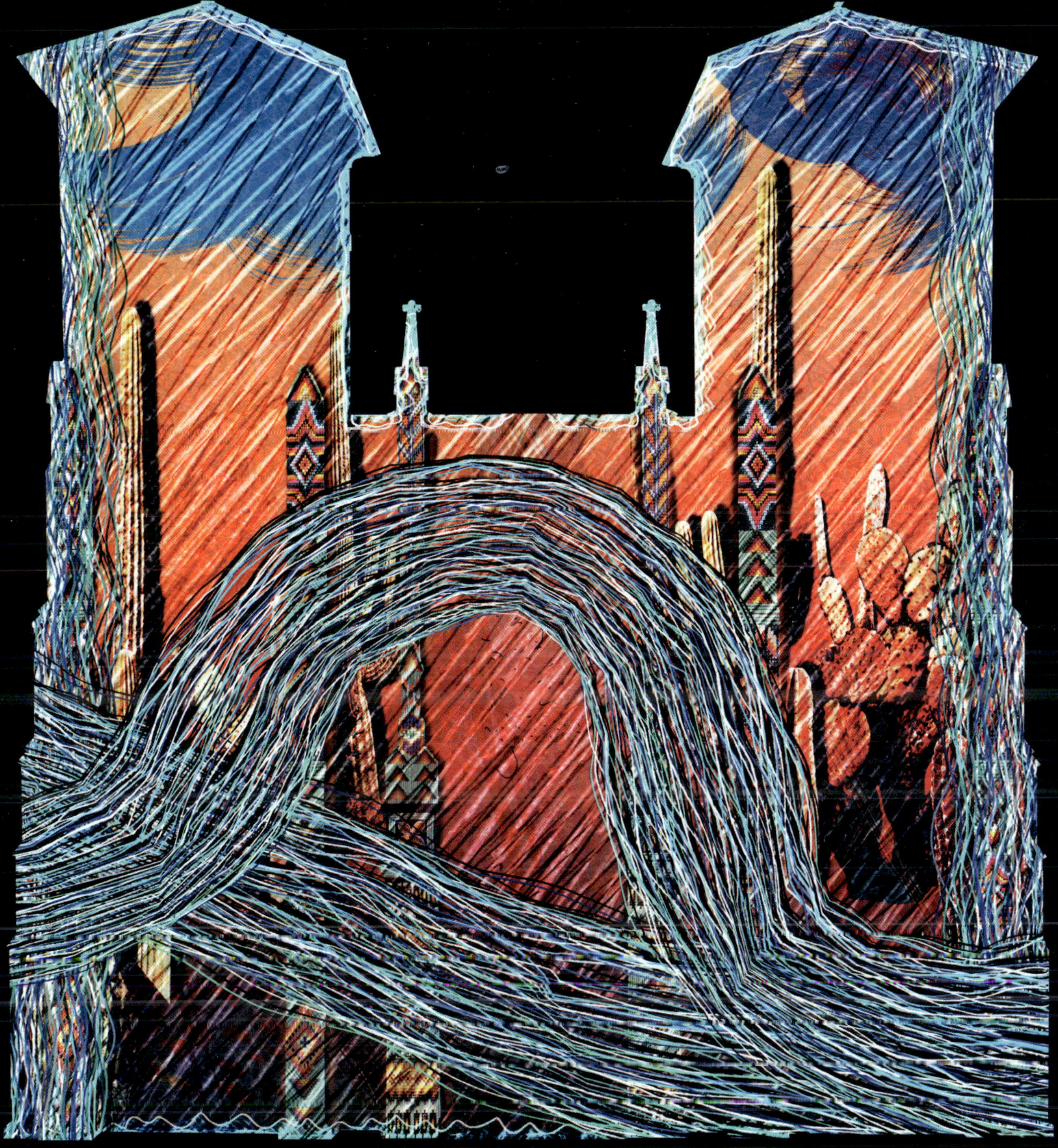

The River

Indian Rain

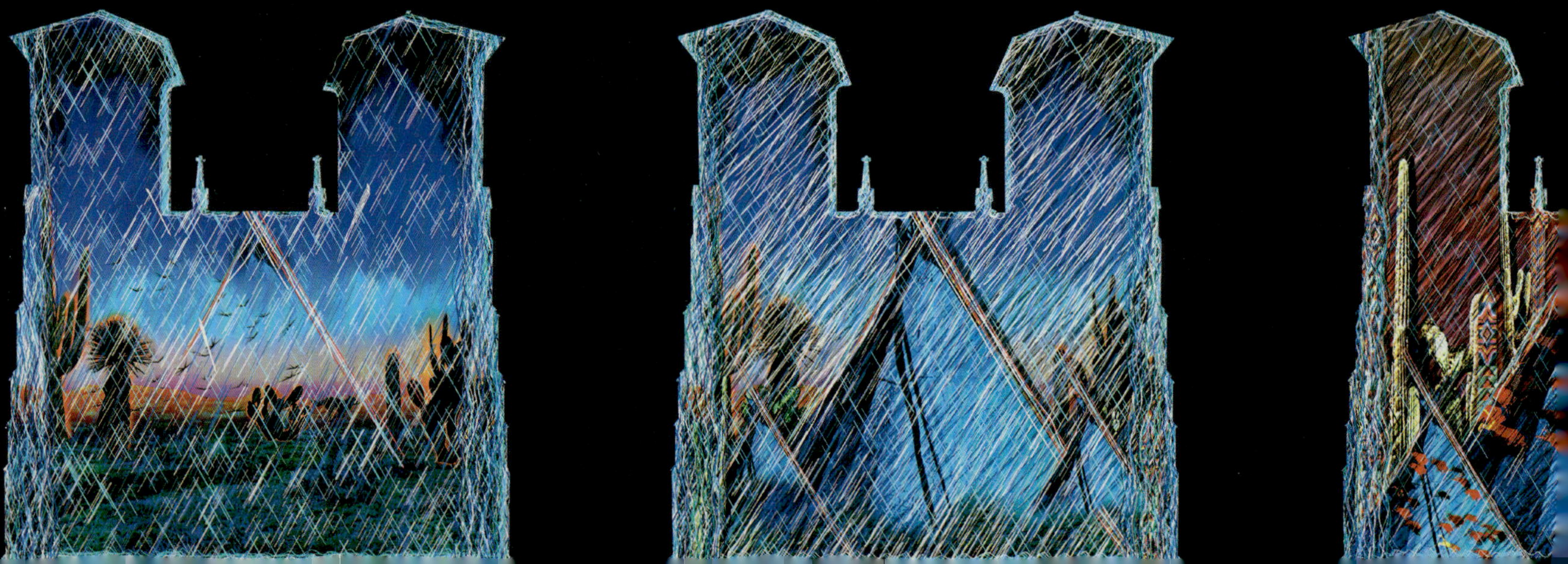

The River

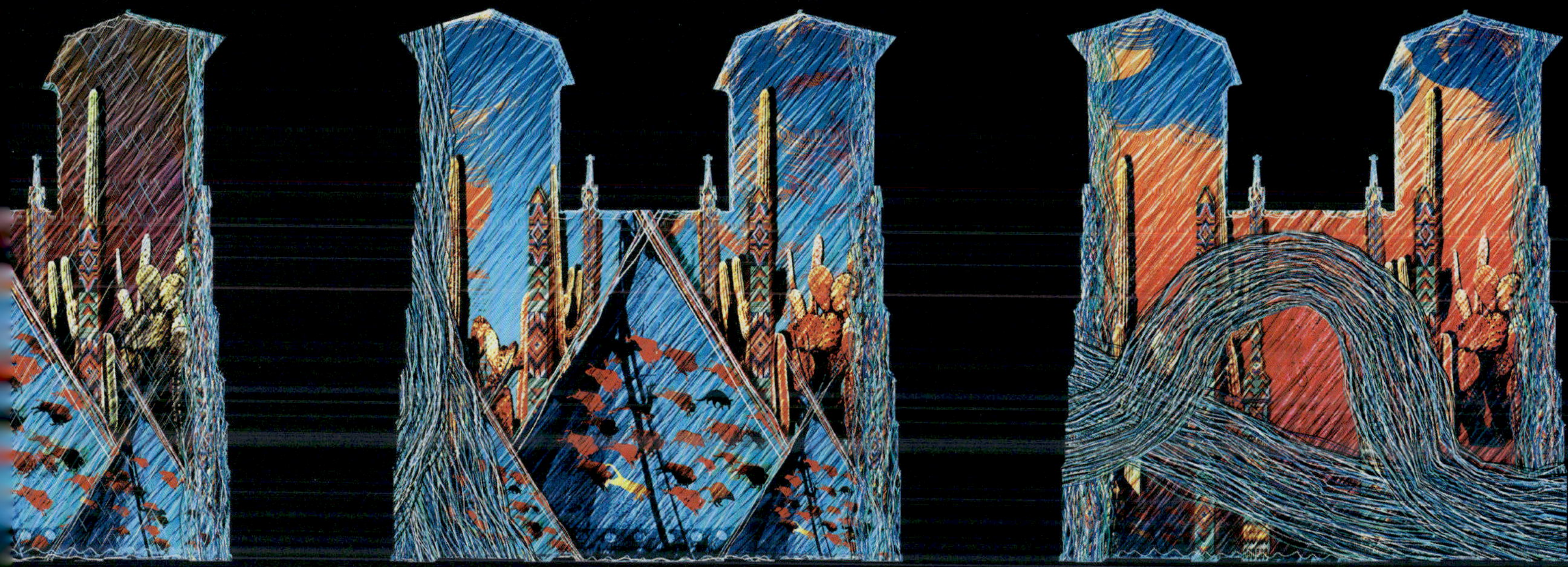

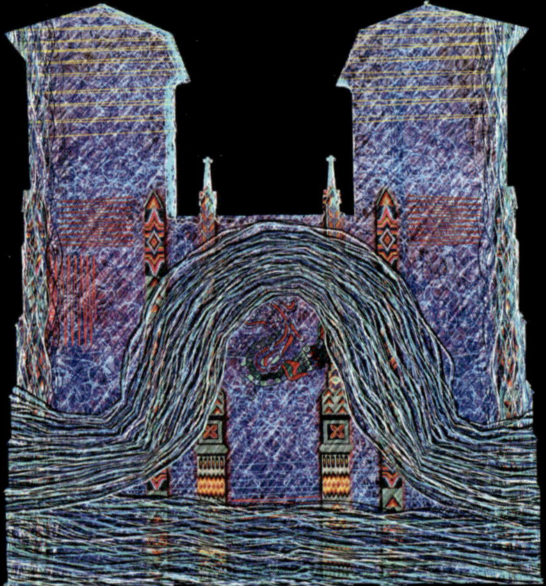

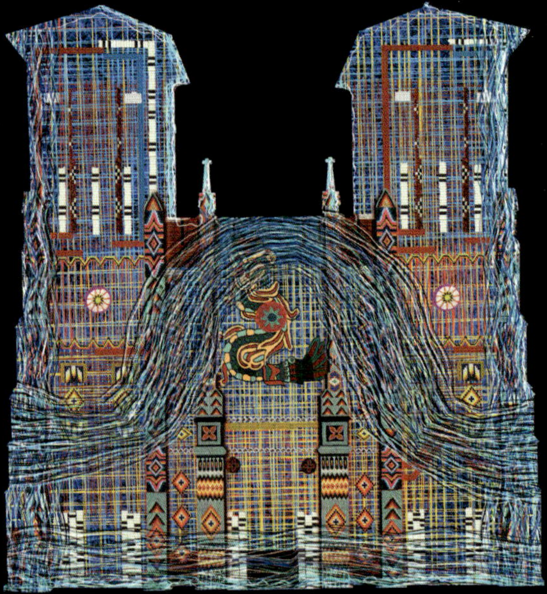

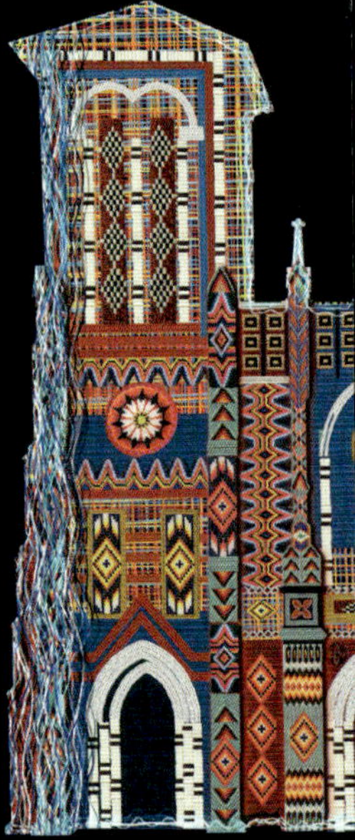

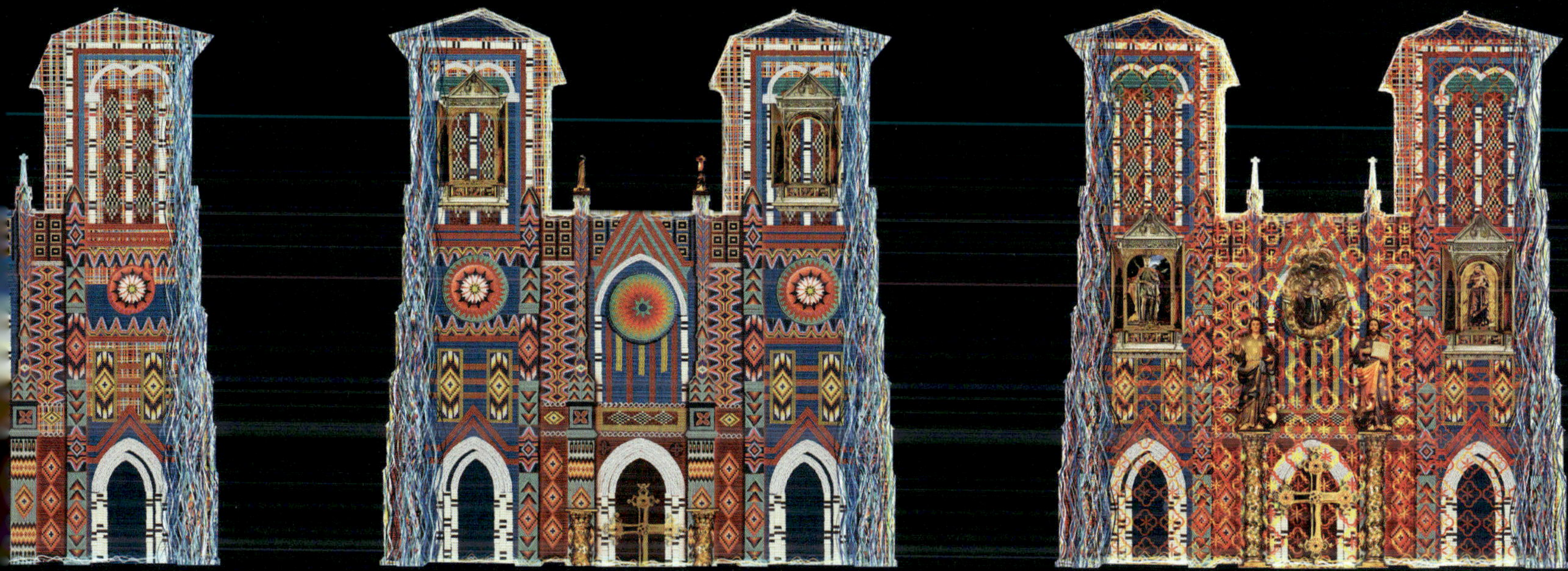

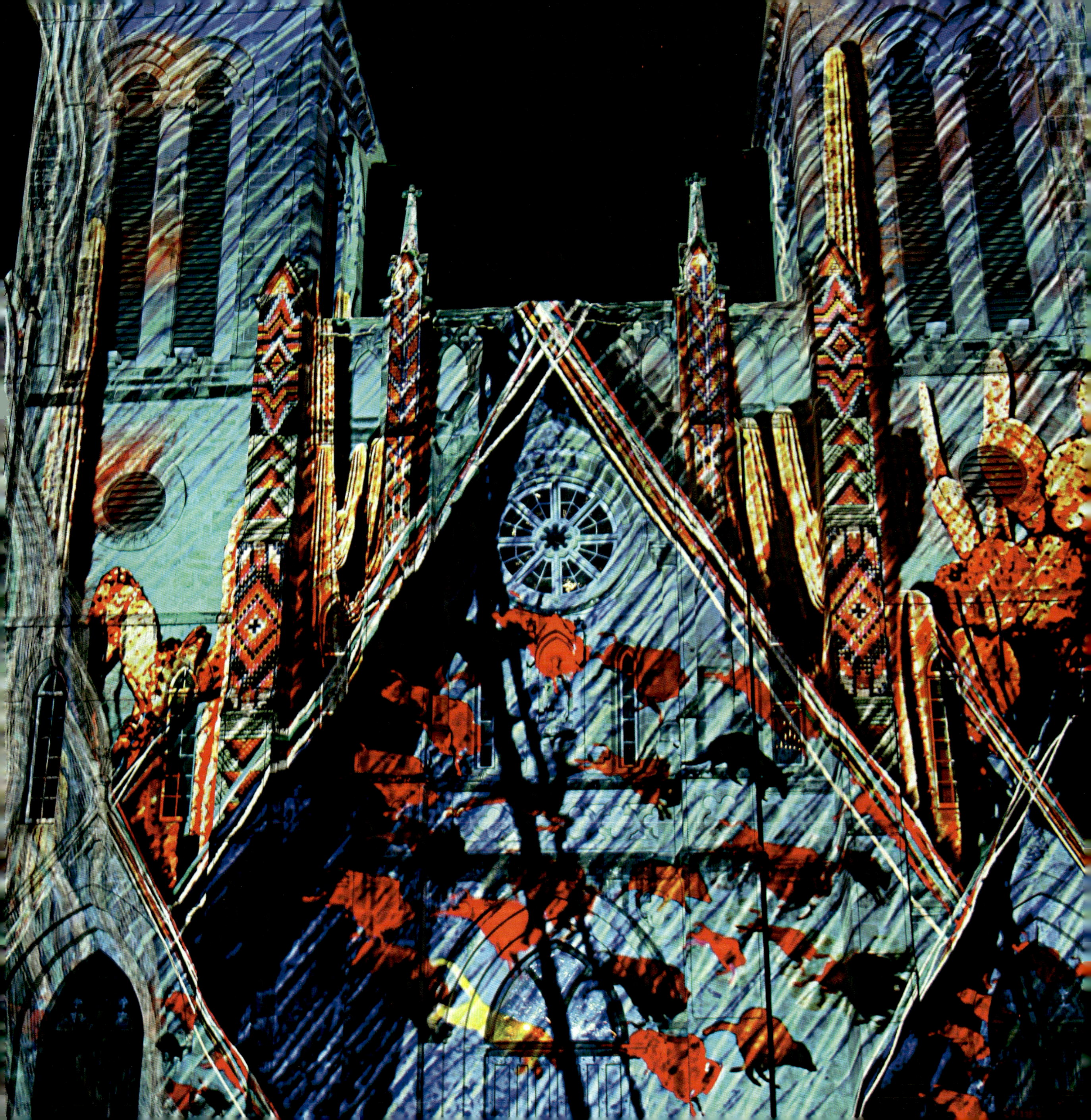

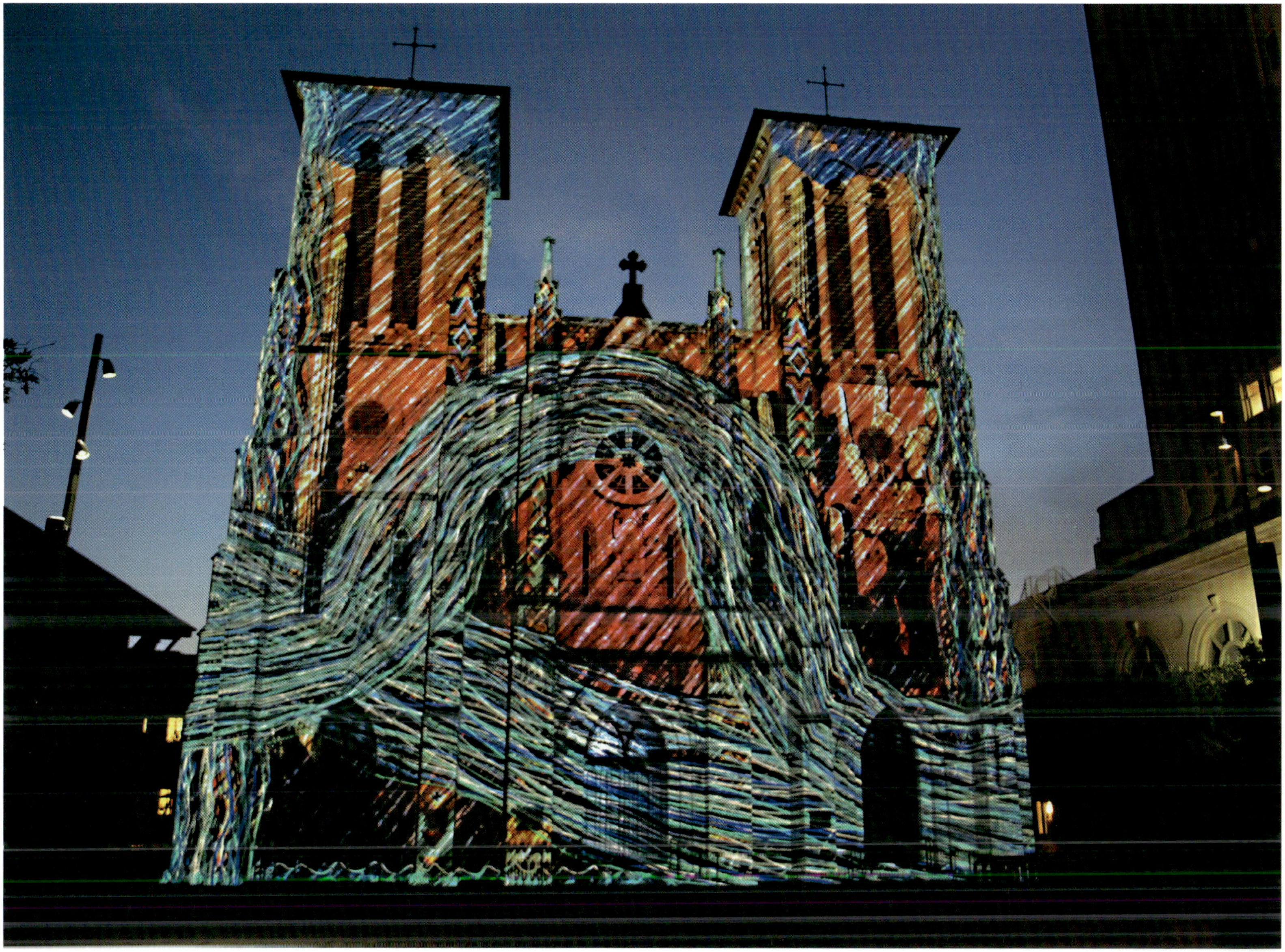

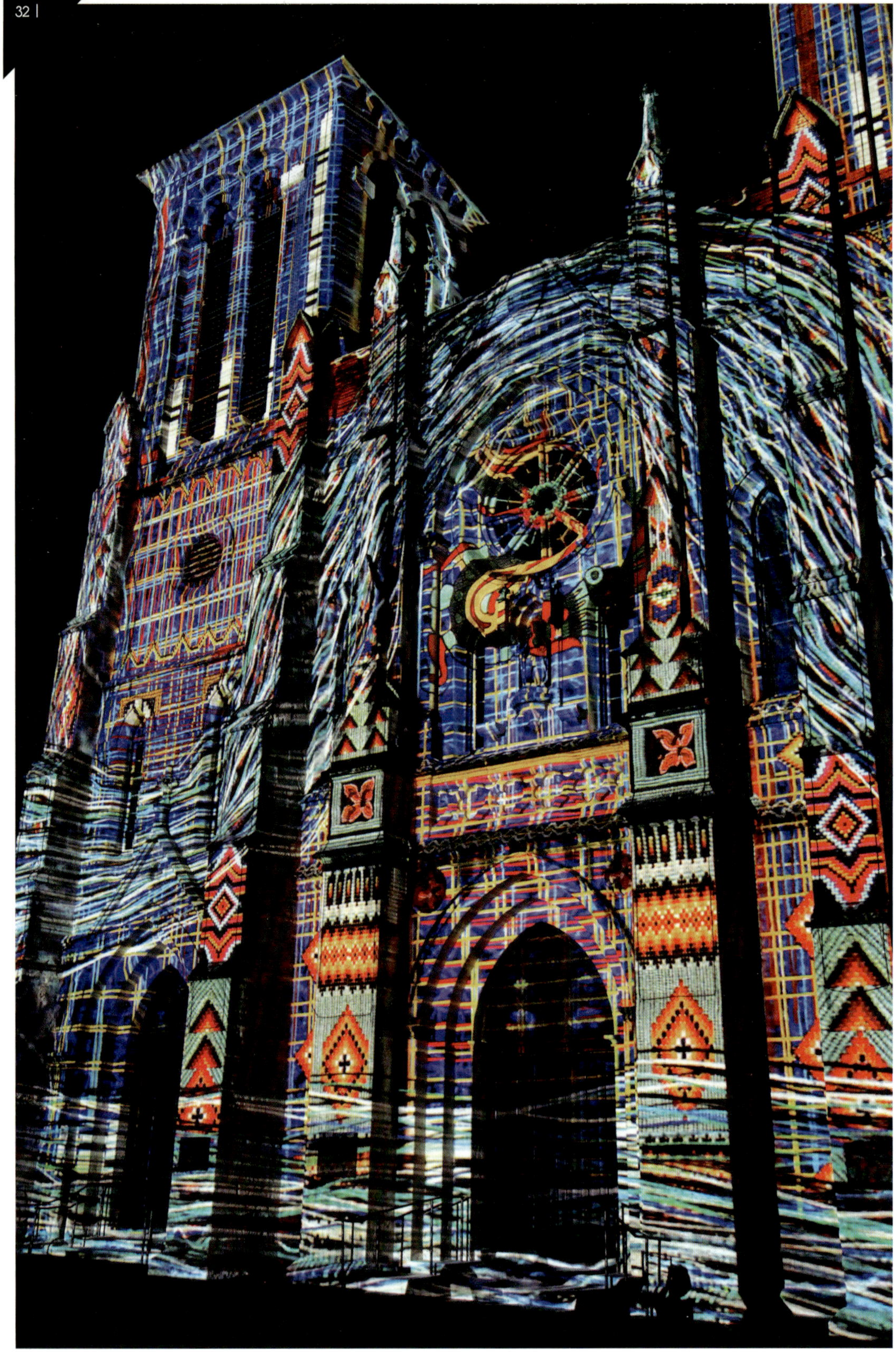

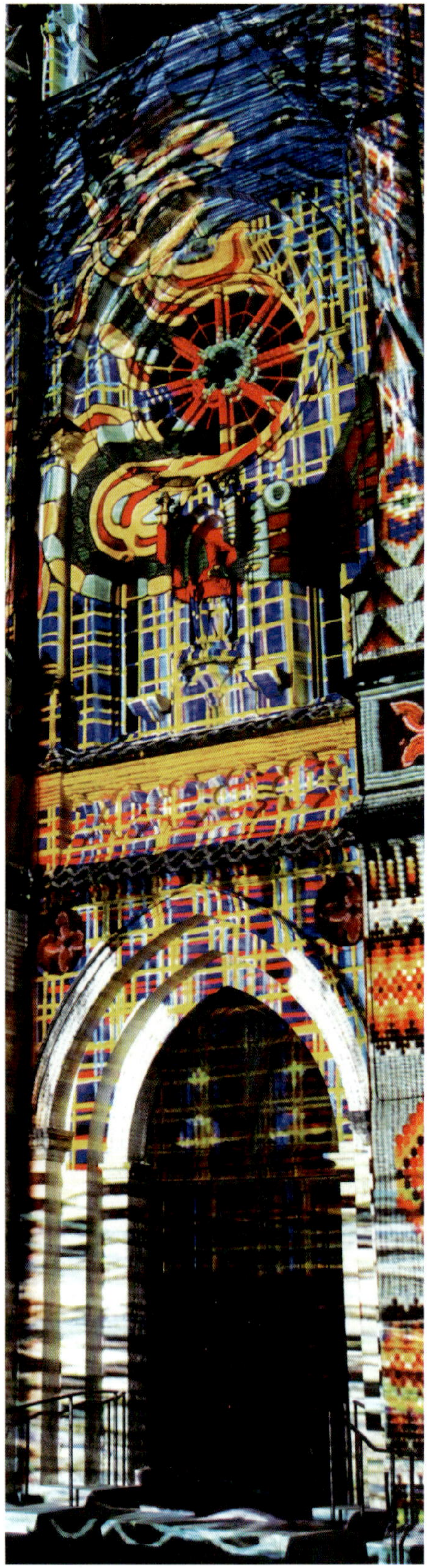

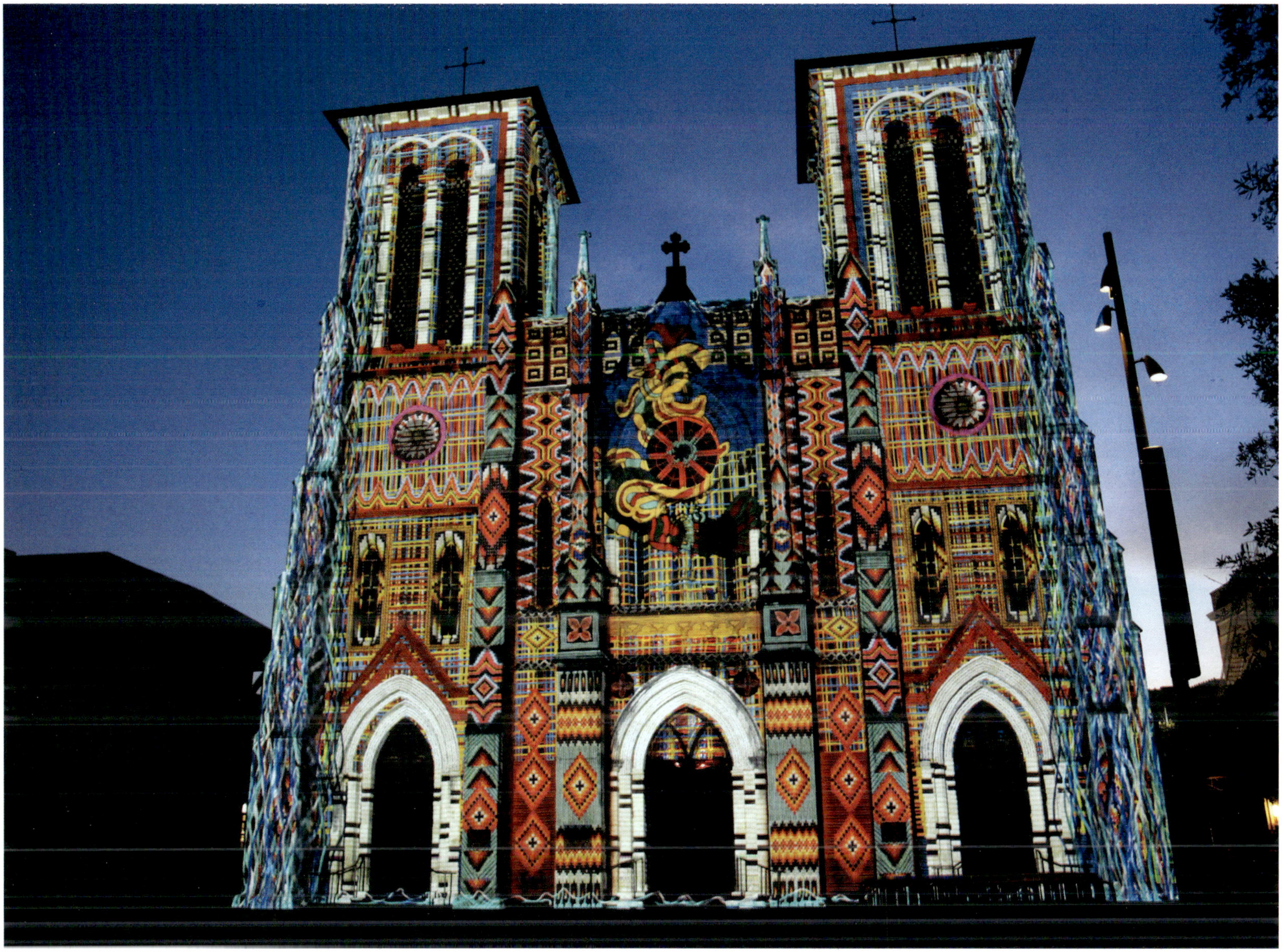

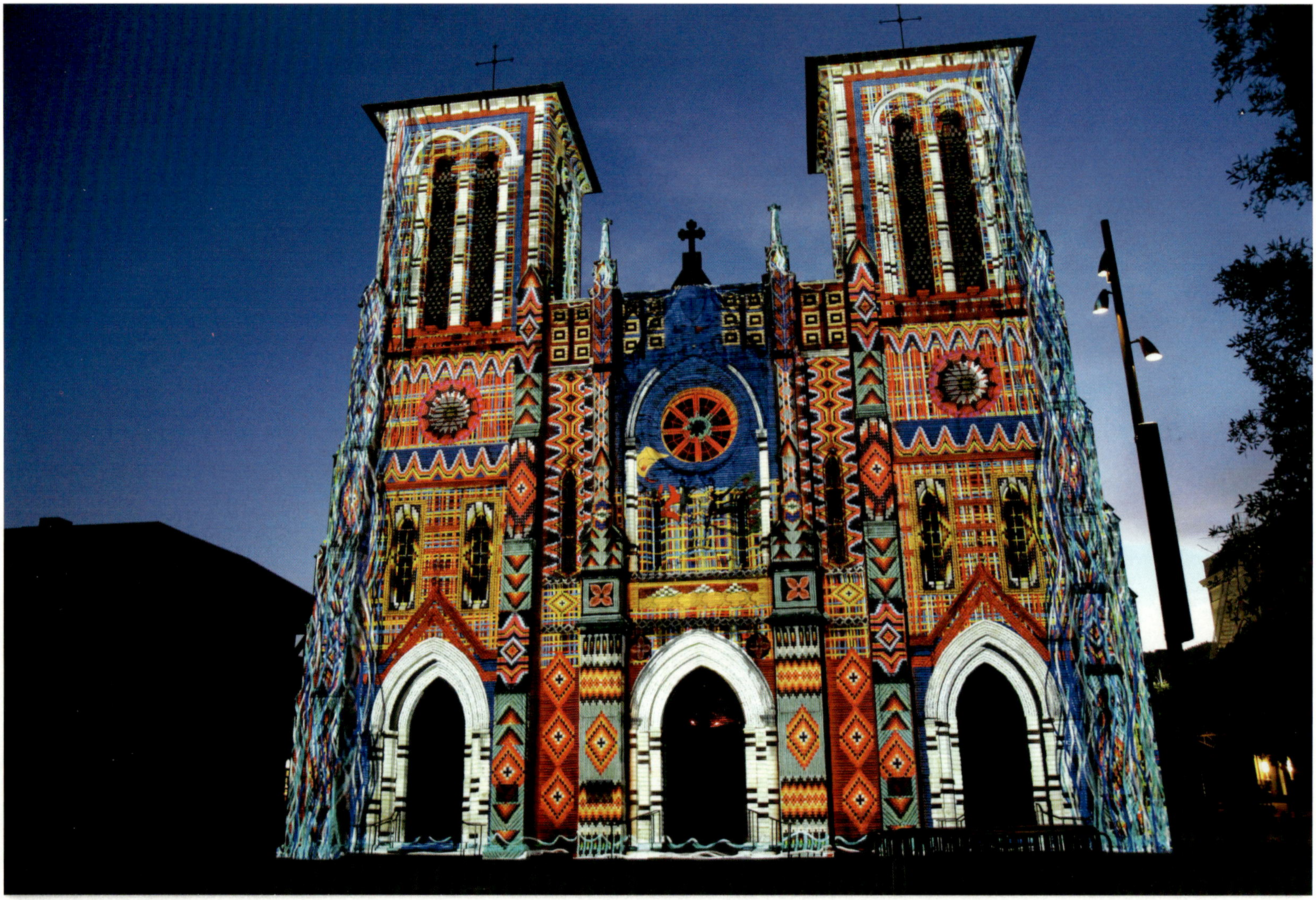

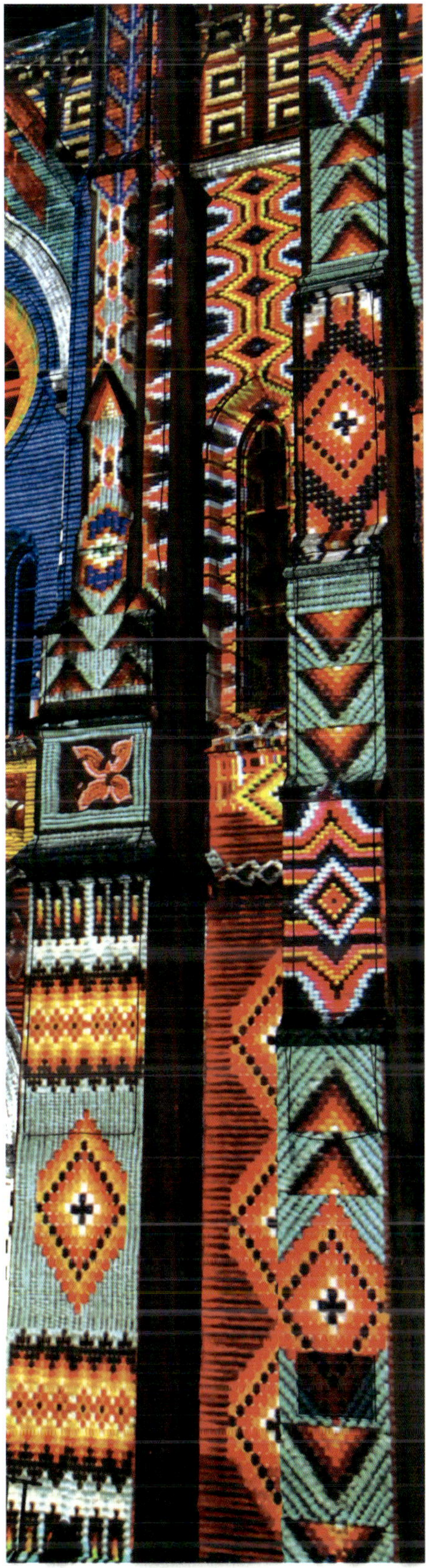

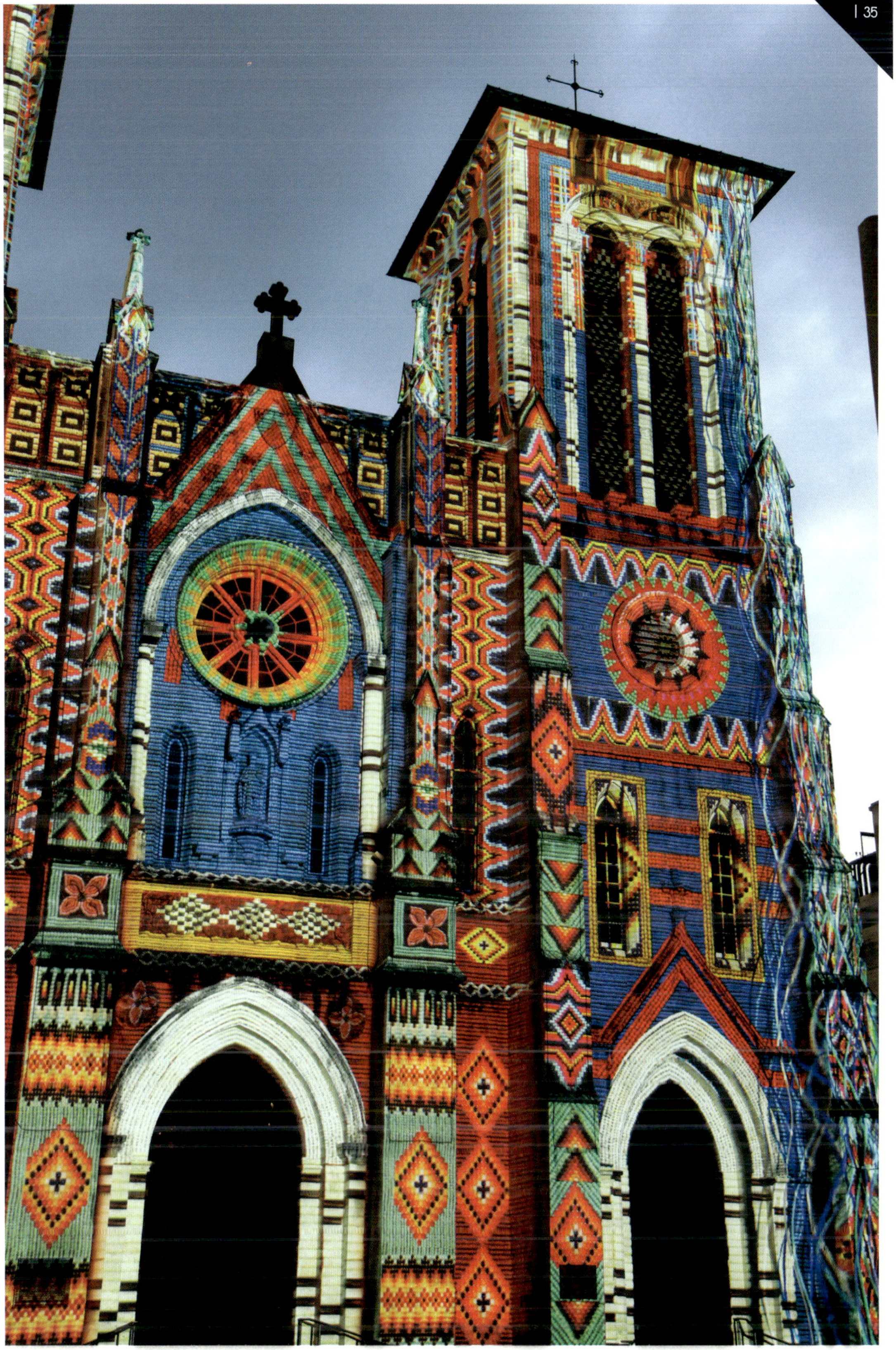

Sequence 3

SPANIARDS

SETTLEMENT

Missionaries enter the indigenous world with Christian representations and symbols. Indian culture is replaced. The river flows along the sides of the Cathedral and leaves space for missions to settle; San José, Concepción, San Juan and *Espada* Missions. Indian pattern melts with Spanish geometrical drawings inspired by San José mission frescoes. Indian and Spanish patterns meet and interlace, assemble, complete to create a new décor. Christian treasures such as; paintings, statues and crosses brought by Spaniards are on the church's façade. San Antonio de Padua polychrome wooden statue appears as a retable referring to *Arnao de Brusellas*.

MISSIONS

The mix of patterns and architectural styles show the vision of a complete mission resulting of establishment success by the Spaniards.

Mission Concepción triangular porch is recognizable on the towers. San José baroque *Rose window* is seen above the Cathedral doors and then the porch appears on the central entrance.

Church composition shown is simple like its masons, missionaries, Indians and first colonists.

GOLDEN CATHEDRAL

However, the power of Spain is total and Mexican gold gradually and symbolically substitutes the colored patterns, showing the power of *Conquistadores*.

The Cathedral becomes gilded as a sign of the Spanish wealth.

NOTE

A Spanish expedition discovers San Antonio site in 1691, on June 13th. The river and the city hold their name from San Antonio de Padua celebrated on day of discovery. Established between San Pedro Creek and the loop of the river, the first Franciscan mission is founded by padre Antonio Olivarès and Isidoro Espinosa en 1718 under the name of San Antonio de Valero (from the name of New Spain Vice King, Marquès de Valero). A few days later, the new governor, Martin de Alarcon has the first government building (or presidio) built just nearby, on the other bank of the river under the name of San Antonio de Bejar (according to the name of Duke of Bexar, Spaniard hero killed during the conquest). The river San Antonio is known in the 17th century by the name of Rio de San Antonio de Bejar.

At the end of the 17th century Texas is the place of a territorial fight between Spain and France, Spanish coming from the South by Mexico City and the French travelling from Northern colonies of New France to Louisiana.

Spanish fears that the French will seize the gold and silver mines of Mexico's central regions. Spain wants to stop France progression towards the west. The French seek the mouth of the Mississippi to establish long-term settlements in Louisiana.

One understands the challenge of Texas territory, Spanish fearing the French expansionism which marked the reign of King of France Louis XIV. The French Company of the Indies seeks for new territories to develop trade routes towards the West and the Gulf of Mexico. Caribbean Islands are very disputed grounds.

The French founded the city of New Orleans during the year in 1718.

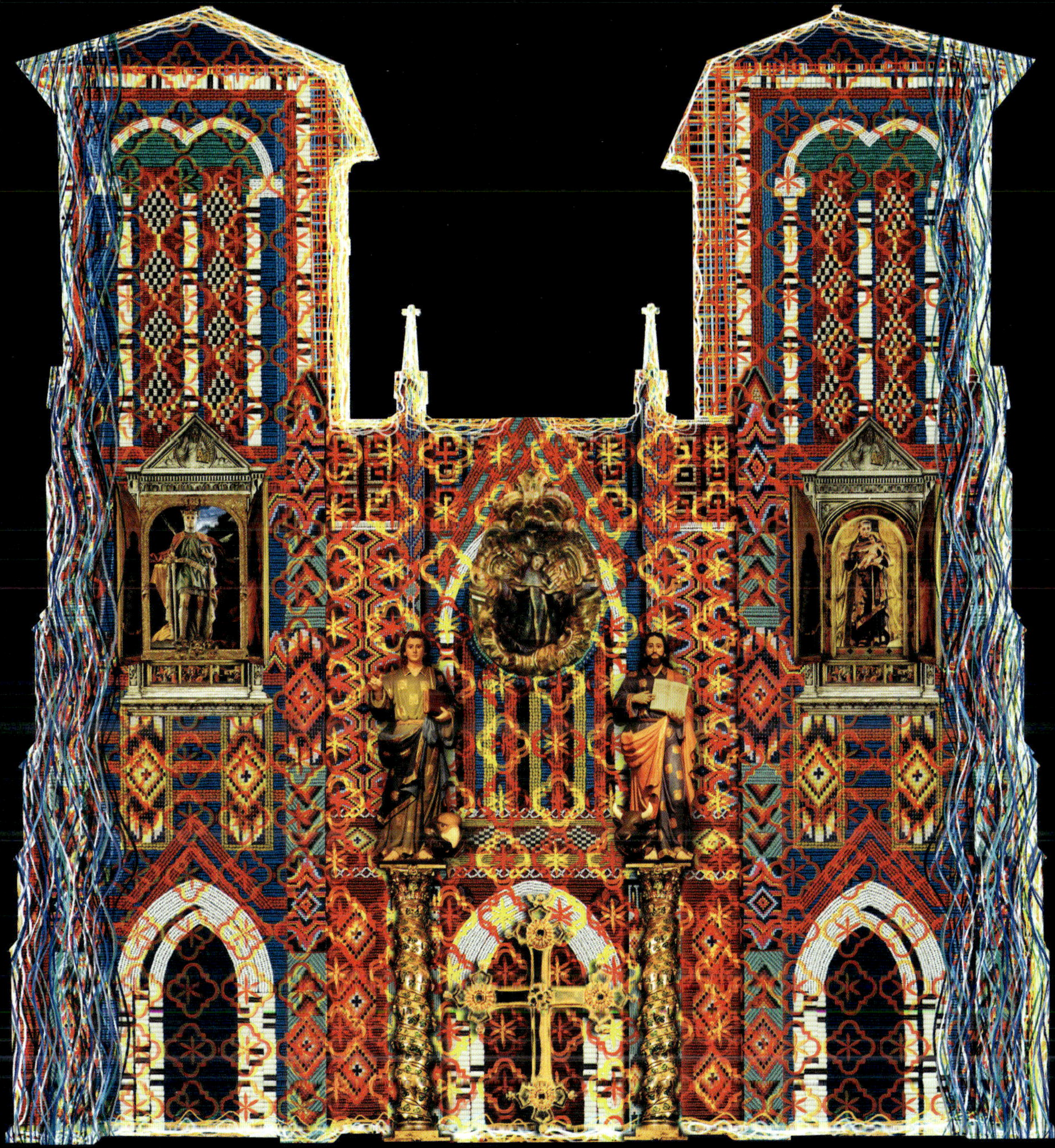

Settlement

Settlement

Missions

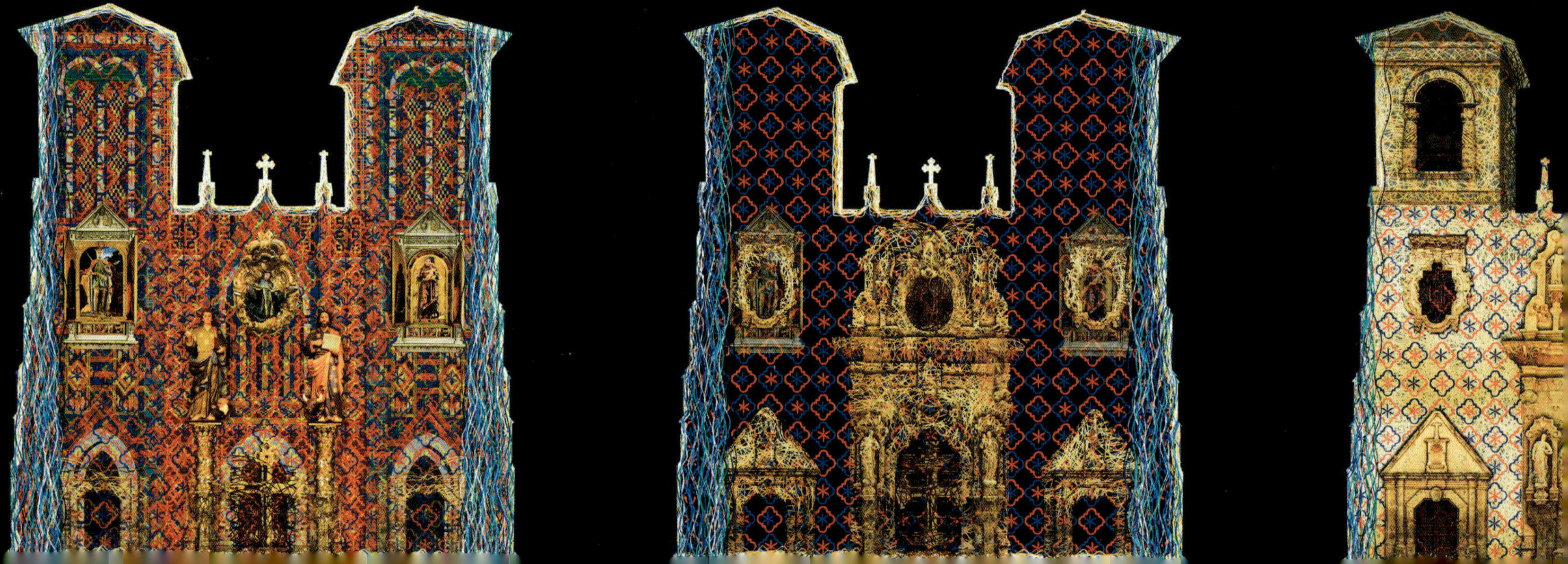

Golden Cathedral

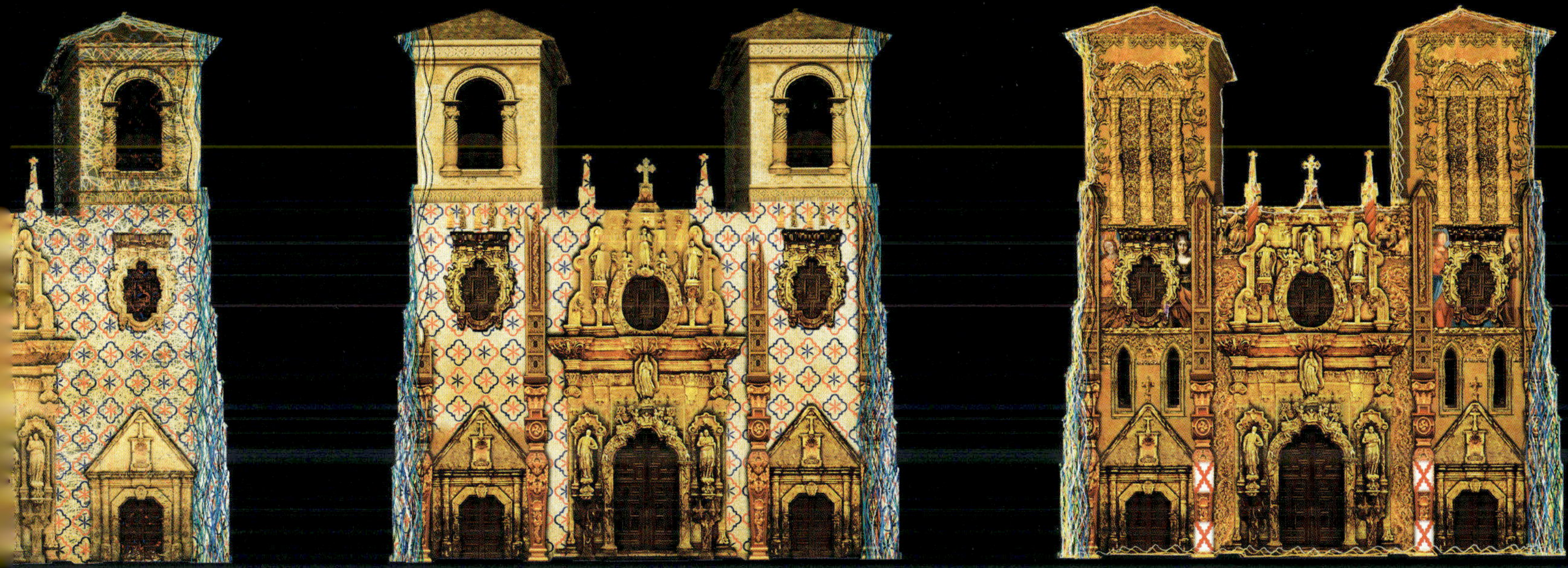

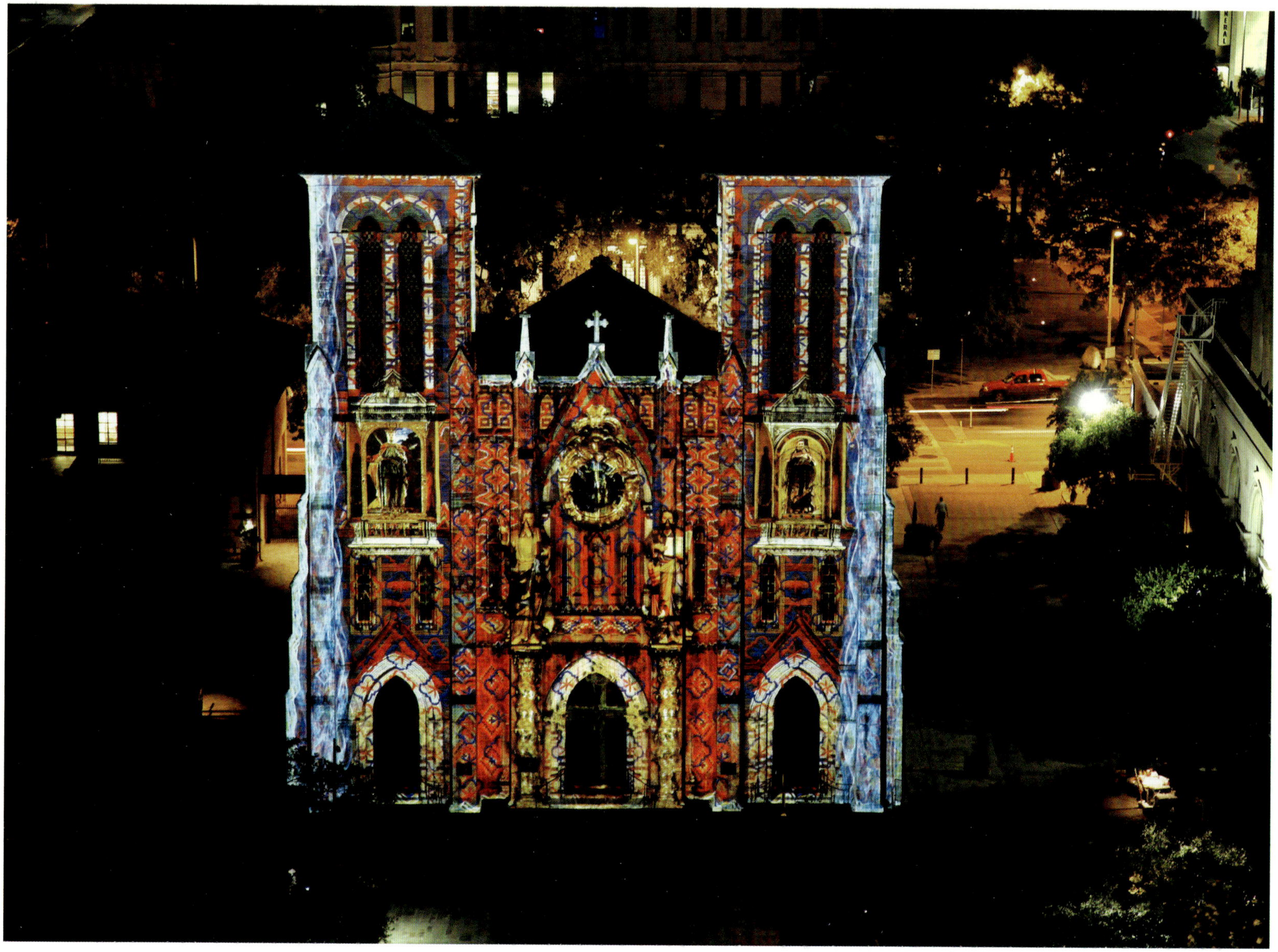

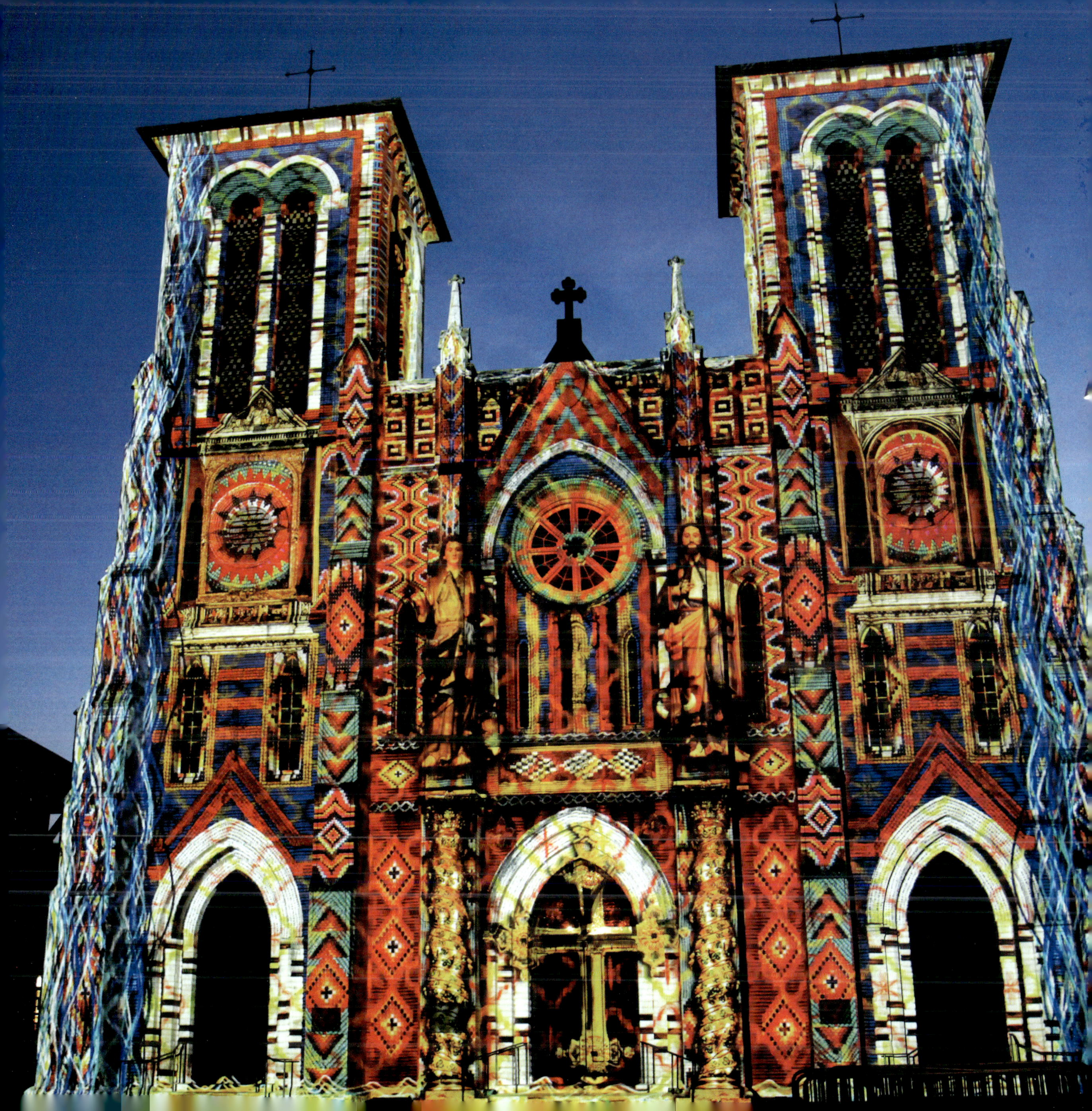

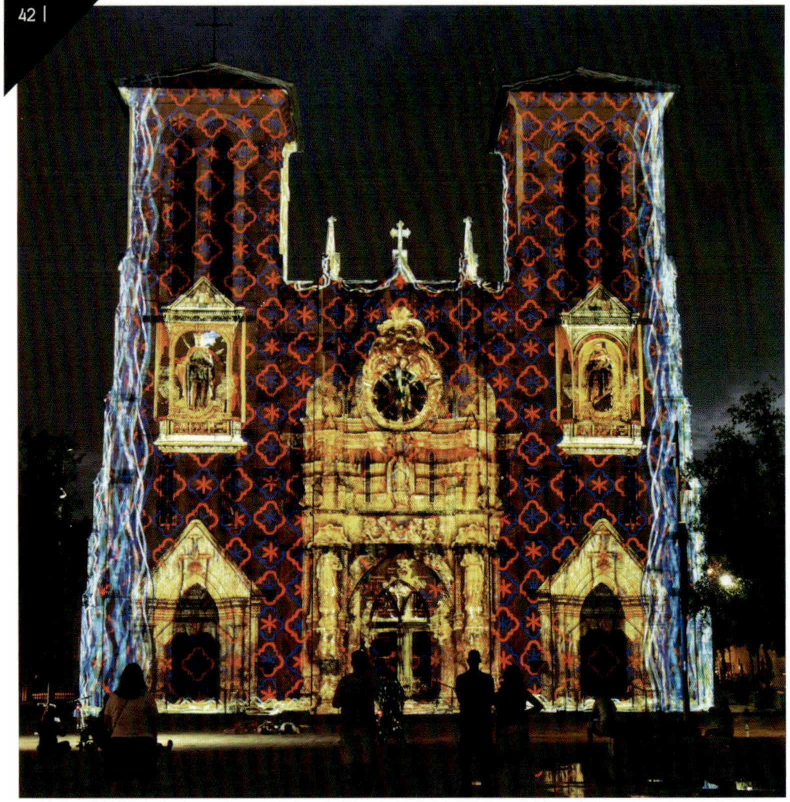

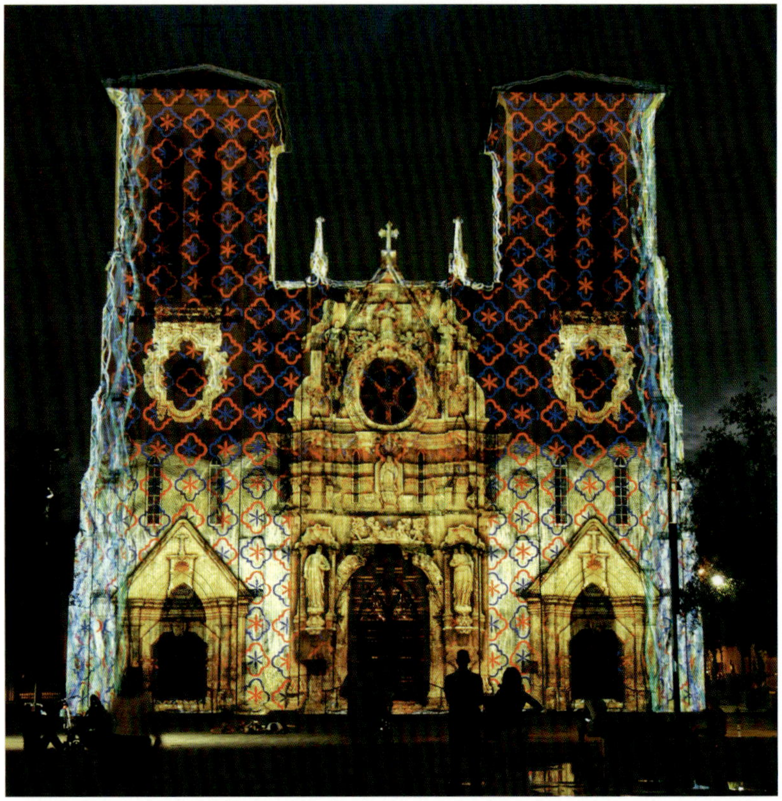

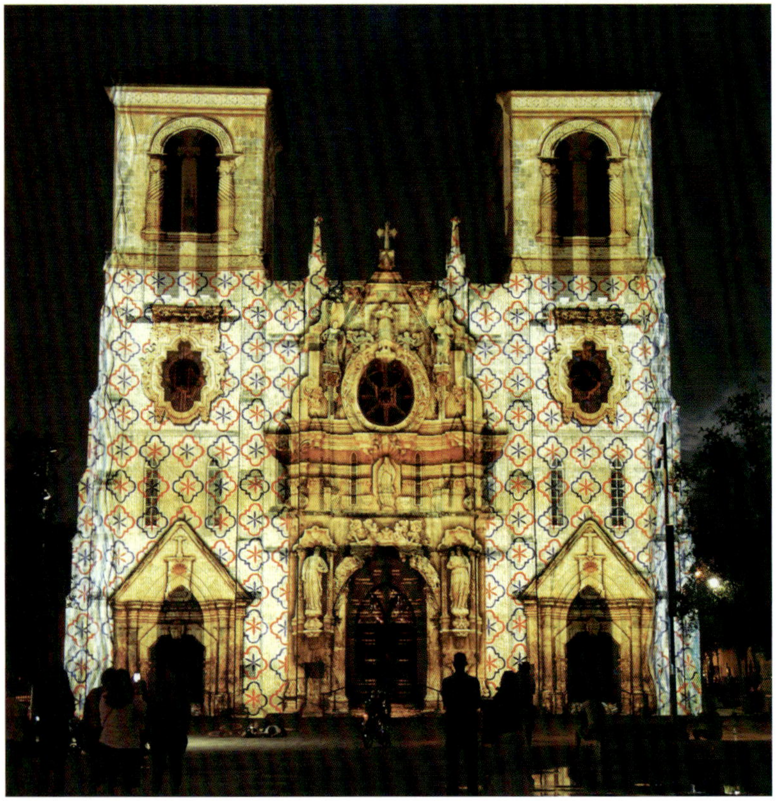

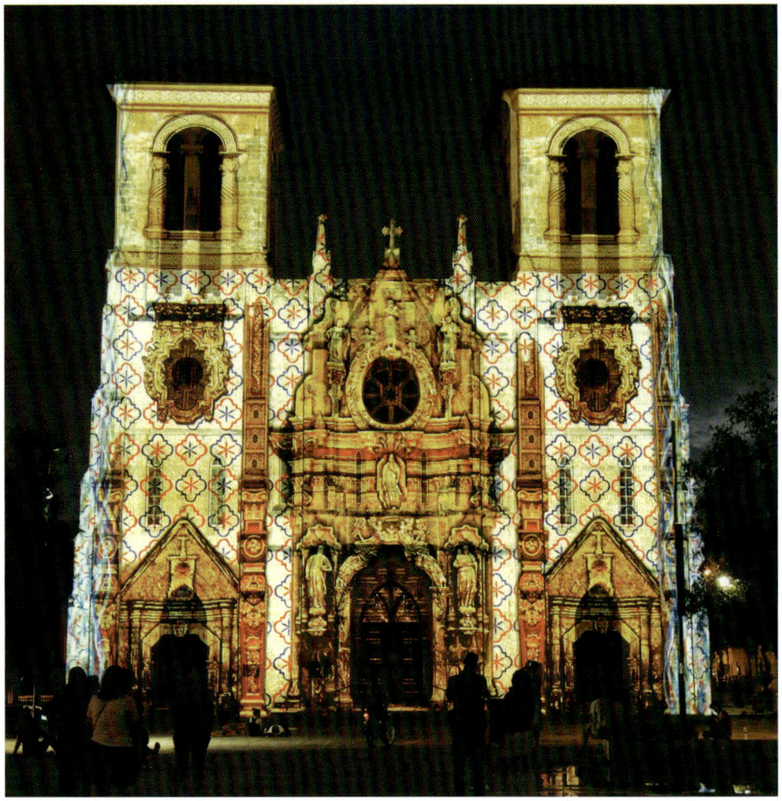

– SAN ANTONIO THE SAGA –

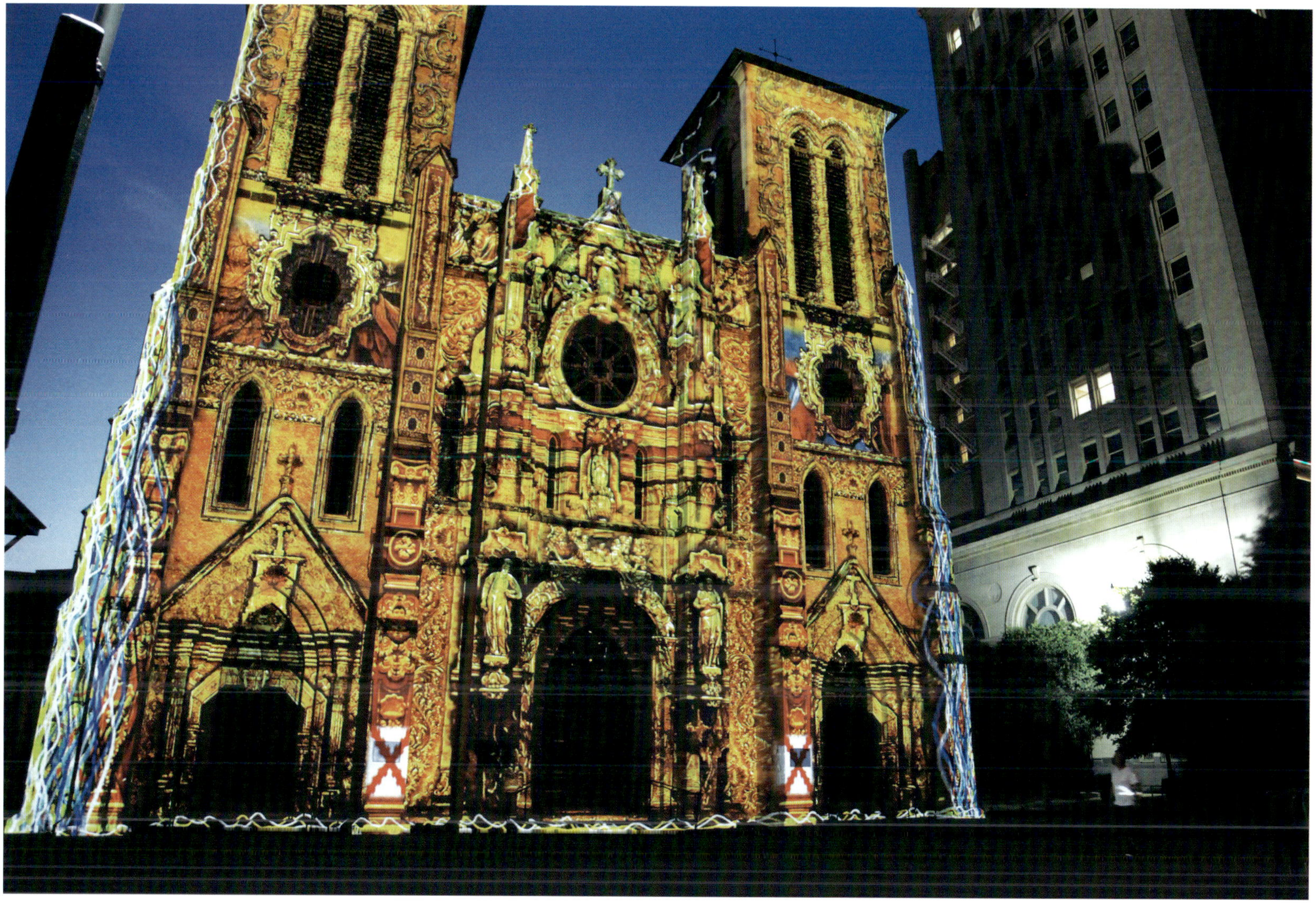

Sequence 4

FOUNDATION OF SAN ANTONIO

NEW SPAIN CROSS

As an emblem of new power, flags of New Spain take place on the pilasters. When the Flamenco music starts, a large red ragulee cross, falls down on the Cathedral at the center of the composition. The golden Cathedral vanishes and the foundation of the city returns.

An ancient map with white houses and Plazas appears as multiple white stones taking part in the layout of the city of San Antonio in 1718. Cartography fills up the façade. The river keeps flowing along the towers.

FATHER MARGIL AND VIRGIN DE LA CANDELARIA

Saint Andrew's red cross straightens in two parts on the tower, framing the new born town.Portraits appear on the church towers; the Viceroy of the New Spain and Fr Antonio Margil, *Franciscan priest founder of many missions.*

Immigrants coming from Canary Islands lay the first stone in 1738 under the patronage of *Virgin Nuestra Senora de Candelaria*. The first cupola at the apse appears on the nave.

QUANAH

Various diseases and repeated attacks by Comanches and Apaches put San Antonio settlement in danger.

Colored feathers fly through the dome to create the headdress and face of Indian Comanche chief Quanah Parker pictured with painted face and jewels.

His huge portrait fills the entire façade.

NOTE

The three symbolic orders of power (religious-military- civil) are henceforth represented in San Antonio, and the first parish belonging to religious order is placed in a protection situation, between civil order of Presidio and military power of the missions. Missions move towards south of the city to extend and protect from possible French intrusions (San José, Concepción, San Juan). San Fernando parish is founded in 1731, on March 9th, by a group of Canary Islander colonists. The name of Fernando is taken from the name of future King of Spain Fernando VI, same name as 11th century Spain Catholic Kings dynasty founder. The throne of Spain is occupied since 1700 by a French dynasty; the Bourbon family. The King of Spain Charles III who reigns in 1731 is the son of Philippe V, first Bourbon King of the Spanish crown.

It is the beginning of the town of San Antonio. Canary Islanders *built the first parish church with some stones brought from Canary Islands, starting in1738. The church is complete around 1755 by mason Ibarra.*
San Fernando Cathedral today is the oldest continuously operated Catholic parish in the United States.

The life is however difficult in San Antonio. The Indian threat is always present even though the colony has organized. Apaches and Comanches attack the missions, they kidnap colonists wives and children.

The population bears also heavy losses among the converted Indians who are not immunized against european infectious diseases. Several revolts take place at that time in the area. Distance to rich colonies of Mexico and territorial competition with the French stop any connections towards the East.

Life is not luxurious in San Antonio.

The colonists sell the few local resources at high prices from their homes to spanish soldiers the garrison.

The town of San Antonio hardly grows. The gold of Spain shines far from Texas. San Antonio has no more than 2000 inhabitants.

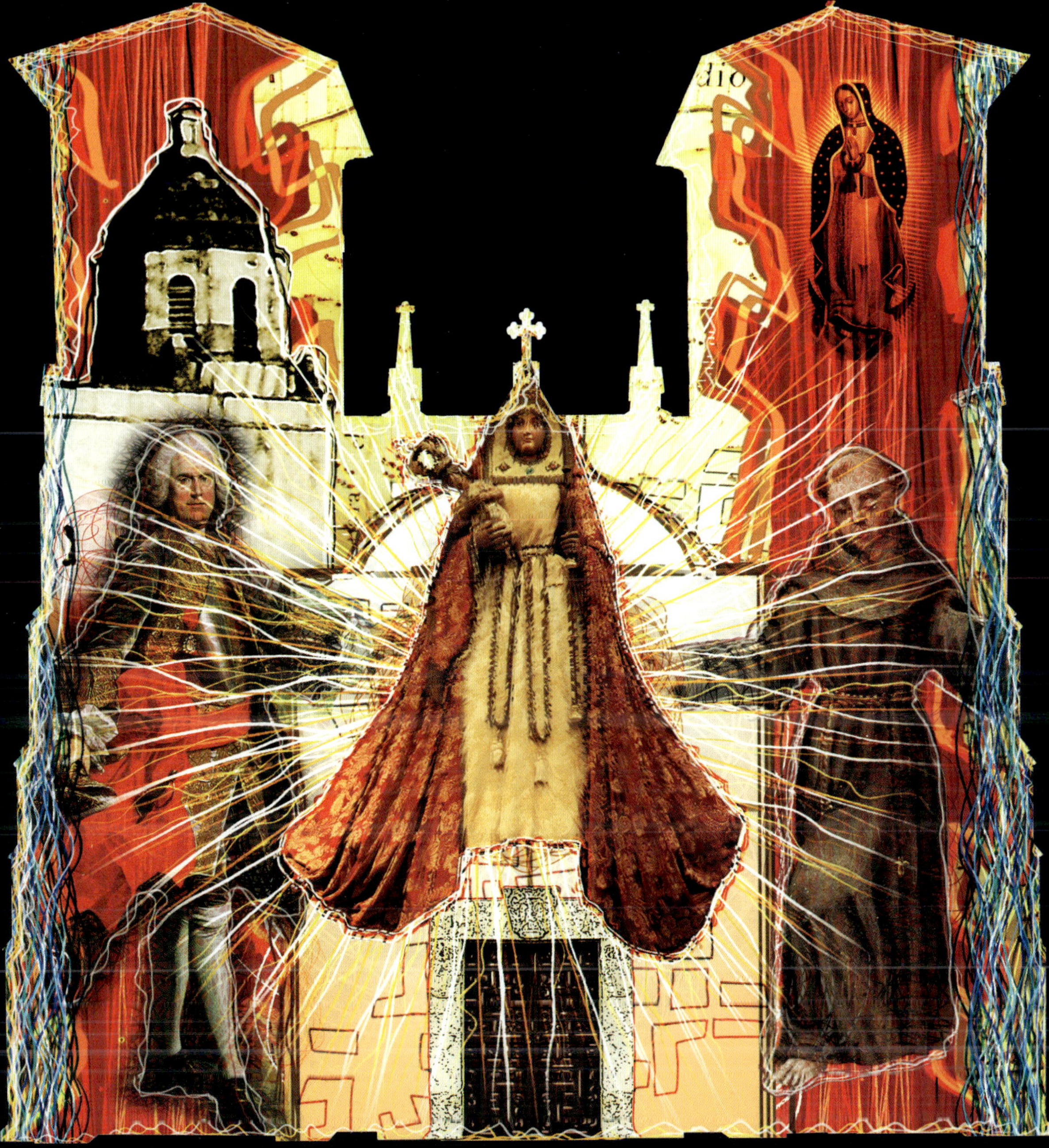

Father Margil and Virgin de la Candelaria

New Spain Cross

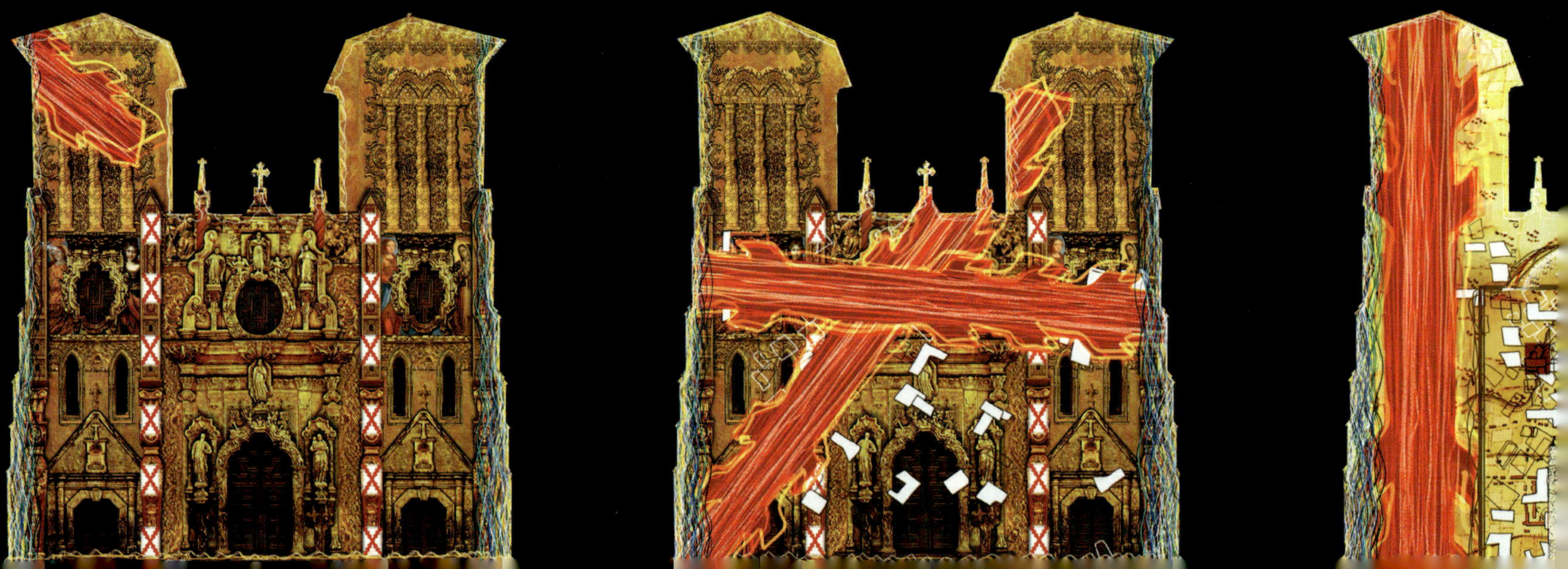

Father Margil and Virgin de la Candelaria

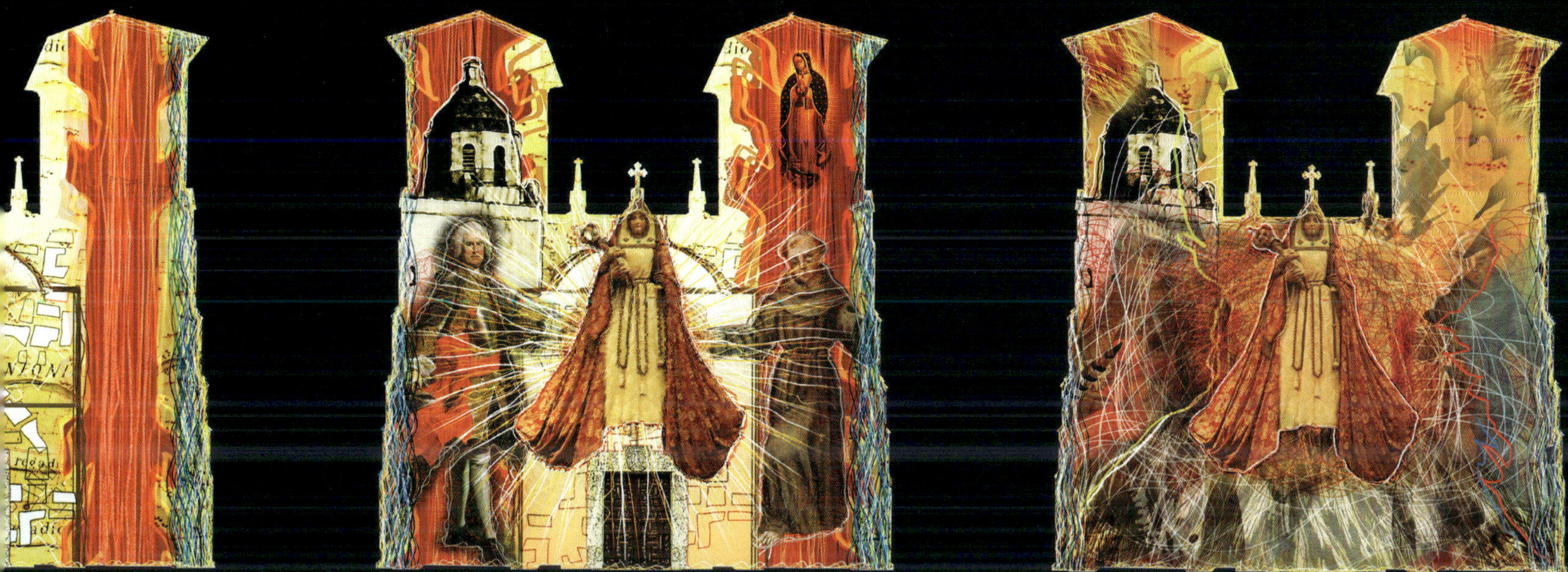

Quanah

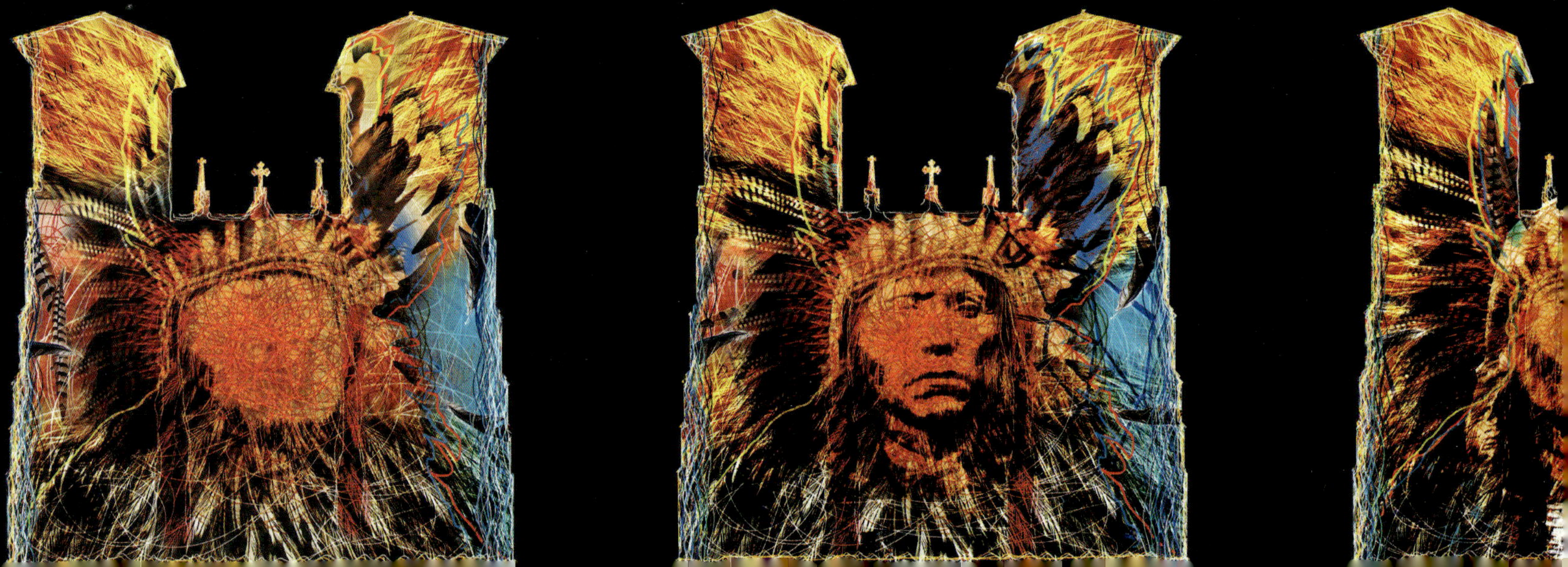

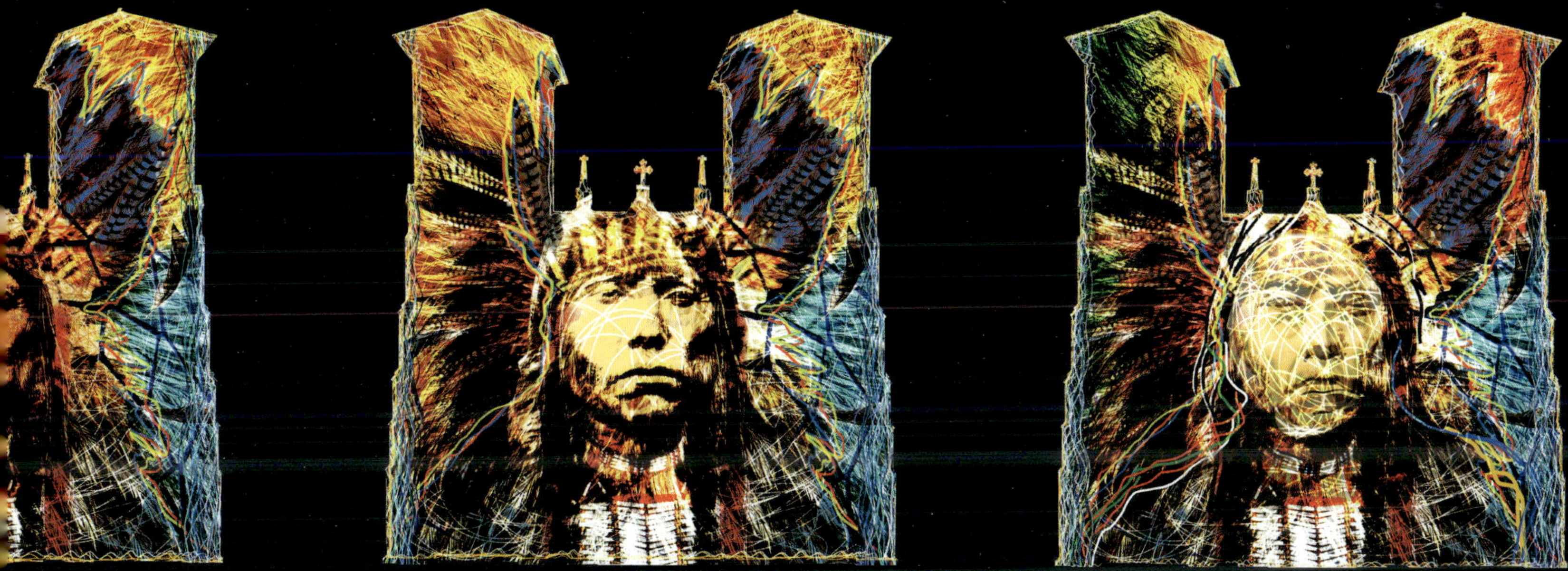

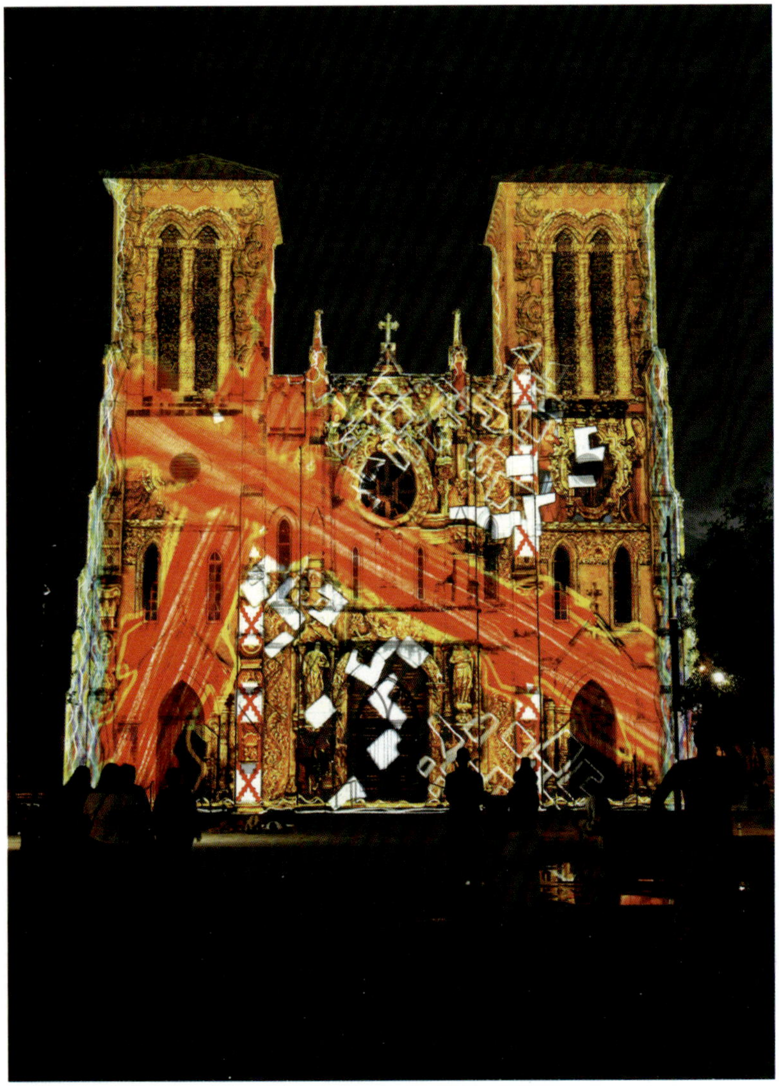

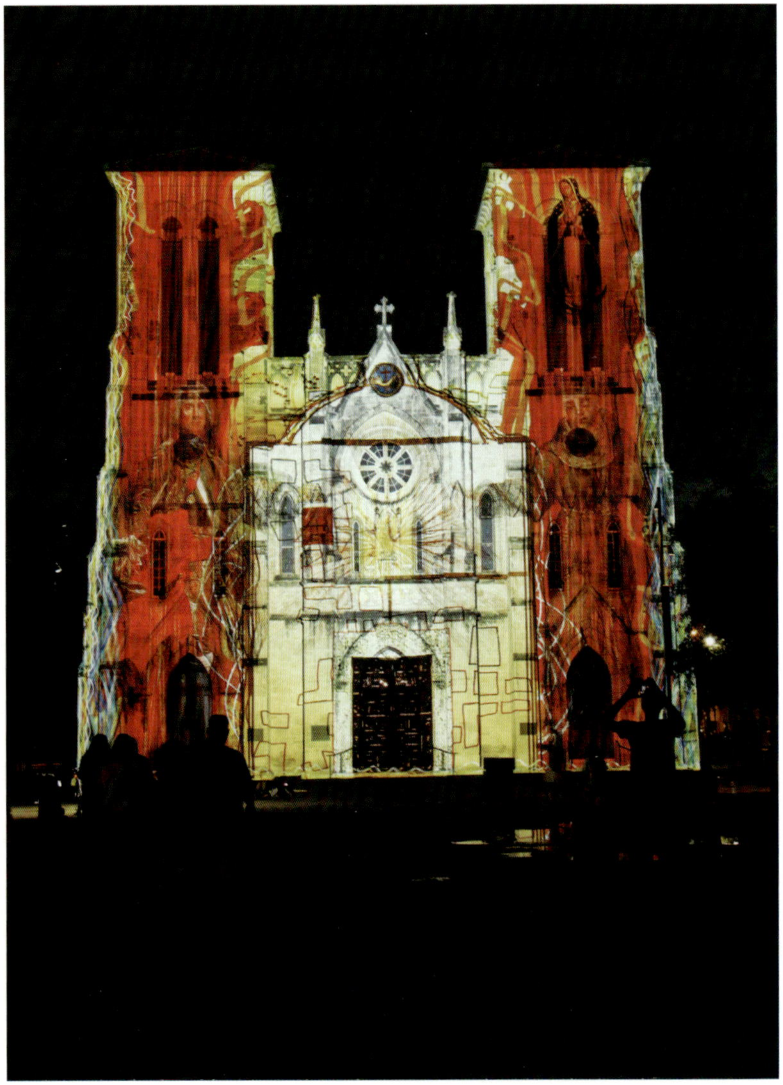

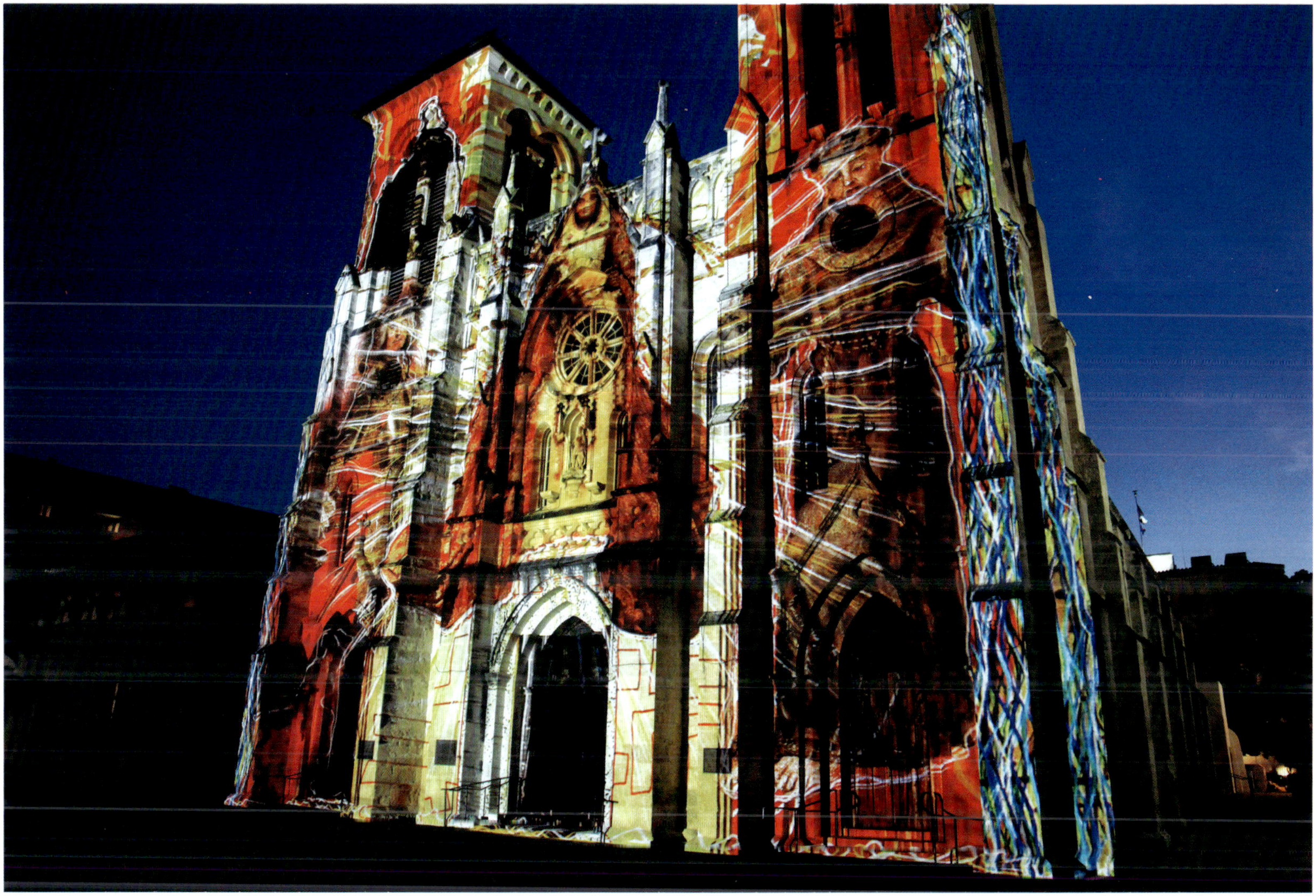

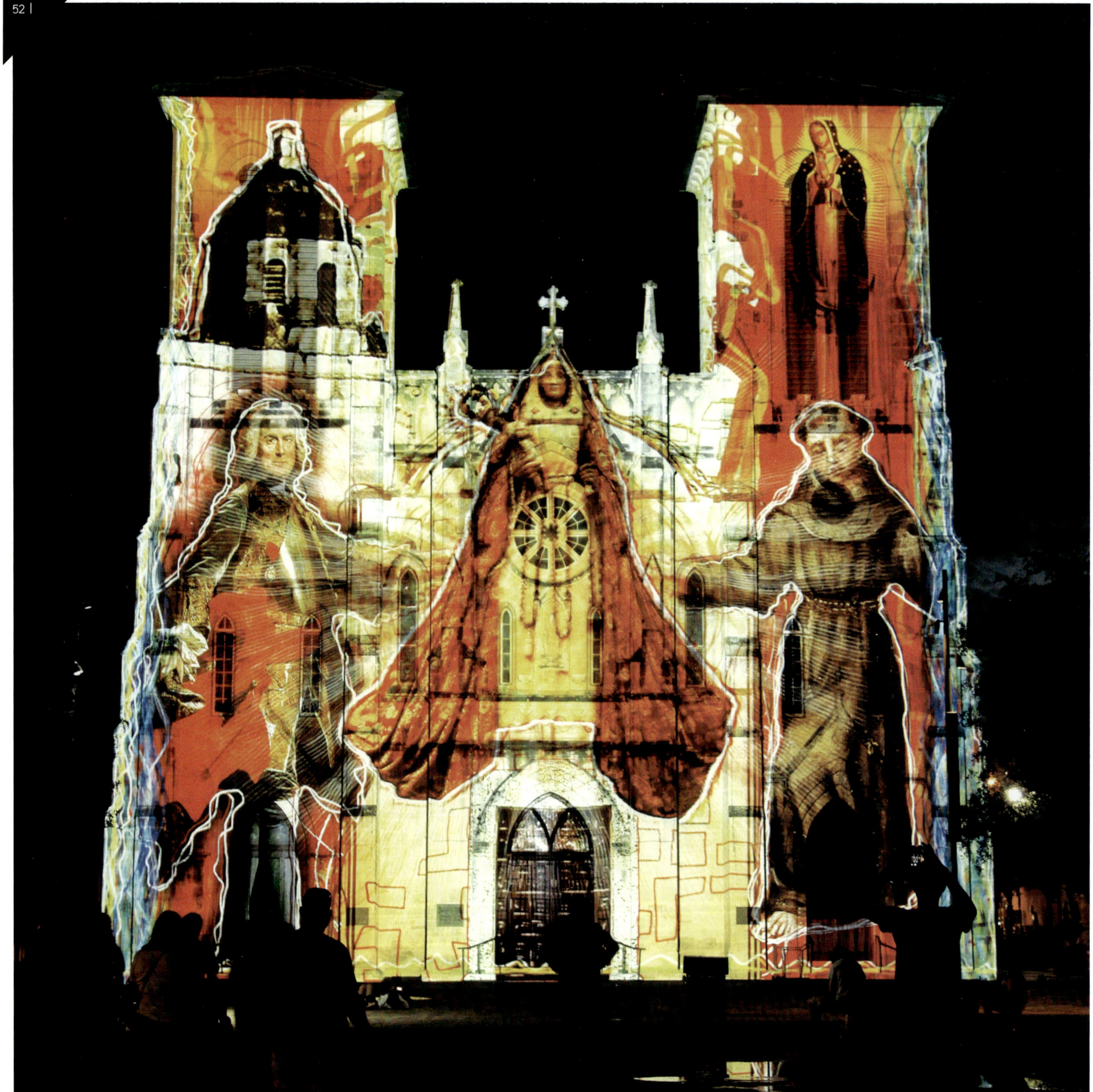

- SAN ANTONIO THE SAGA -

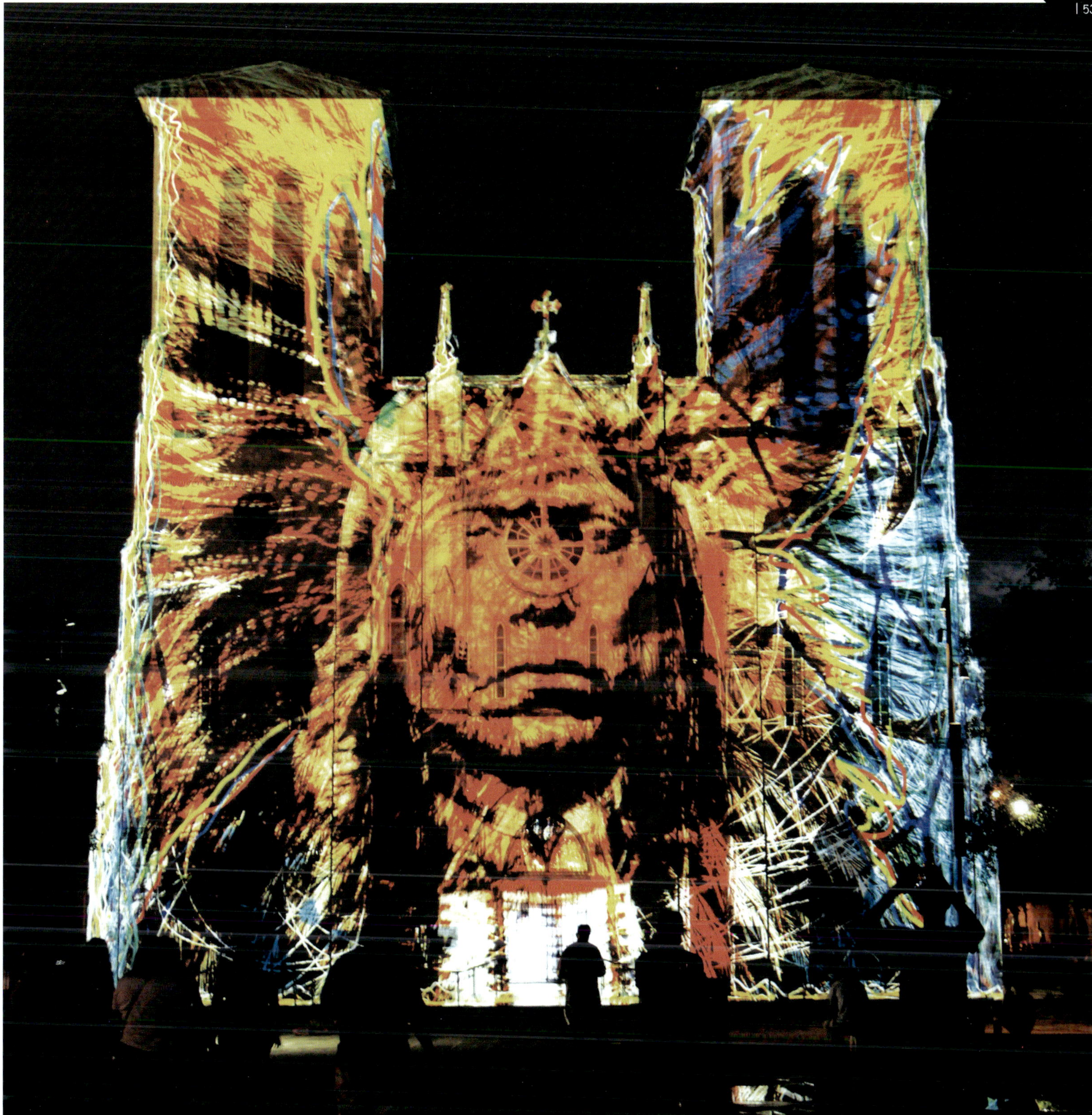

- SAN ANTONIO THE SAGA -

Sequence 5

ALAMO

FR. M. HIDALGO/ATOTONILCO

Gently the face of Quanah transforms into a *Mexican Catholic priest who called for revolution against the Spanish on September 16, 1810*. Fr Miguel Hidalgo his portrait rallied with Agustin de Iturbide and Antonio de Santa Anna. The Indian feathers change to colors of Mexican flag.

The Cathedral carries the colors of *Atotonilco, Gto,* a town near *San Miguel de Allende* where Hidalgo took Virgin de Guadalupe's banner as the rebels symbol.

Basilica of Atotonilco frescoes cover the walls of San Fernando.

THE FIGHT (ALAMO)

Texas belongs to Mexico but Texans do not accept the supervision of Mexicans. Frescoes are replaced by a rebel army gathered at Alamo mission. Among them Travis, Bowie, Bonham and Crockett. Two armies pictured as two groups of soldiers are now facing on the two towers, an American rebelious force on the left side, the Mexican legitimate army on the right side. The picture composition refers to Michelangelo's last judgement in the Vatican. Texan troops are outnumbered and without orders. Cathedral's towers move to clash and push back. Groups shiver in slow translation, shake in movement and smoke. Alamo defenders are pushed beyond their walls, the crowded Mexican army defeats the texans. Tower on right-hand side crushes the left side, Santa Anna is victorious. The music is quiet, the flute is alone.

HEROES

A catafalque is laid in front of the ruined fort.

At dawn four white marble statues appear from under the ground as four caryatids carrying the red white blue flag with the lonestar of the first Republic of Texas.

NOTE

The movement of Independence of Mexico under the banner of the Virgin of Guadalupe held up by the priest Hidalgo causes the revolt of 1810. Spaniards bring rebellion. A first attempt to independence of Texas is carried out in 1812 by Bernardo Guttierrez de Lara under the green emerald flag of free Texas that floats during one year. The crown of Spain put an end to this rebellion by crushing the Texans at battle of Medina, on August 8th, 1813, killing more than 1400 soldiers - symbols of Texas diversity, Americans, African Americans, Apaches, Texans, Spaniards.
The bases of the independence of Texas are however thrown. The independence of Mexico takes 11 years to be carried out and it is only in 1821 that the Mexican flag floats on the former Spanish colony.
Mexico wins independence and a constitution of Texas is signed in 1824 with the Mexican government. The Anglo-American population feels like owning these lands that they have cultivated and defended for years. Moreover the Mexican authorities starts the process of slavery abolition and it is not appropriate to Texas colonists.
The Texans assert the ground that they occupy and rebel against the Mexican authority. In October 1835, they organize the assault of San Antonio defended by Mexican General de Cos. The city is taken on December 9th 1835 and General Martin de Cos, brother in law of President of Mexico General Antonio Lopez de Santa Anna is constrained to abandon the city. He returns to Mexico after having promised to never return to Texas.
The pioneers of rebellion led by Jim Bowie and William Travis decide to strengthen San Antonio and Alamo in spite of the request for destruction of American General, Sam Houston.
General Santa Anna returns with important troops to besiege the rebels in violating the oath of Cos. The siege of Alamo lasts one month.
The Texans are crushed and Alamo falls on March 6th 1836. Bowie, Travis, Bonham, Crockett and more than 200 men are killed by Mexican army which thereafter executes 300 prisoners in Goliad. Shortly after, the Texan General Sam Houston defeats Santa Anna on April 1836 at battle of San Jacinto and obtains independence. The first Republic of Texas was born.

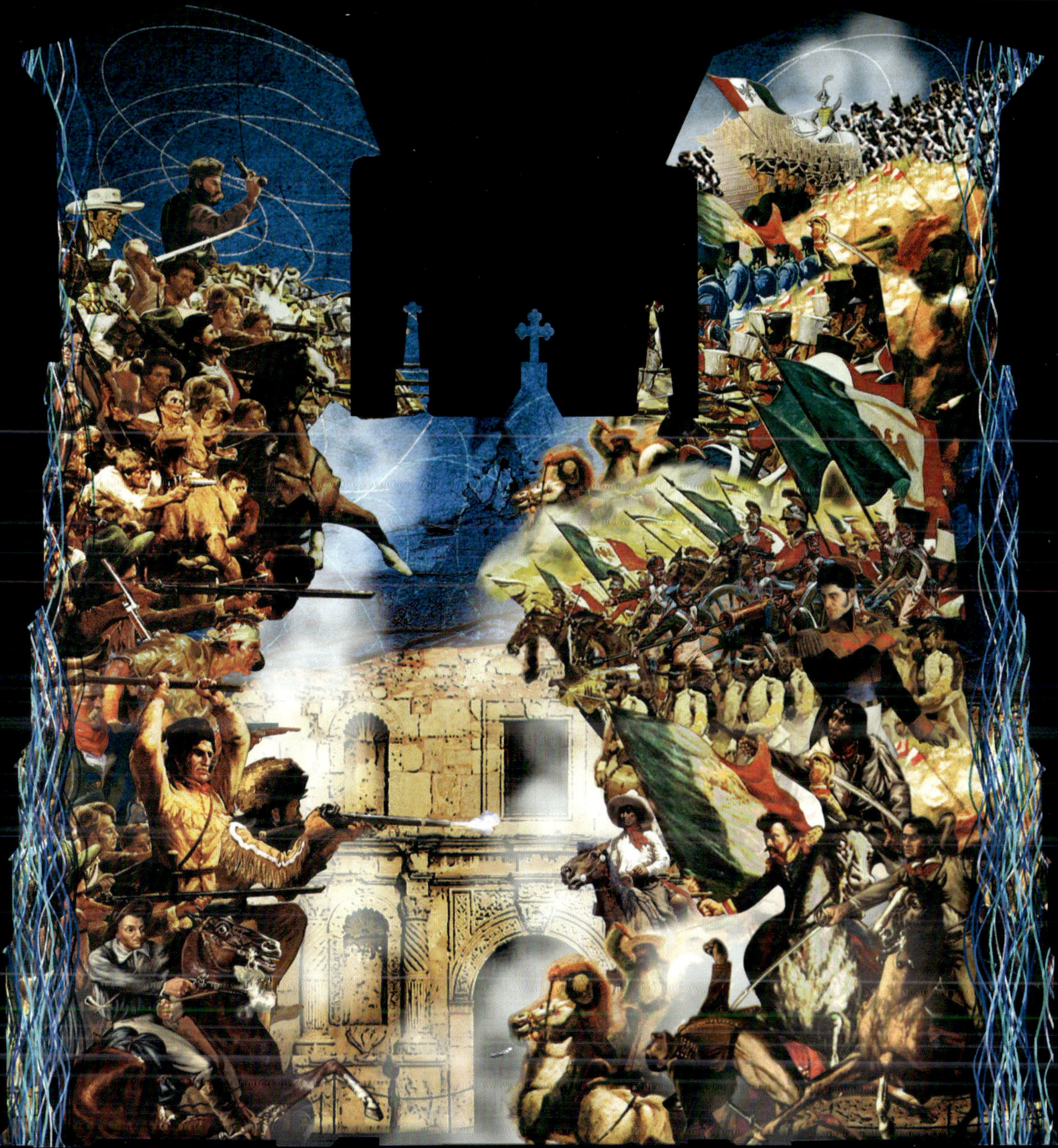

The Fight (Alamo)

FR. M. Hidalgo/Atotonilco

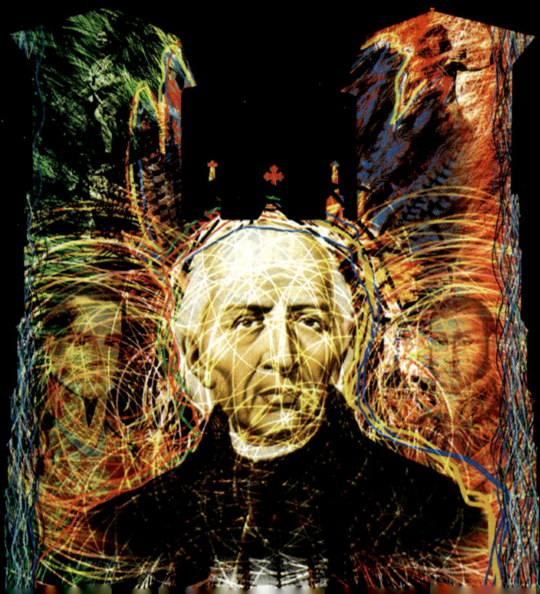

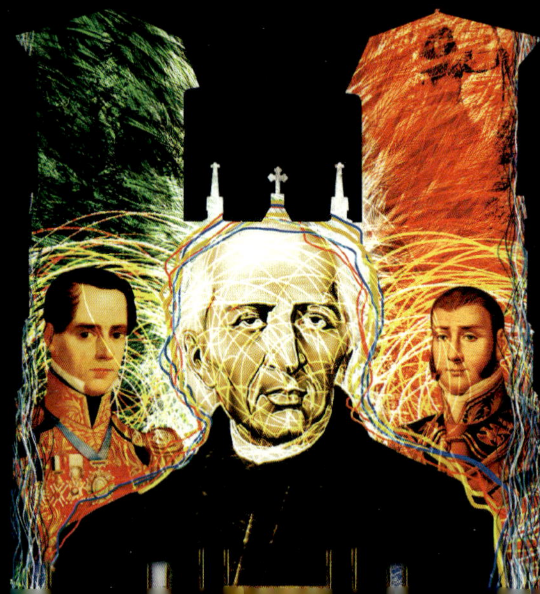

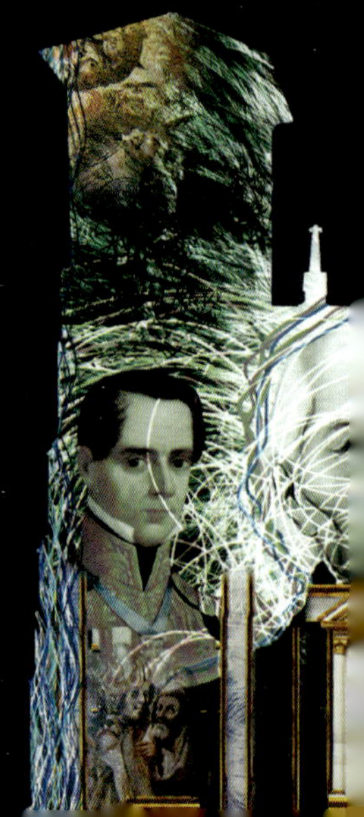

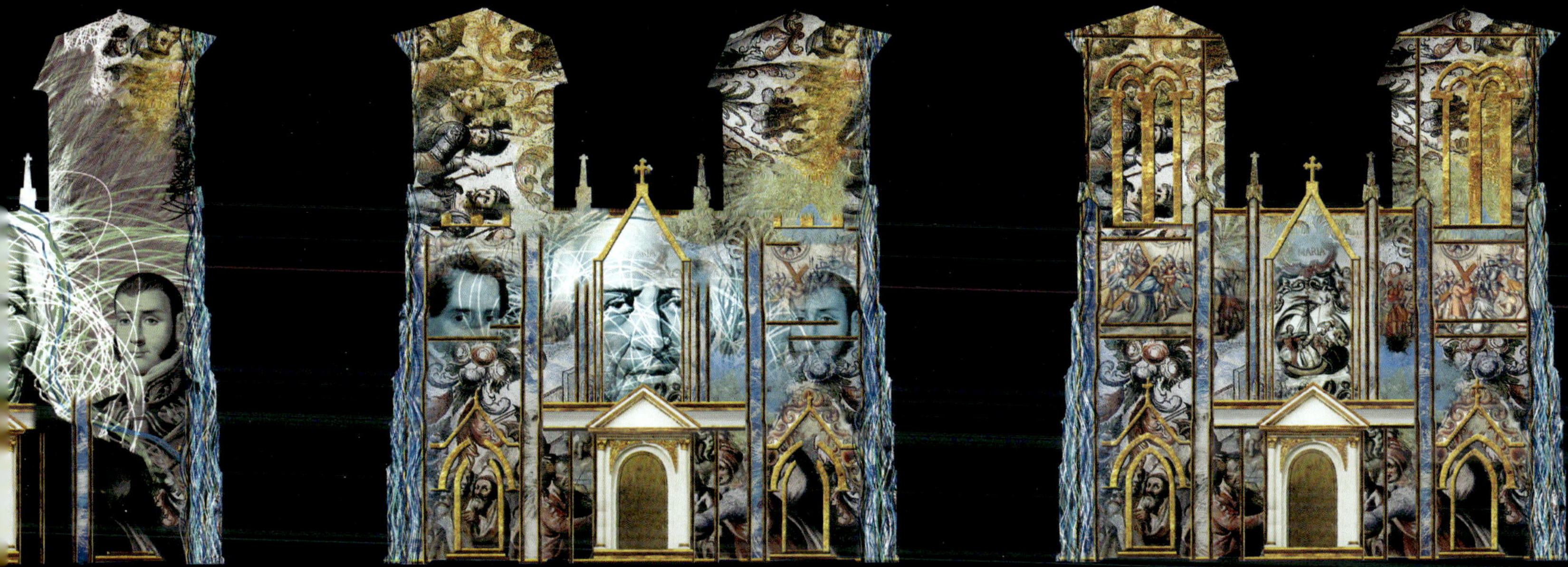

The Fight (Alamo)

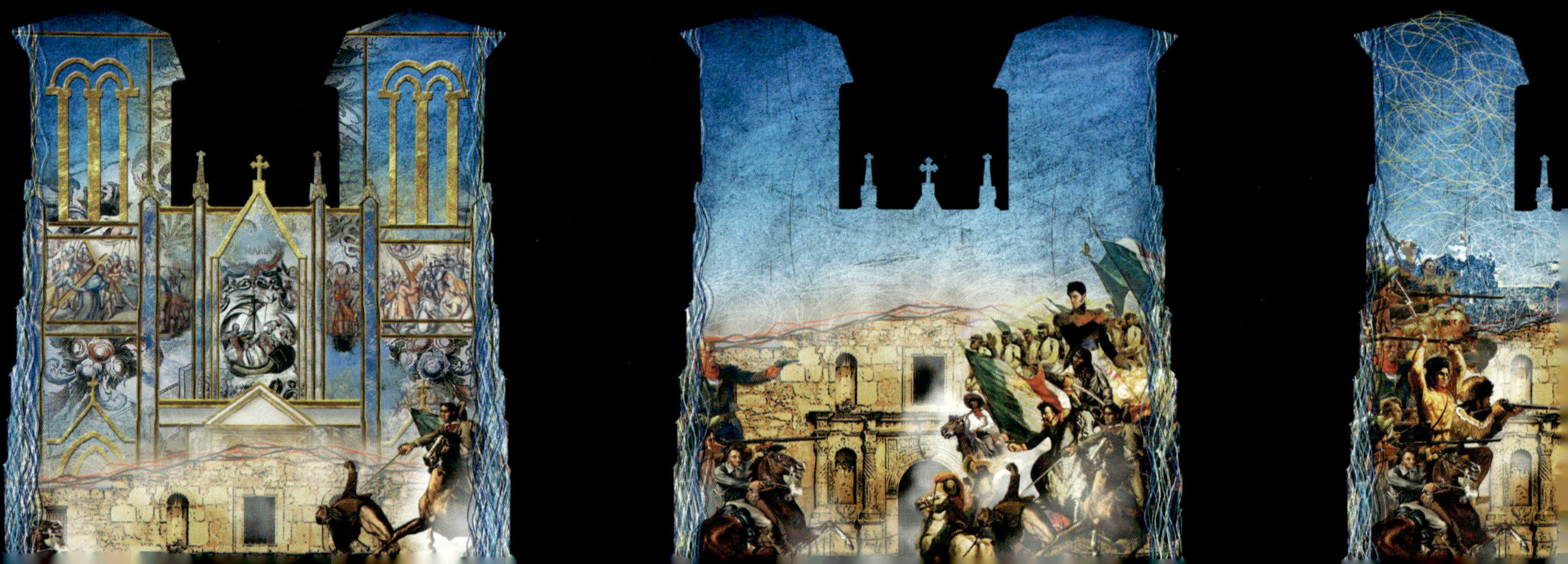

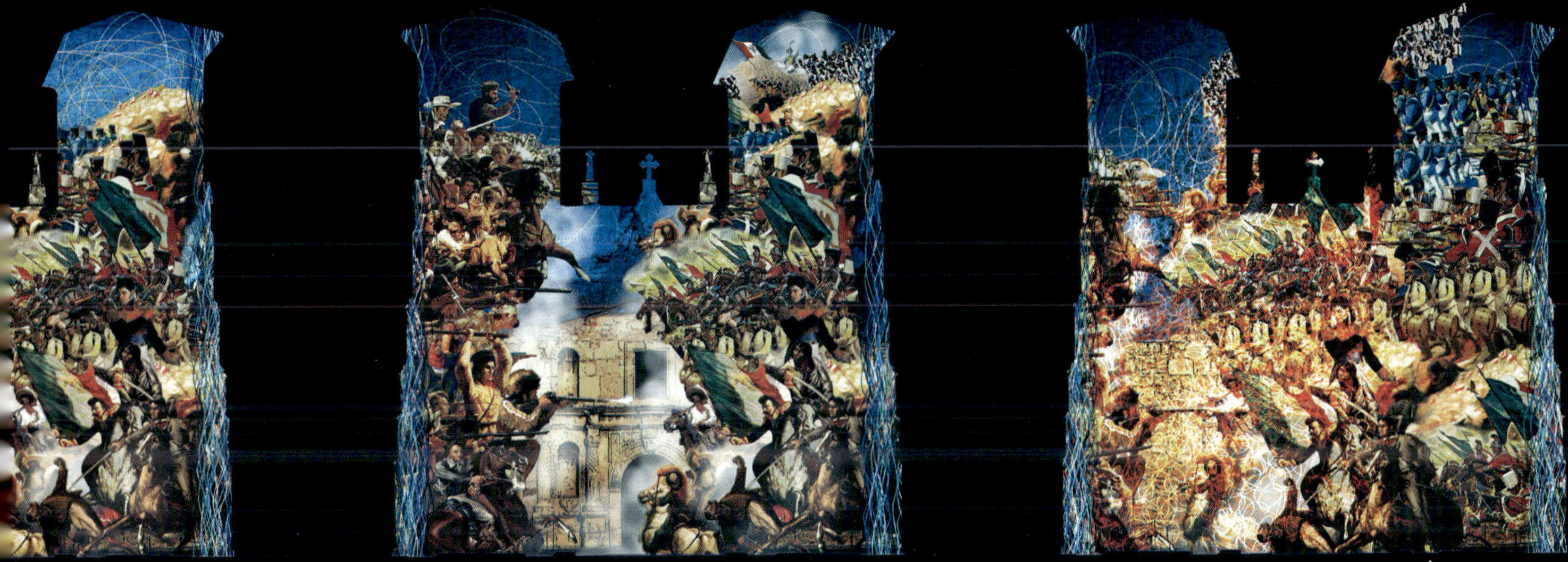

Heroes

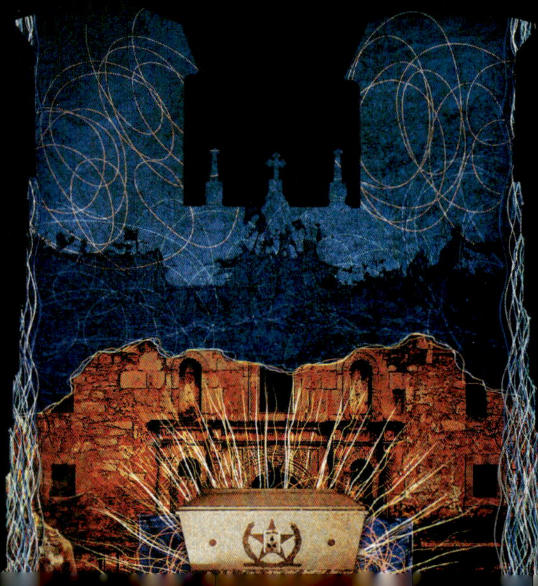

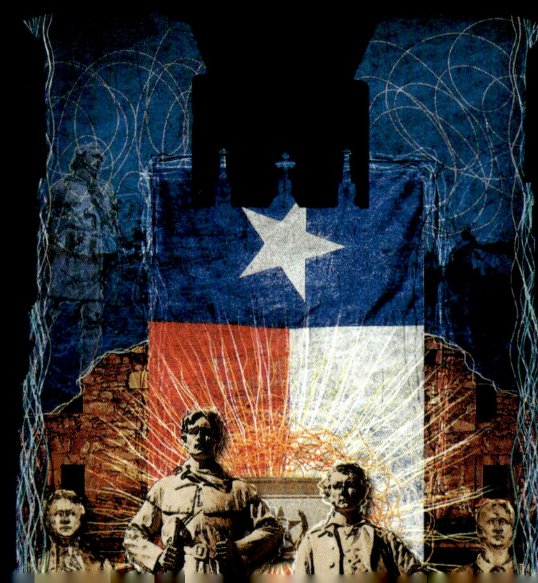

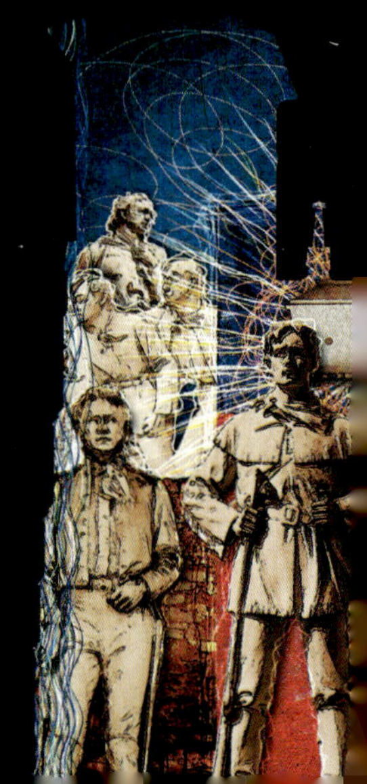

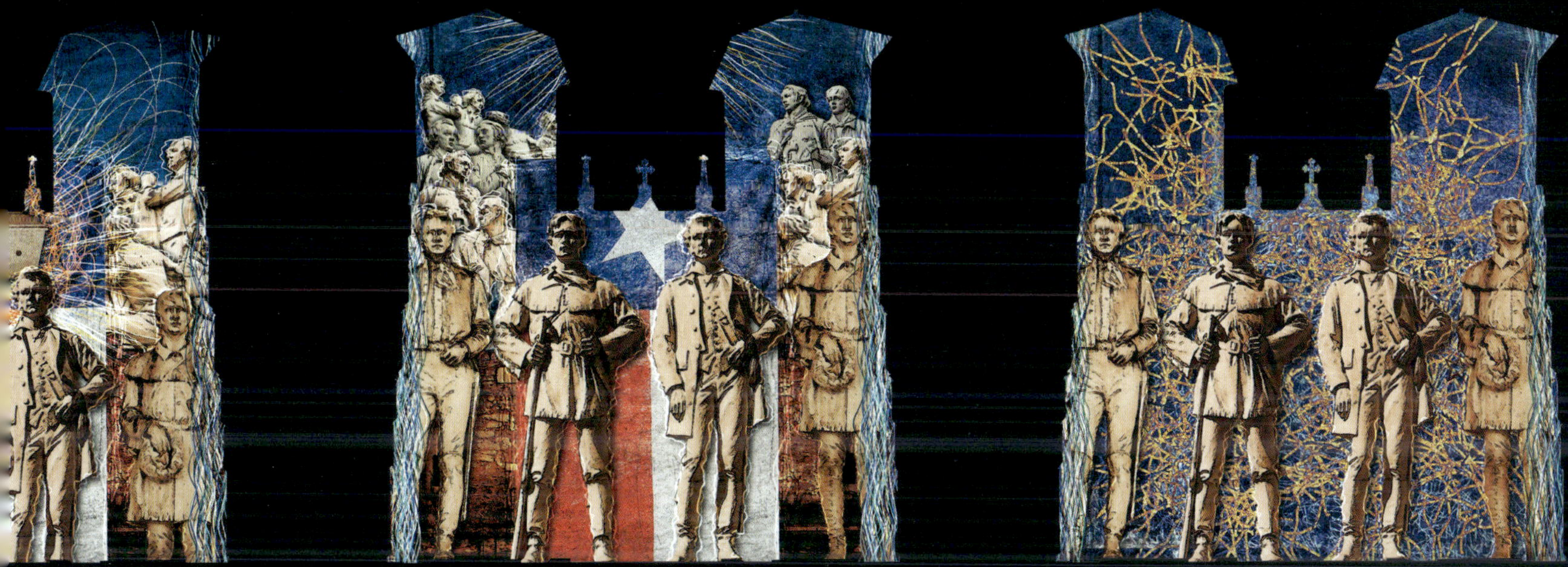

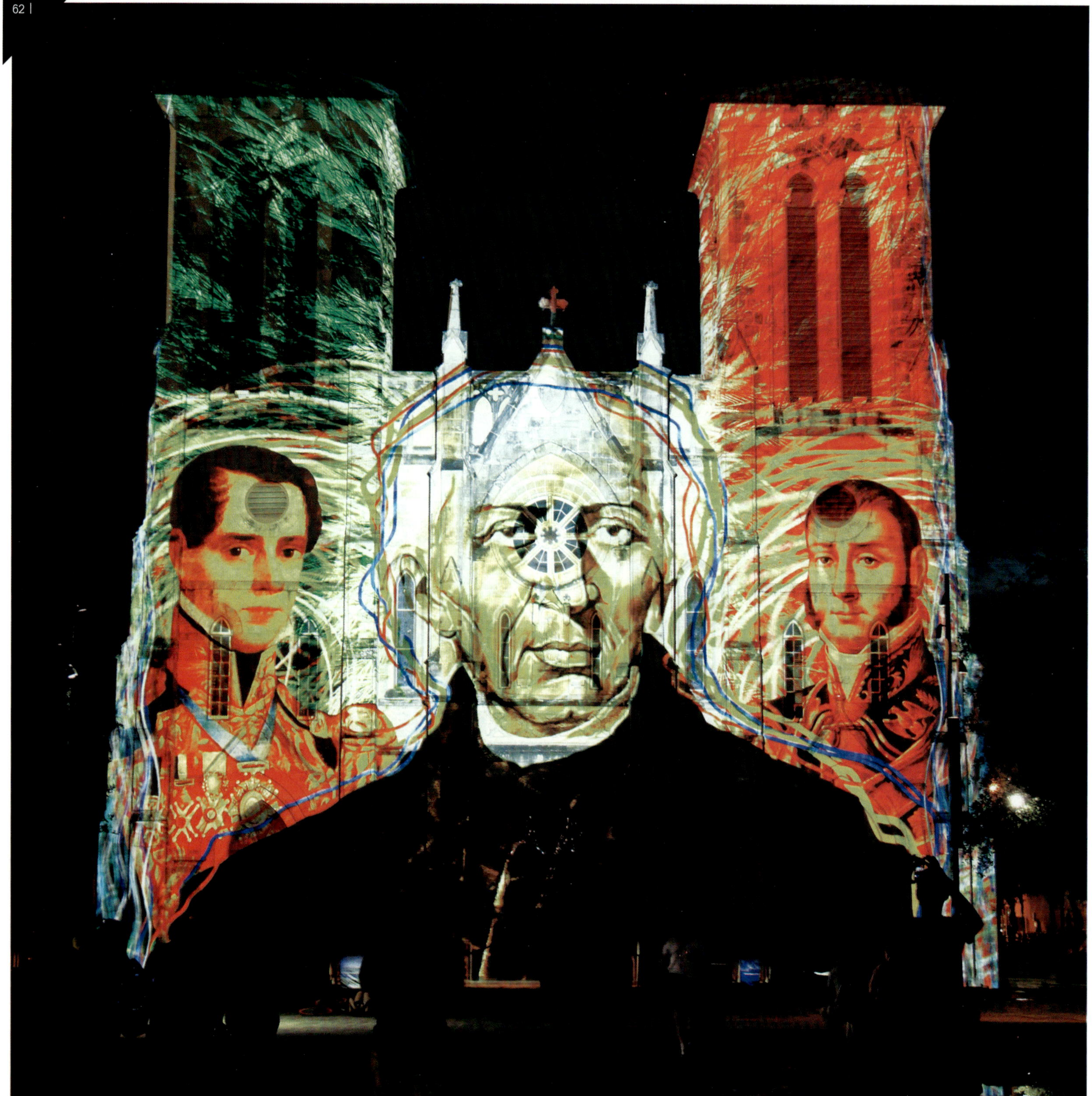

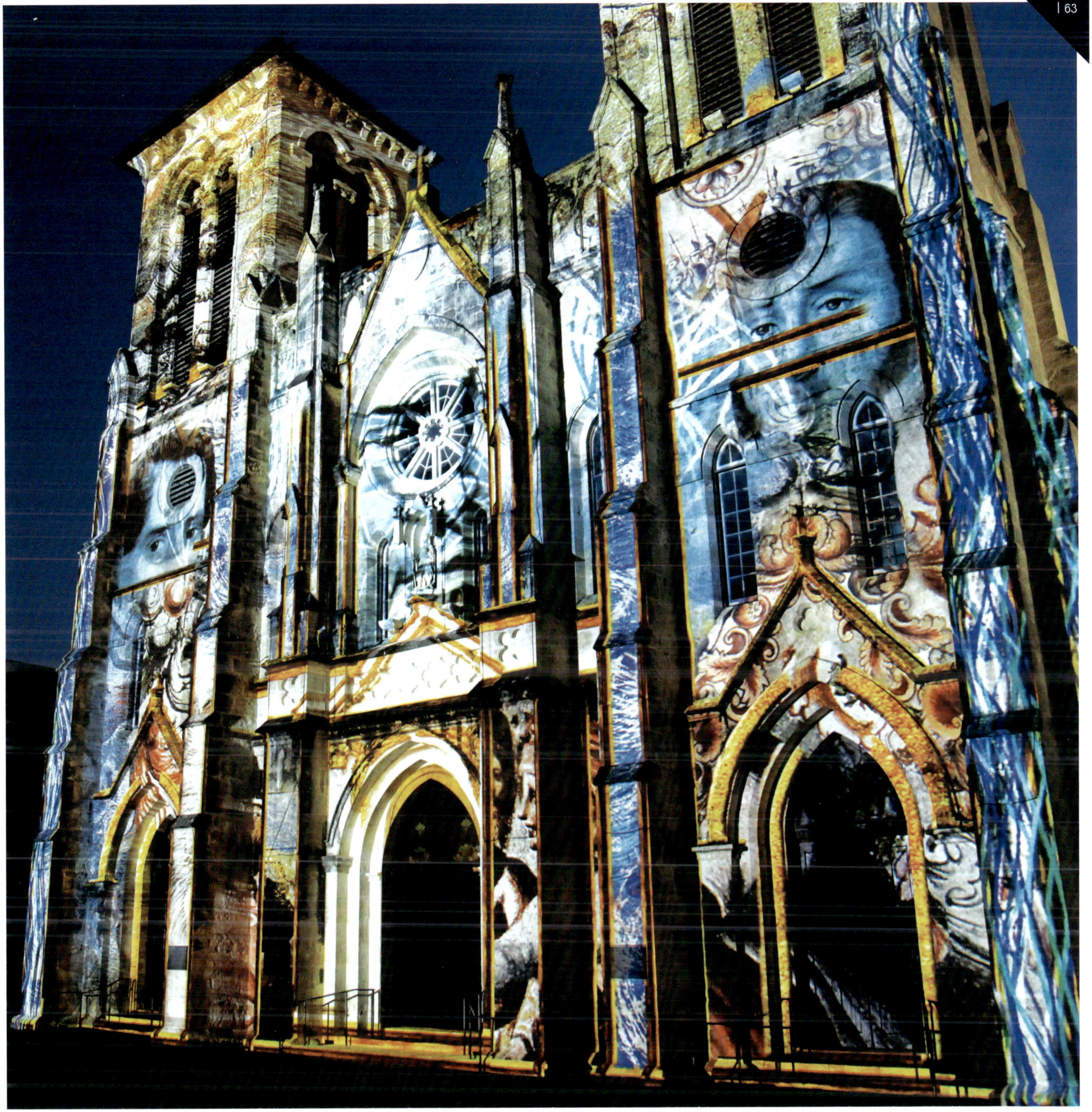

- SAN ANTONIO THE SAGA -

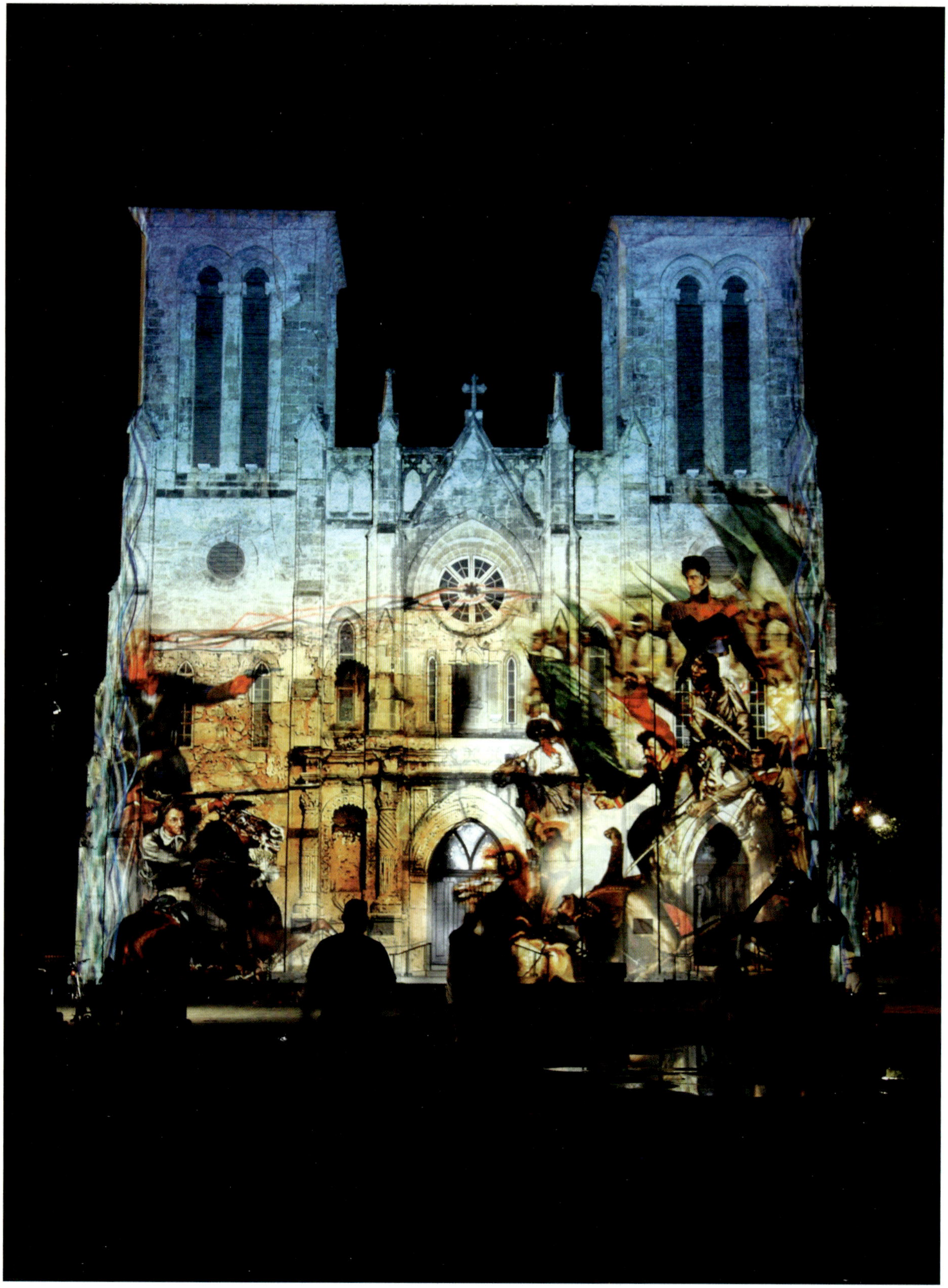

- SAN ANTONIO THE SAGA -

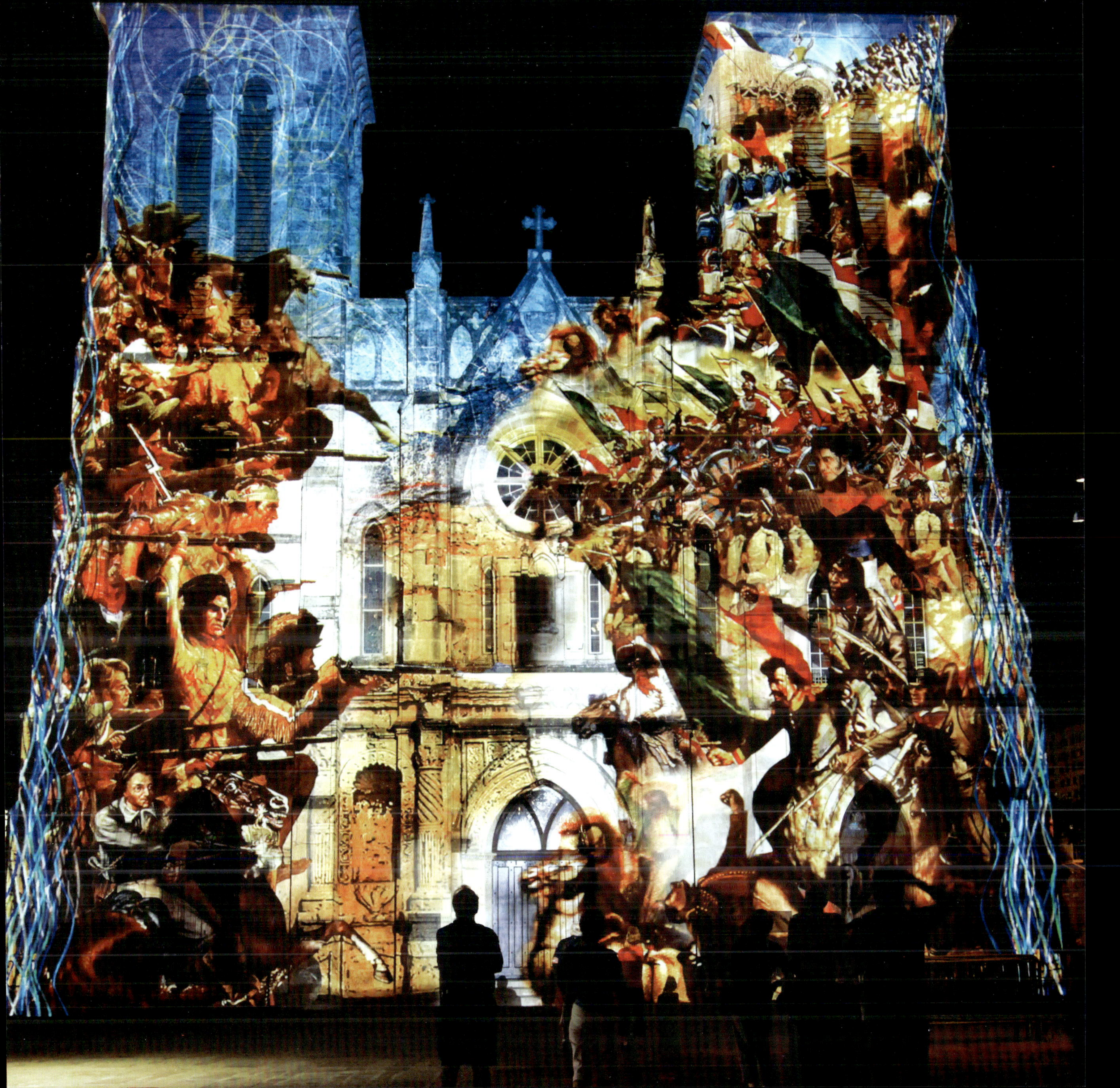

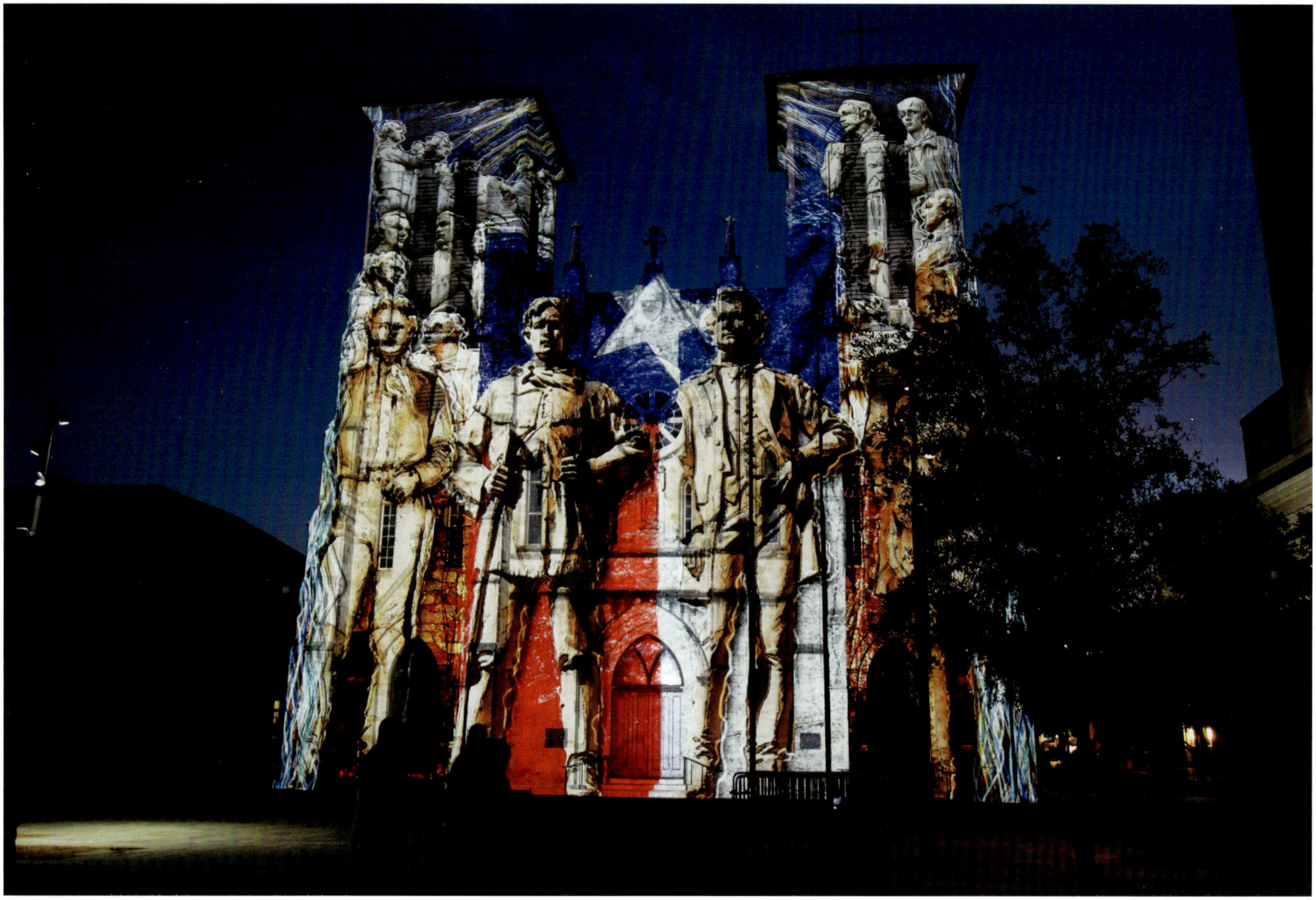

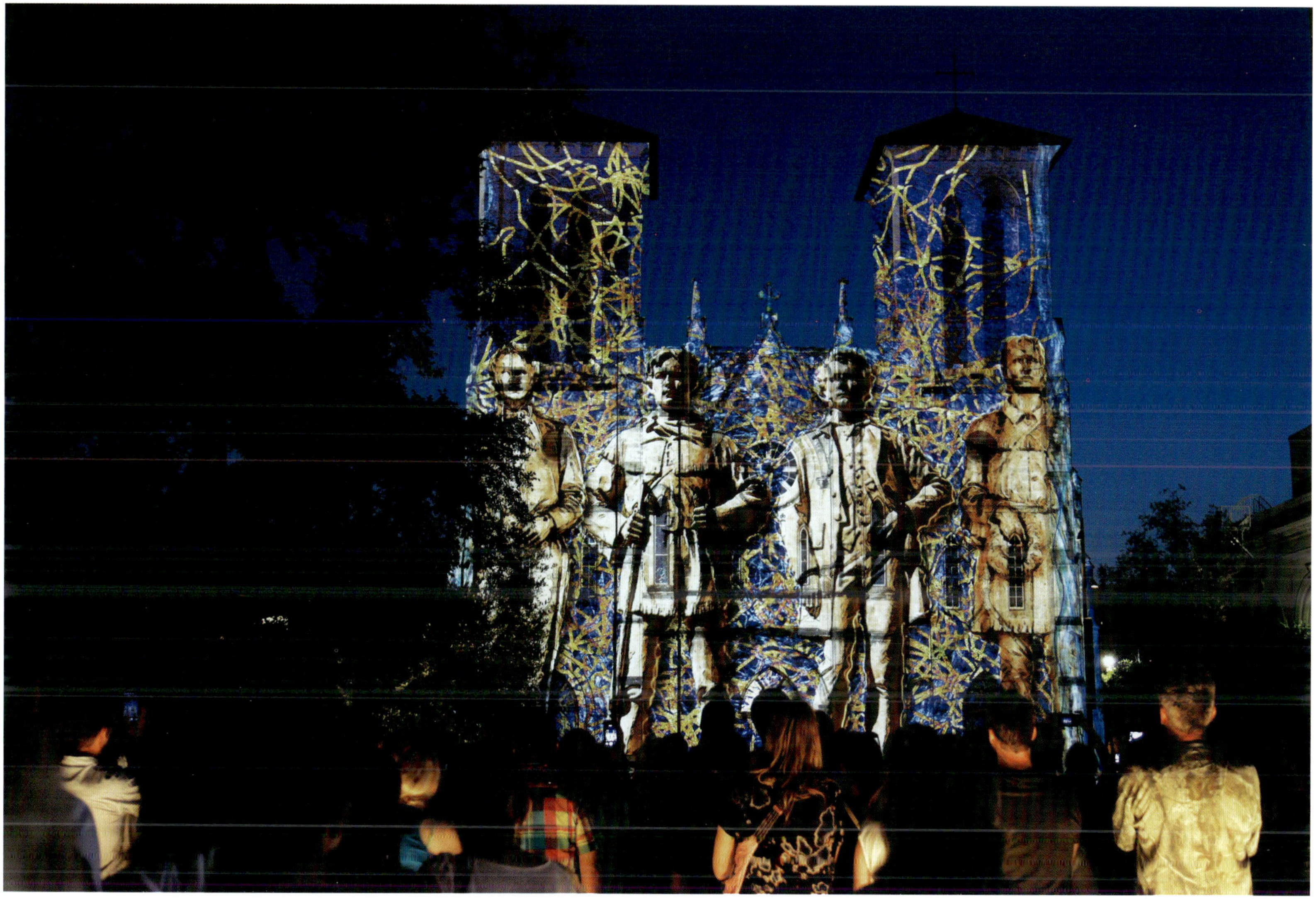

Sequence 6

CIVIL WAR

LINCOLN

The *Lonestar* Republic of Texas joined the states of the Union in 1845 to avoid the Mexican attempts to recover the Texan territory.

The blue and white stripes mix with stars to celebrate the union of the United States. White and blue gather with red to represent the 1860 flag.

Stars and stripes of the American banner organize and shape the United States of America.

Figure of Abraham Lincoln appears on the church's façade.

STRIPES AND BARS

With secession of Texas and other Southern states, the starry red cross of the Confederate flag rips through the American banner.

Stripes and bars are fighting about slavery, the country is devastated.

Buttons of uniforms and colors show separation between North and South.

Portraits of General Robert E. Lee shown on Cathedral right tower and General Ulysses S. Grant on left tower, shine back and forth. Northern stripes fight against Southern Crown of stars among heavy chains.

FREDERICK DOUGLASS

Frederick Douglass appears on the center of the southern battle flag, surrounded with chains and faces. He was a prominent American abolitionist, author and orator. Born slave, Douglass escaped at age 20 and went on to become a world-renowned anti-slavery activist.

War is over Chains are broken.

Stars and Stripes recompose the American flag while *Johnny goes marching home.*

Stripes are the basis for construction of a new country.

NOTE

Texas leaves the Union in 1861 after Abraham Lincoln is elected President of the United States of America in November 1860.
Civil war is quite fatal killing more than 600,000 in the two fields. It reveals a heavy economical competition related to slavery between the North and the South of the United States.
Lincoln's will to abolish slavery is an imperative reason for Southern secession.
The two sides flags wear the same colors, red, blue and white and contain white stars.
The flags are Stars and Bars" in the South and "Stars and Stripes" in the North.
The Union flag did not remove stars representing secessionist states, considering the confederation as illegal.
The confederate flag will count from 7 to 13 stars and will serve between 1861 and 1865.
The confederate flag carrying a spangled cross with 13 stars posed on a Saint Andrew cross is a war flag. It has similitude with the cross of New Spain.
The flag with the crown of stars is the original confederate flag.
Texas definitely joined the Union in 1870.
The music, "The Battle Cry of Freedom" was written by George Frederick Root during the war and was used by both armies... the lyrics were adapted with different words.
The song about "When Johnny Comes Marching Home" was also common to both sides.

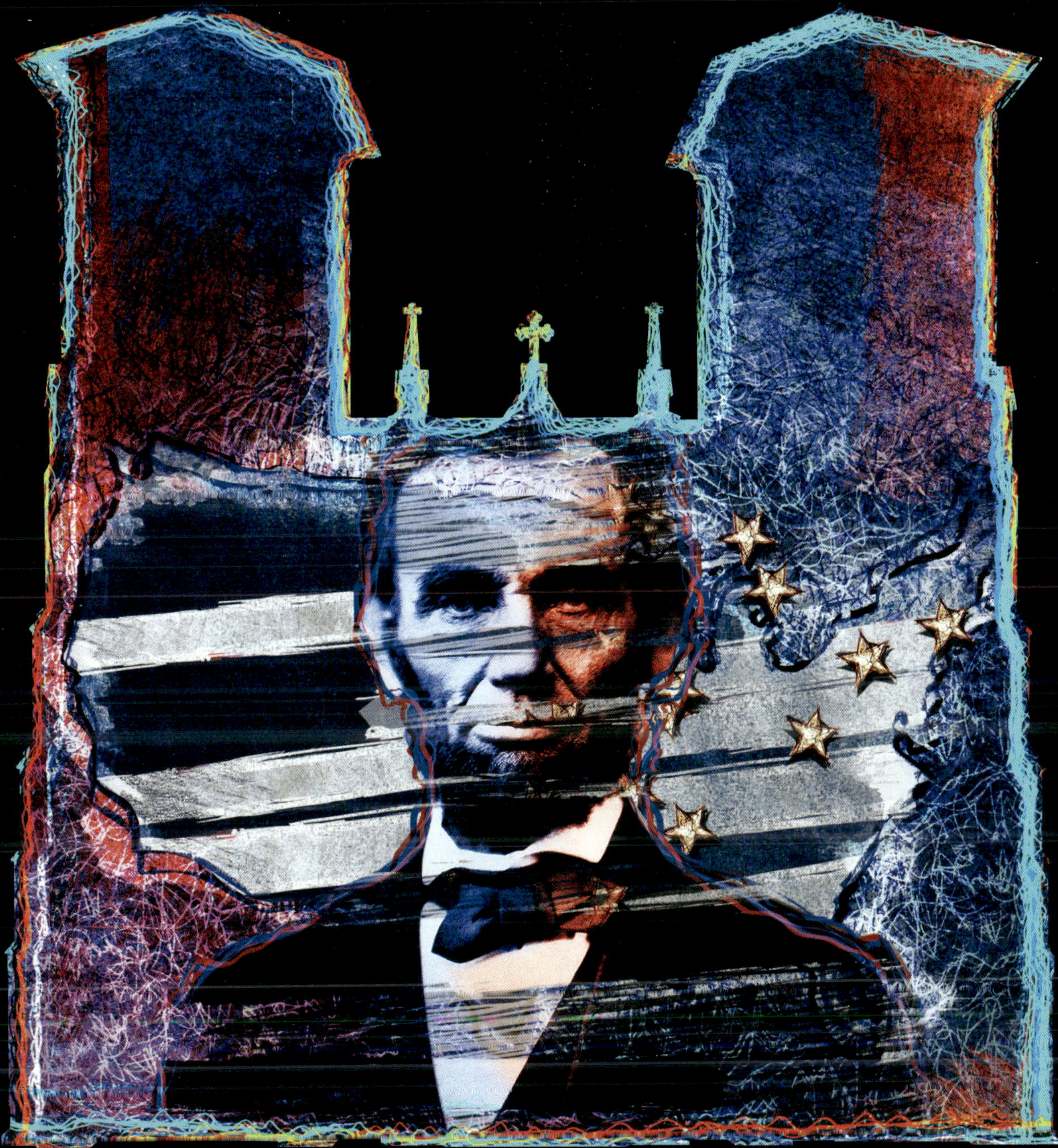

Lincoln

Lincoln

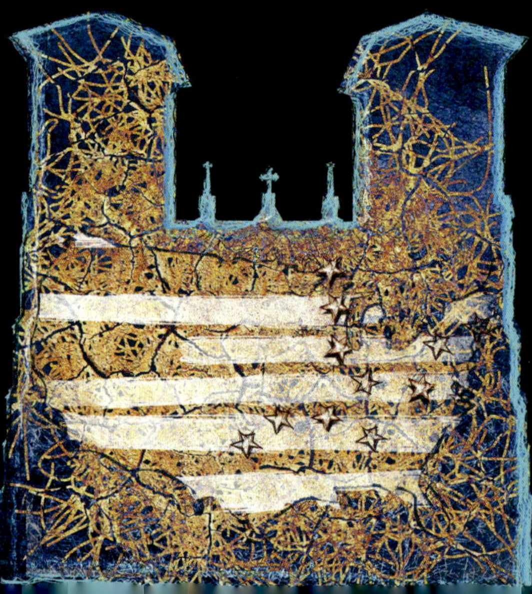

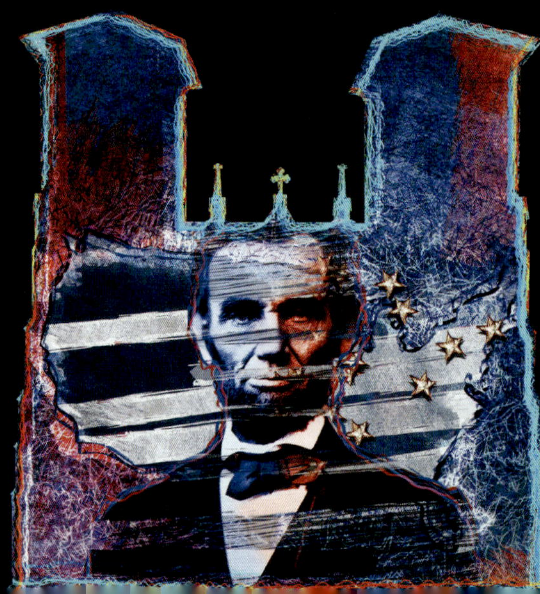

Stripes and Bars

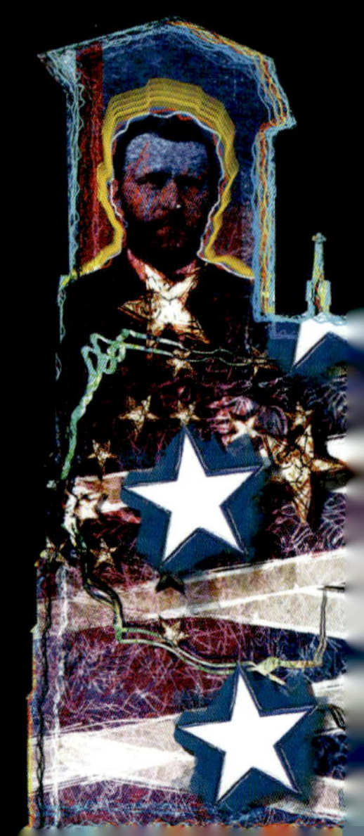

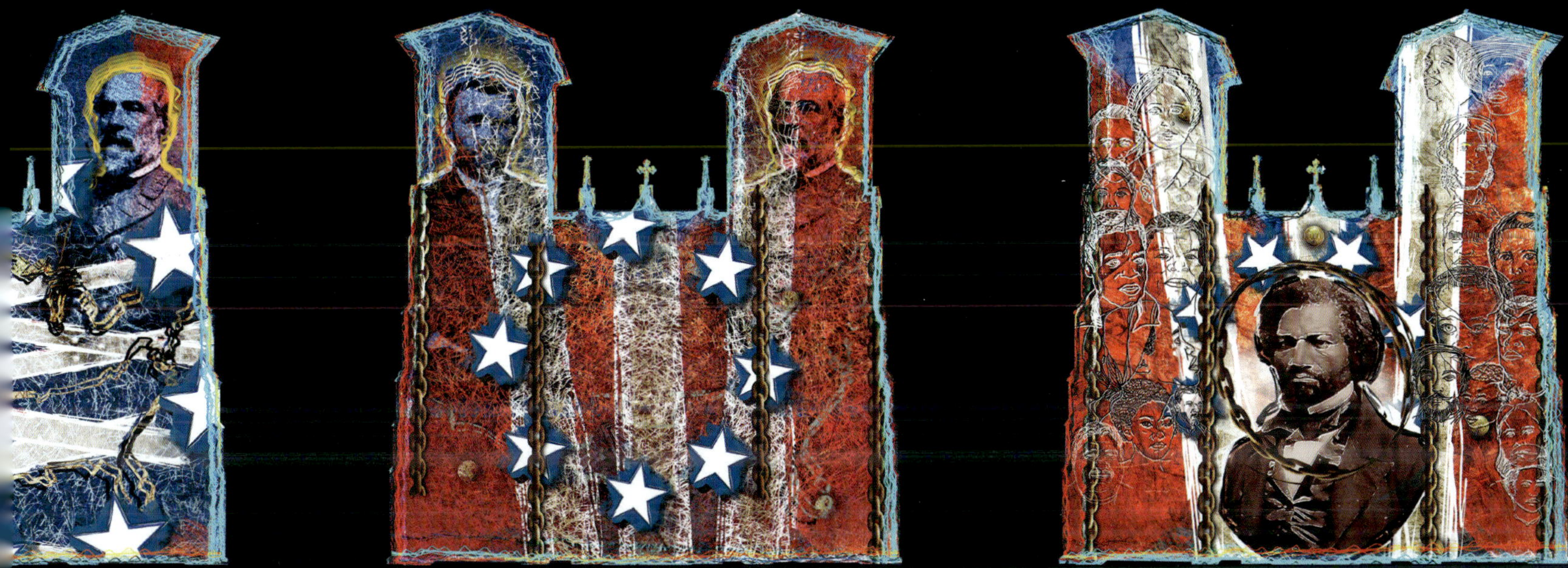

Frederick Douglass

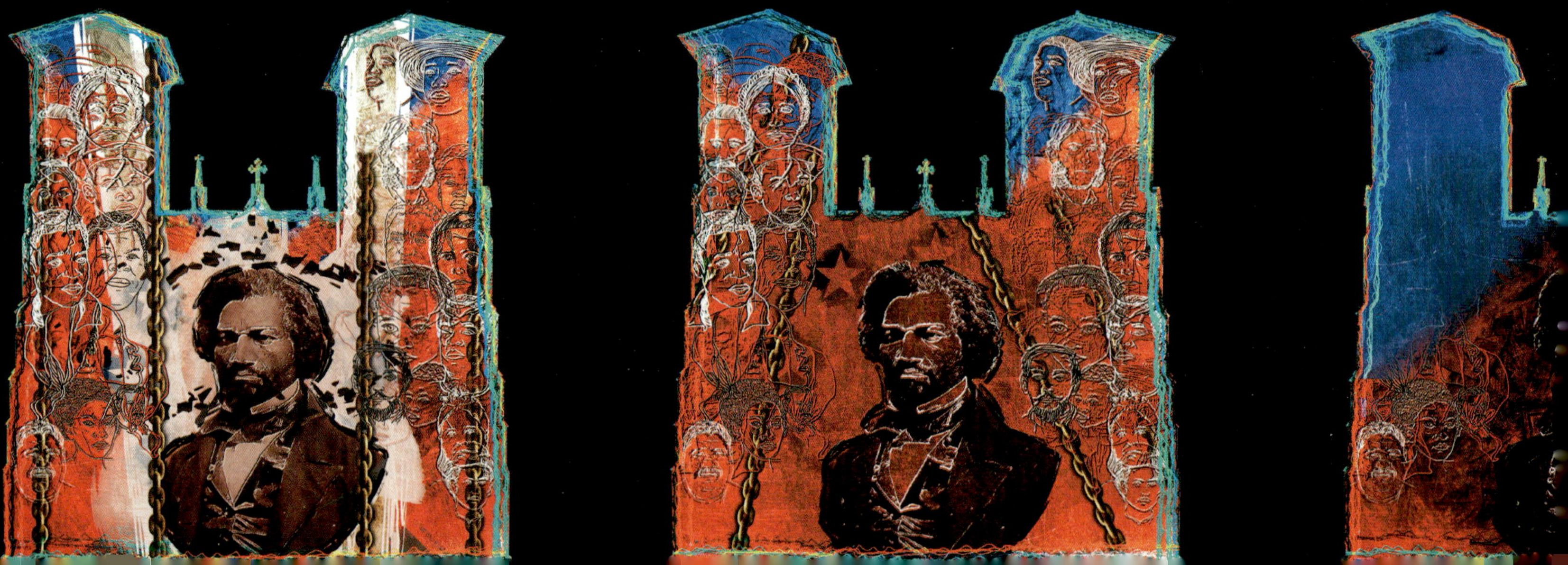

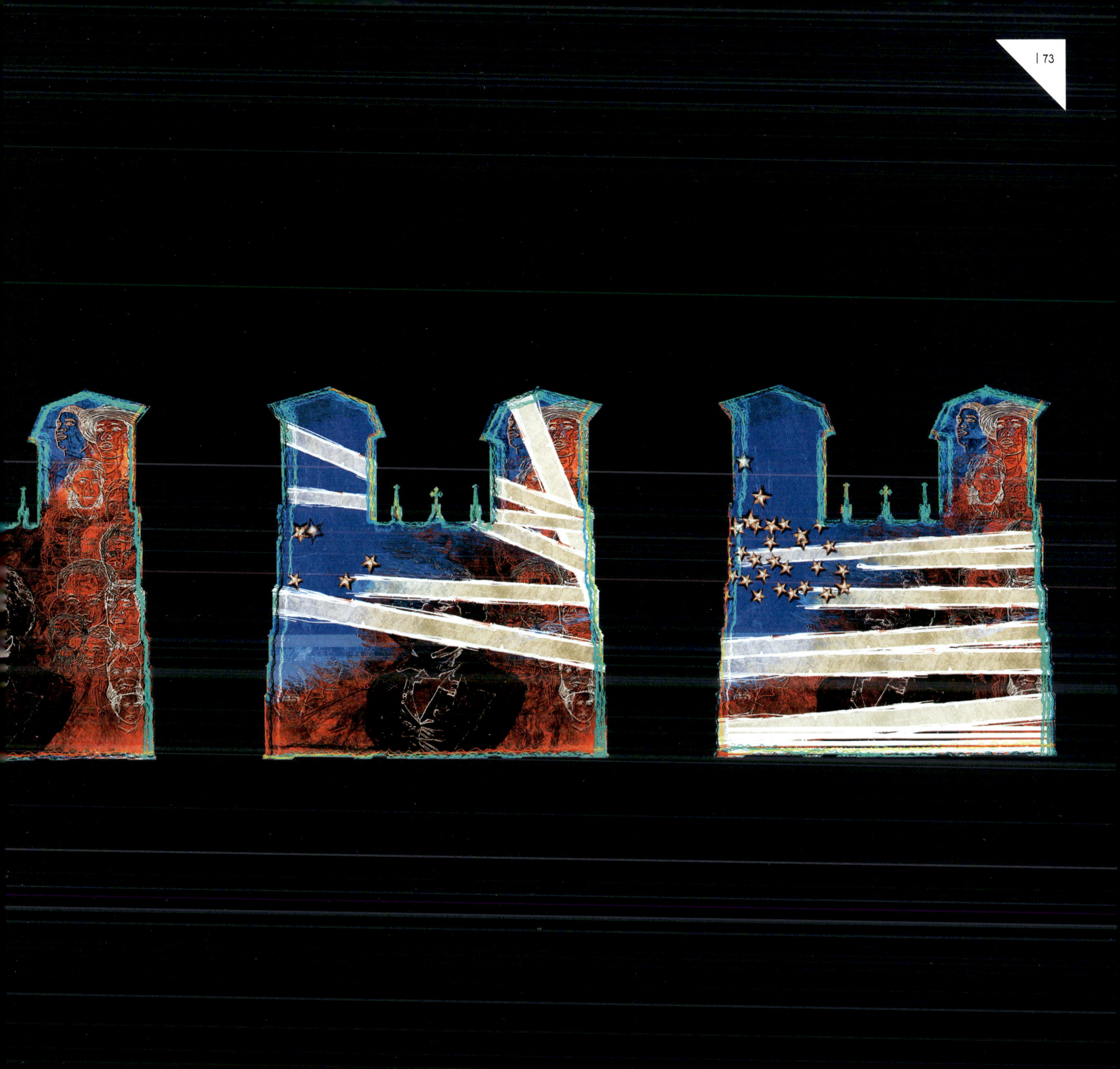

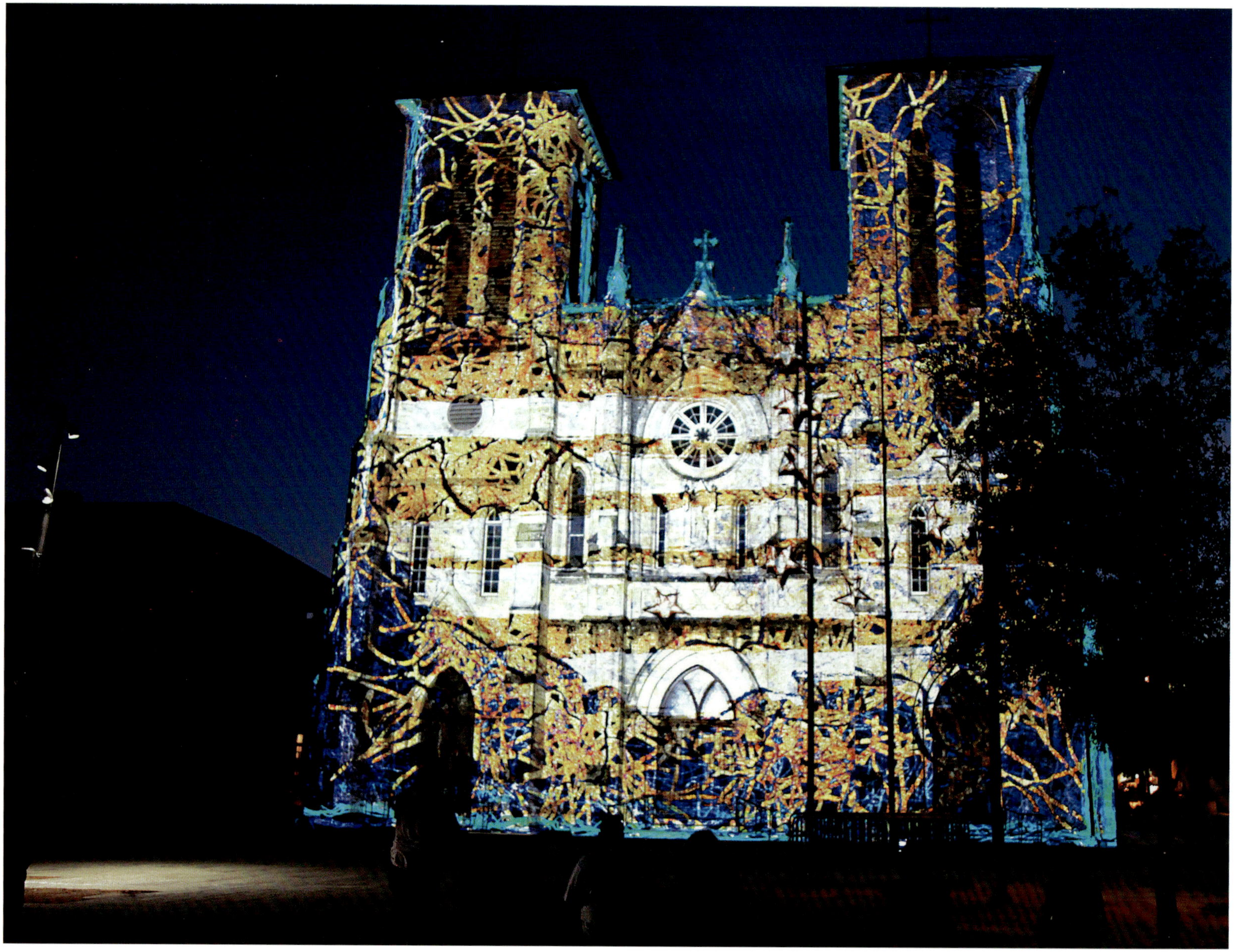

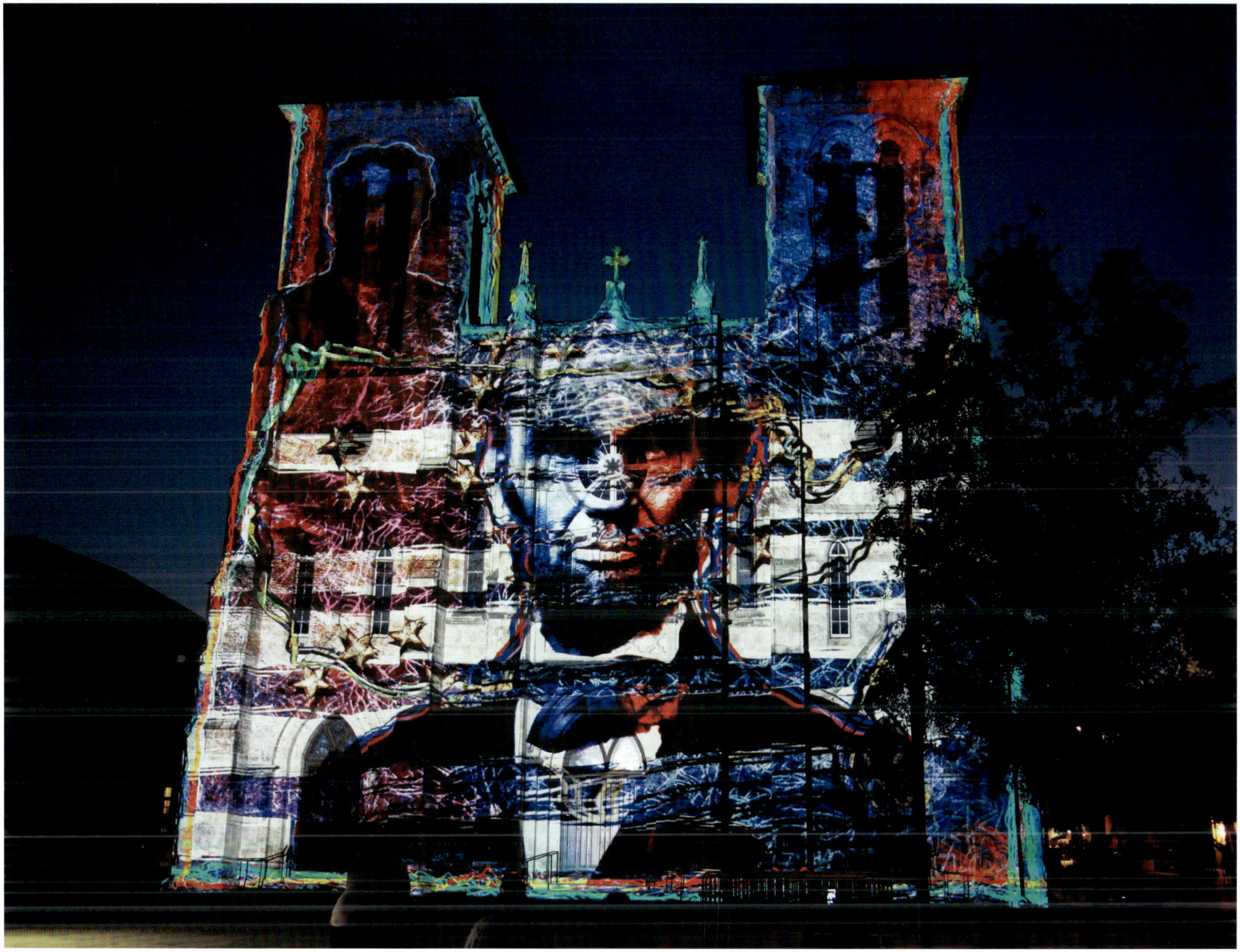

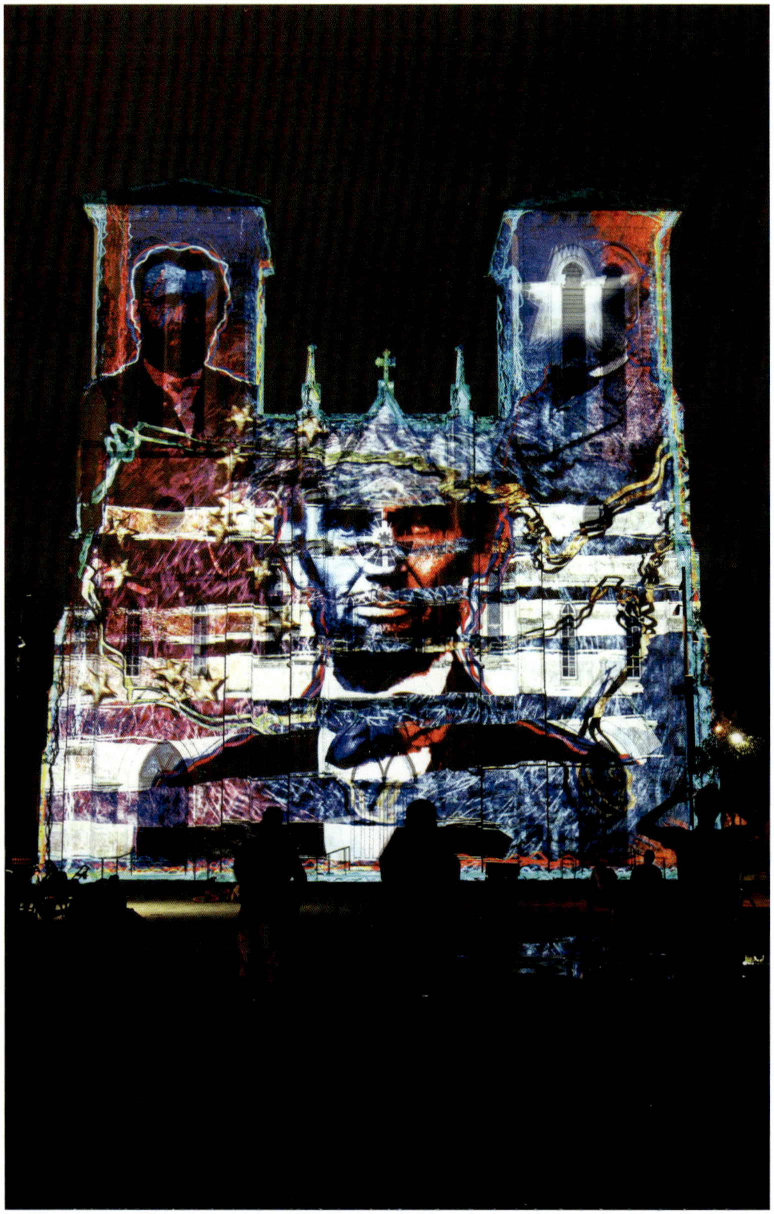

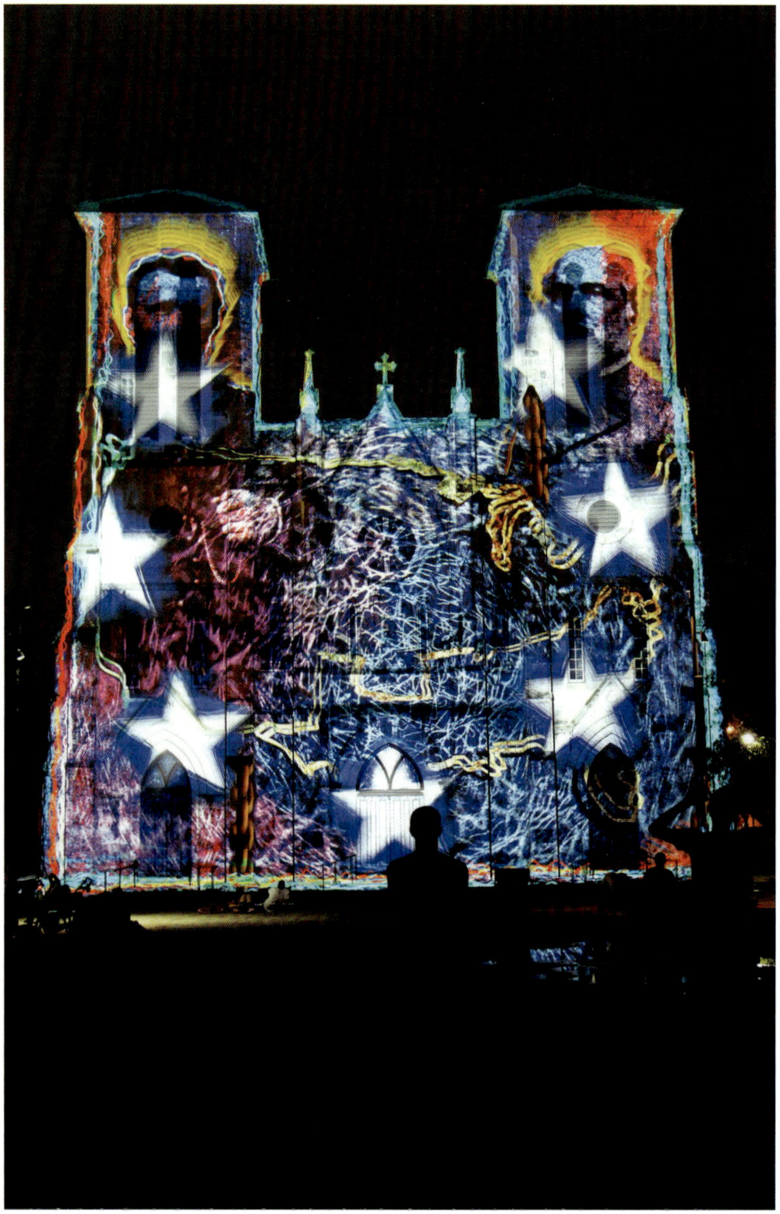

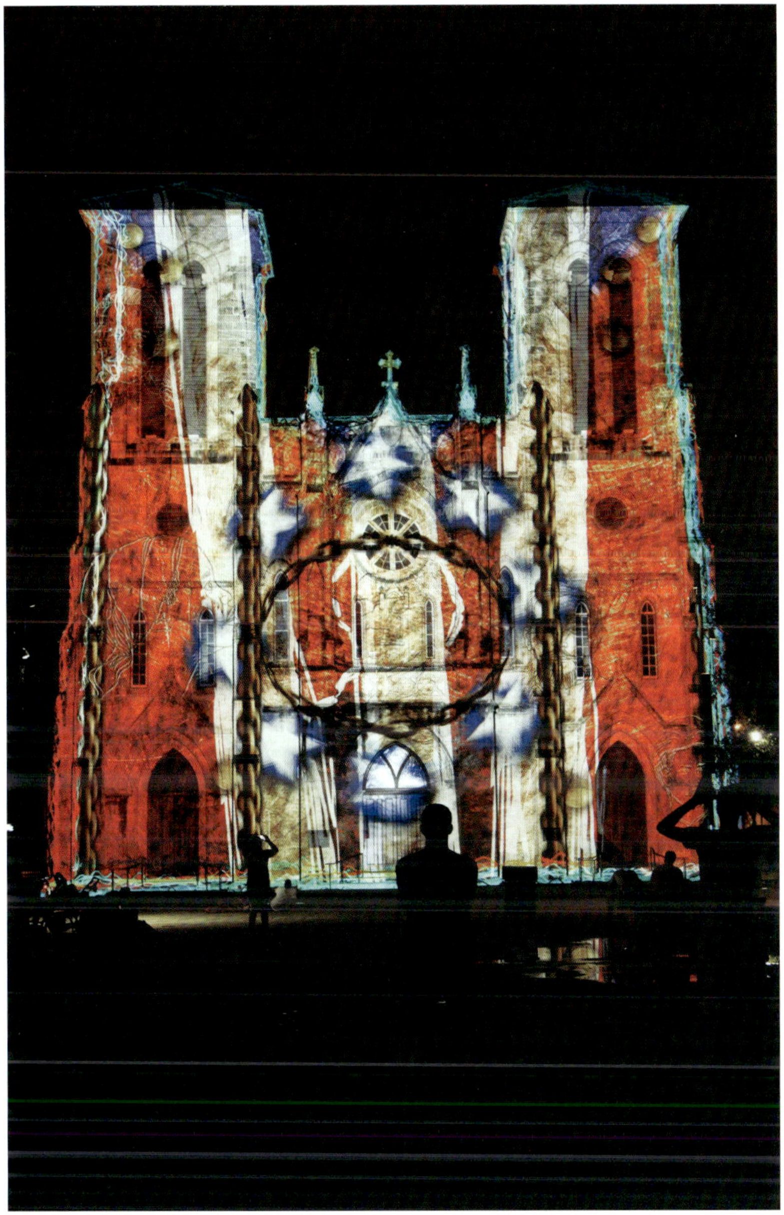

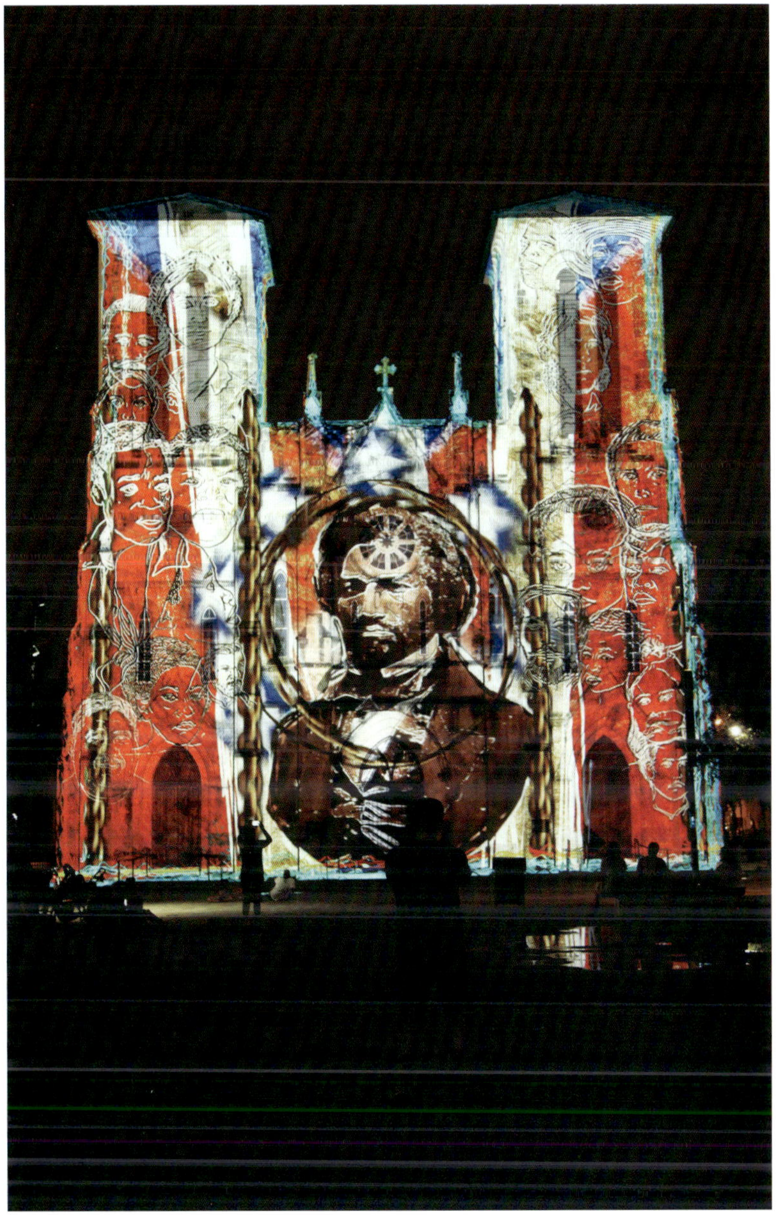

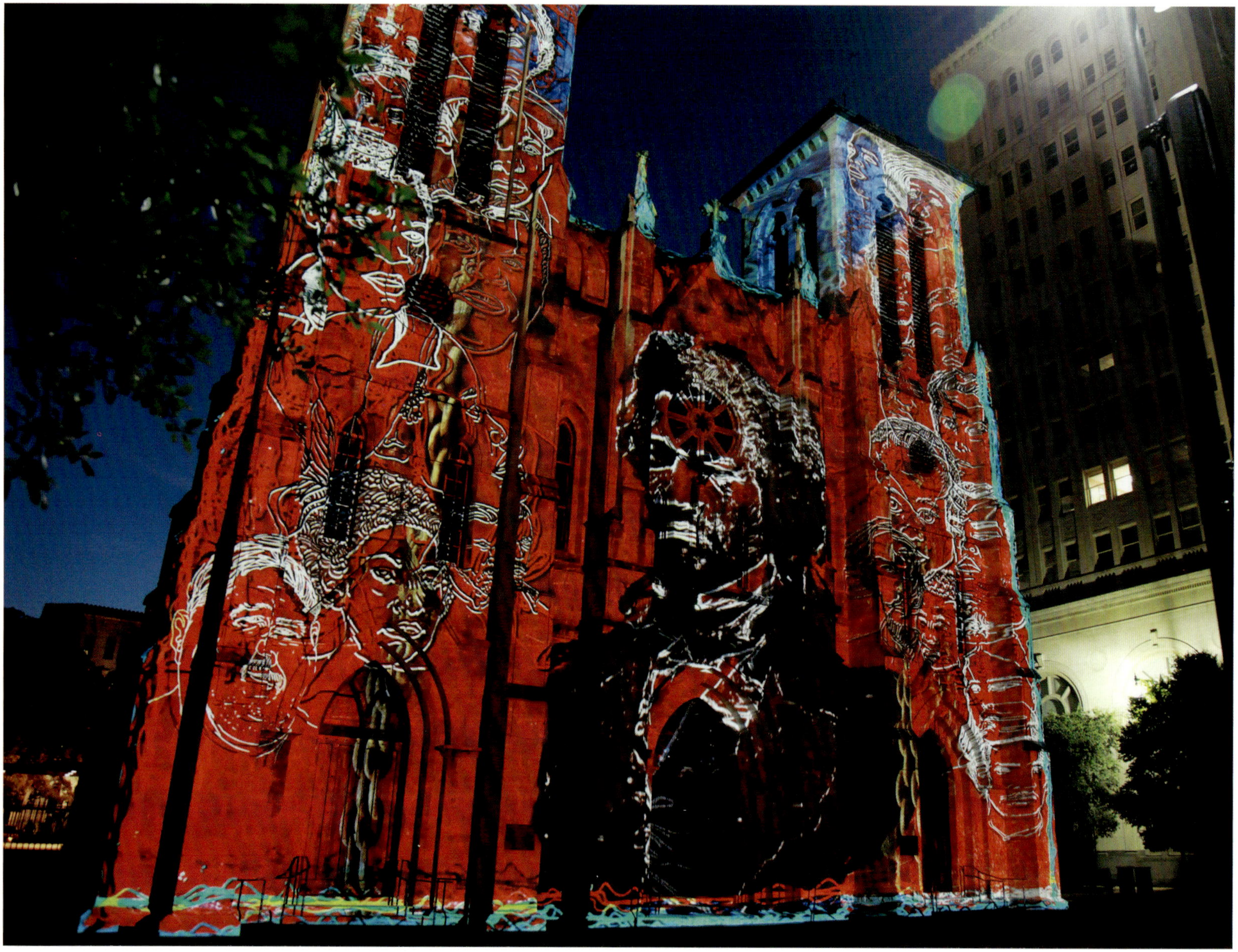

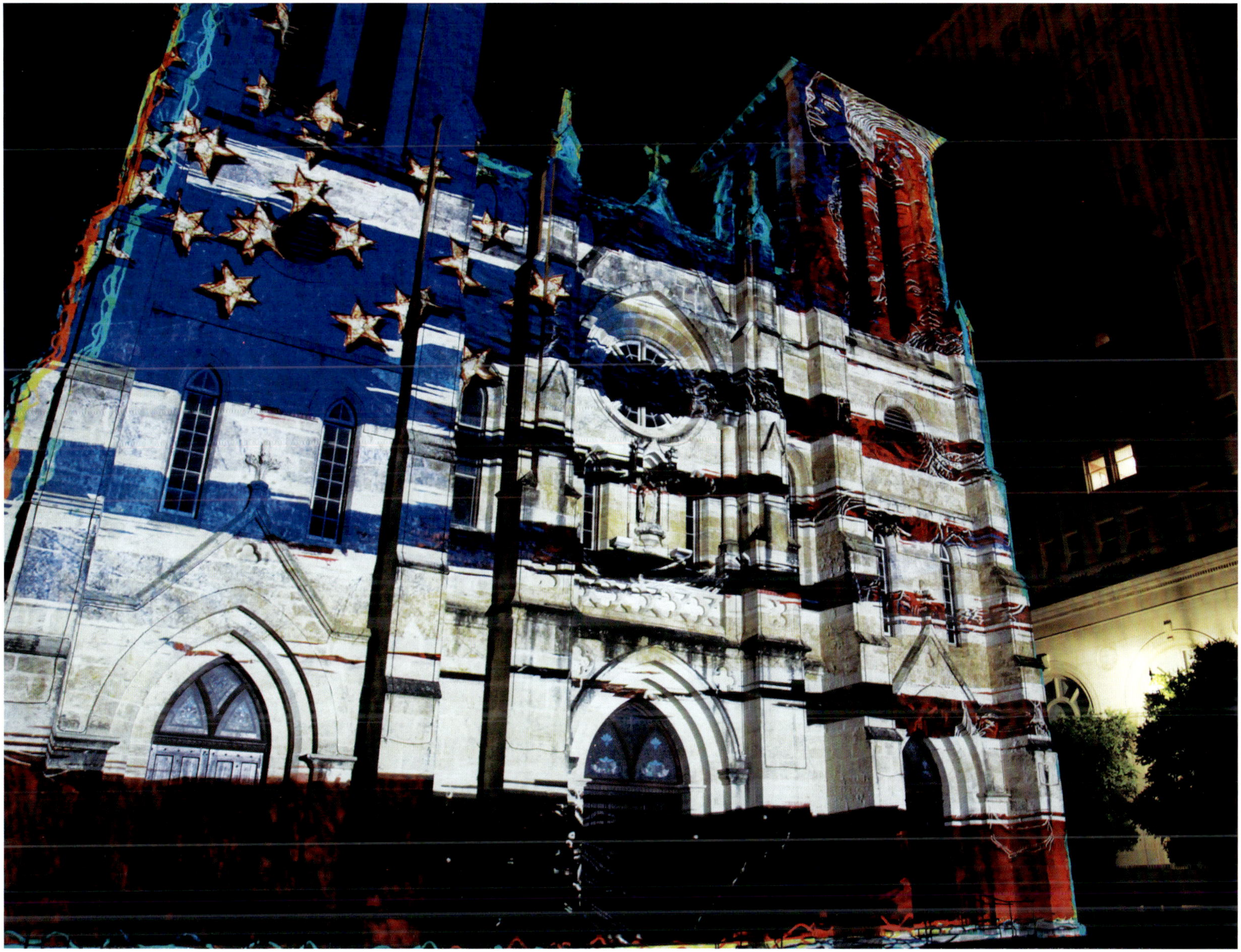

Sequence 7

IMMIGRANTS

NAVARRO HOUSE

Immigrant settlers are families coming mainly from Europe to populate Texas.

Nationalities form groups, each group builds its own villages according to their own know-how from original memories.

They created regional colonial style houses, wood and stone were used as construction materials.

Navarro house is a limestone model of historic regional architecture.

CASTROVILLE AND GRUNE

Cultural groups preserve their own traditions by displaying their national colors and flags floating across the doorways.

Doors, windows, balconies, posts and turned wood embellishes the architecture resulting of a Texas Cultures Mix; German, French, Irish, English, Scottish, Swedish, Norwegian, Greeks, Italian as well as Chinese and Korean.

Alsatian community of Castroville reminiscences of *Strasbourgian* architecture, quickly adapted to local architecture, wood and color give it, its full scope.

With festive traditions the population gathers in the villages, fiestas, beer is flowing. This is the West. Music quotes the songs of Tyrol an Alsace, accordions from Germany, *bandas* or trumpets of *Mariachis*, "Bier Fest" becomes popular.

MERCADO

At the end of the nineteenth century Hispanic population meet at the produce Market in an authentic colorful Mexican environment.

Mexican food is served by *Chili Queens*, also called *Marias*.

In the streets, cattle is passing through San Antonio.

The city is isolated from the East coast because the railroad system has not been built.

Thousands of *Longhorns* and carriages cross downtown.

NOTE

In 1820 immigrants increase under the impulse of Moses Austin, american who obtains from dying Spanish royal authorities the authorization to allow the installation of 300 Anglo-American families in Texas. Colonization is propagated. Government of Texas establish in San Antonio in 1823.
The new Mexican authorities agreeing on the establishment of these new inhabitants, Americans spread in Texas and, Hispanics exceed quickly in numbers.
In 1824, Mexican government creates a large state in North Mexico made up of Texas and Coahuila, with Saltillo as a capital and called Coahuila y Tejas.
A strong international immigration settles in Texas in the middle of the 19th century, between 1840 and 1870, they are European families attracted by settlement programs with land.
Thus, towns as Castroville (1844) were created and populated by the Alsatians, Grune (1872) and Fredericksburg by German settlers. This colorful and cosmopolitan immigration brings a strong mix of society.

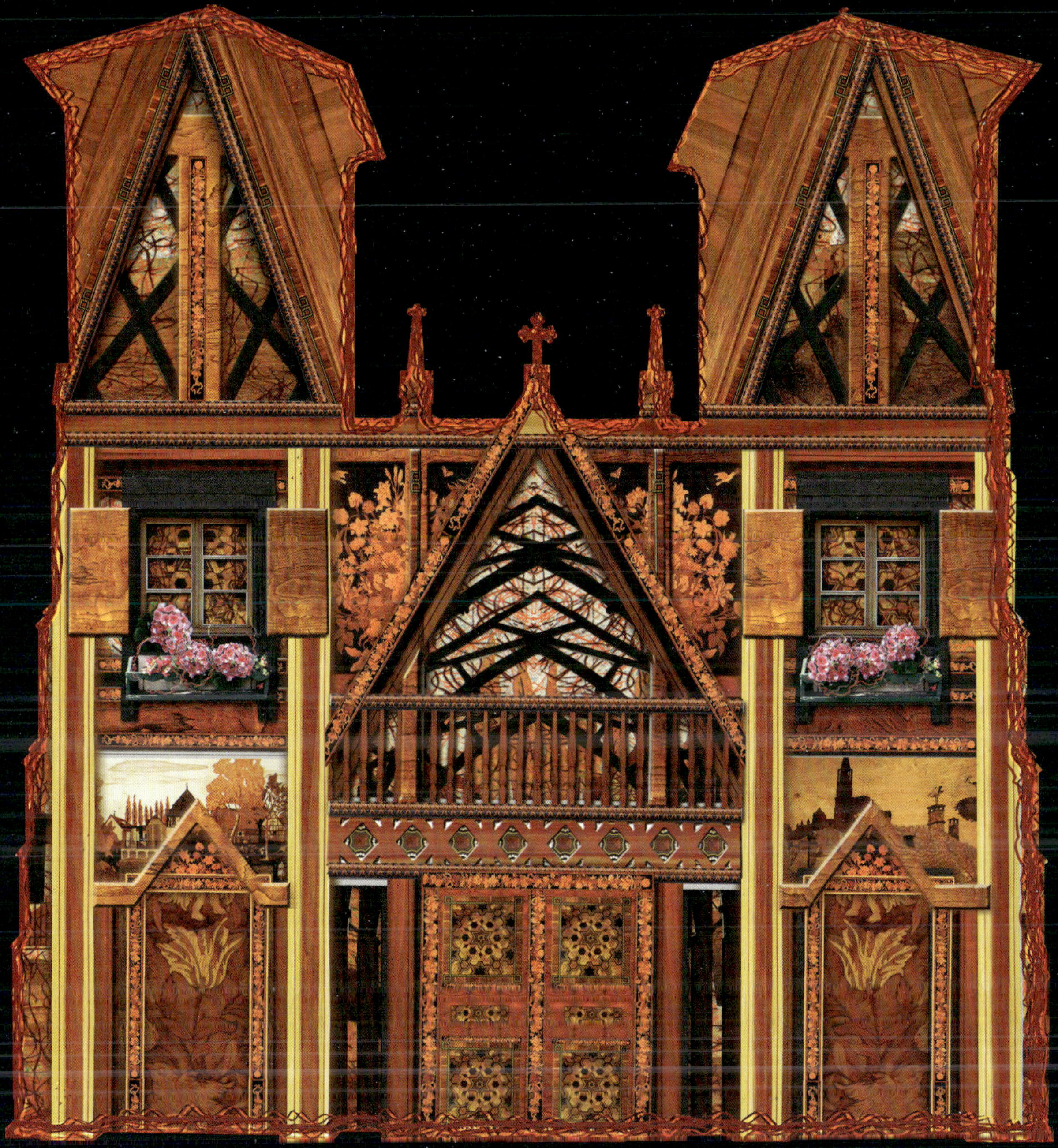

Castroville and Grune

Navarro House

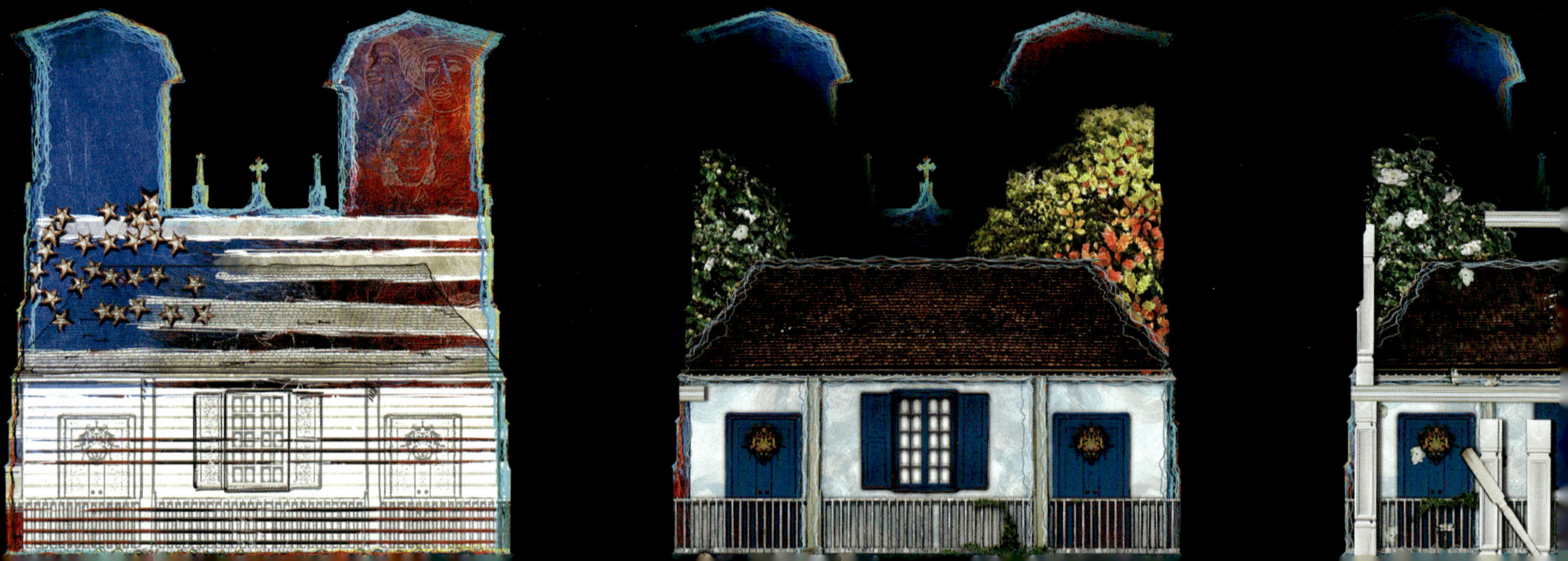

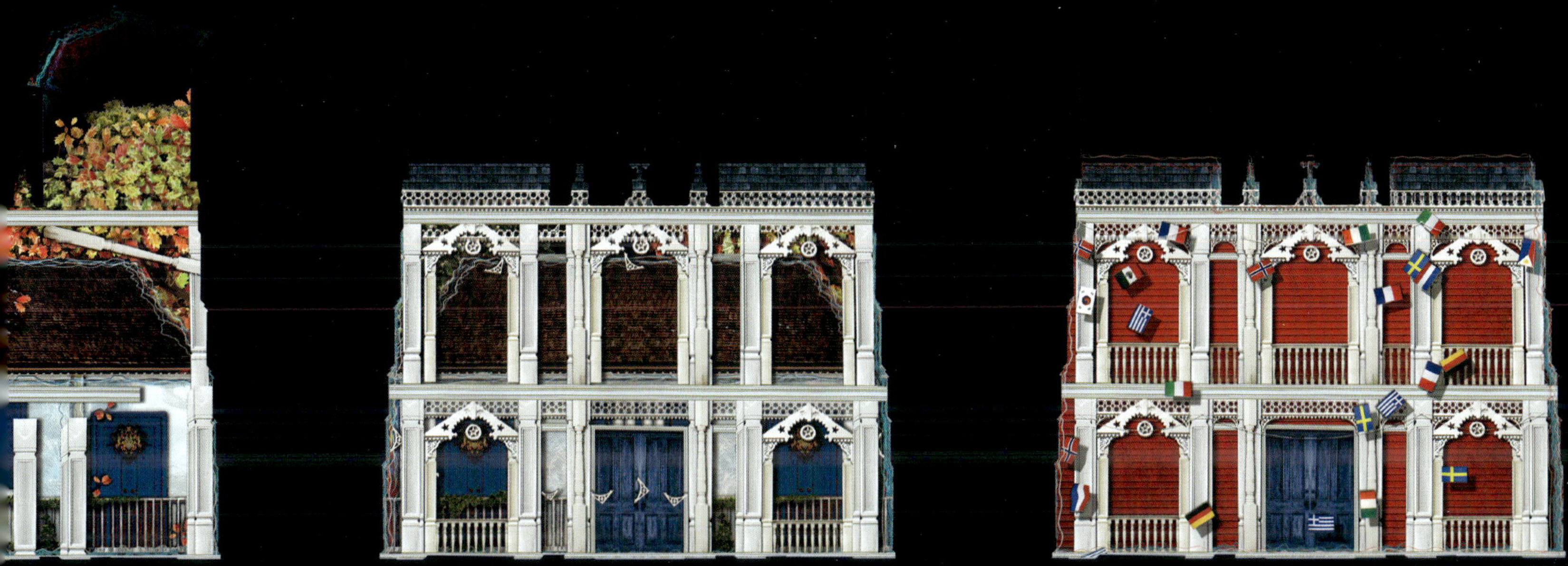

Architectures

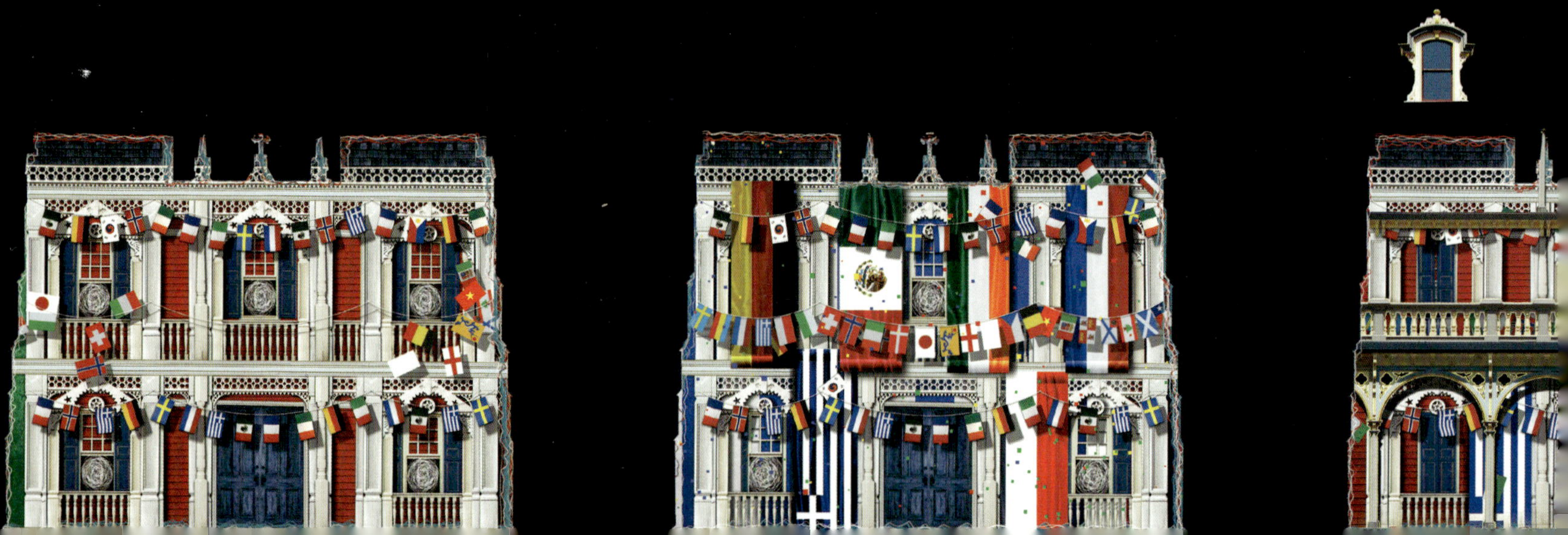

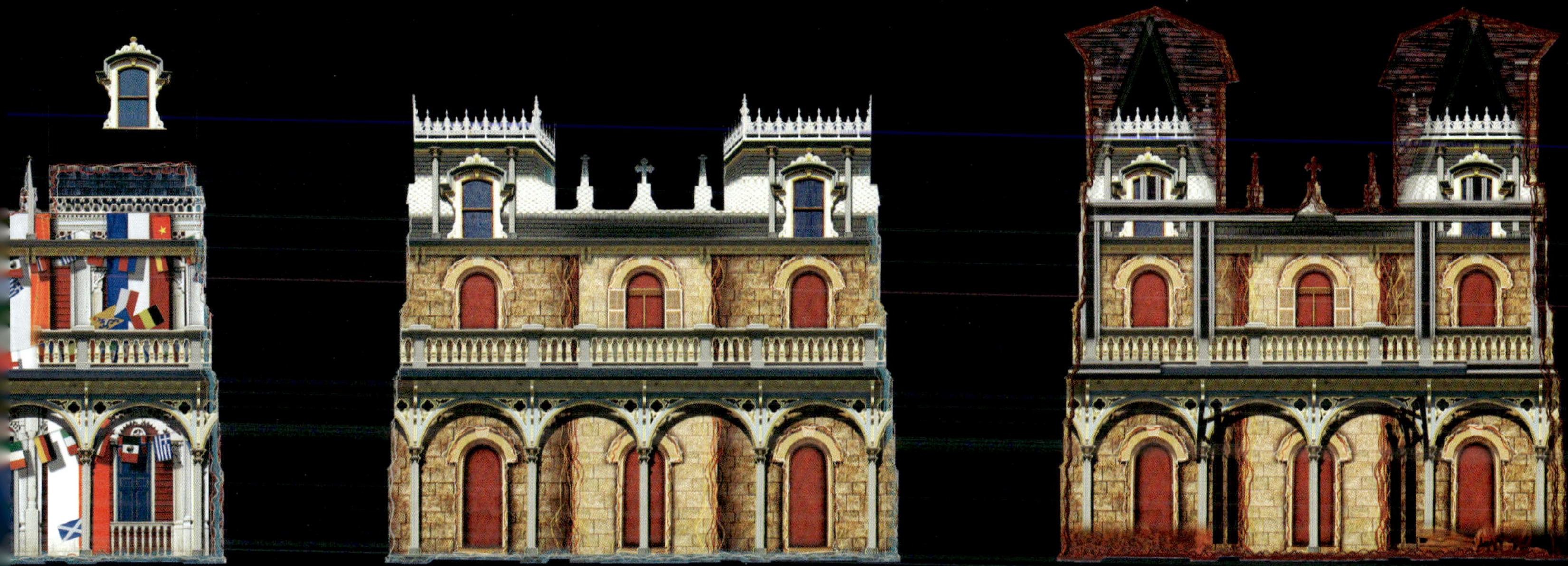

Castroville and Grune

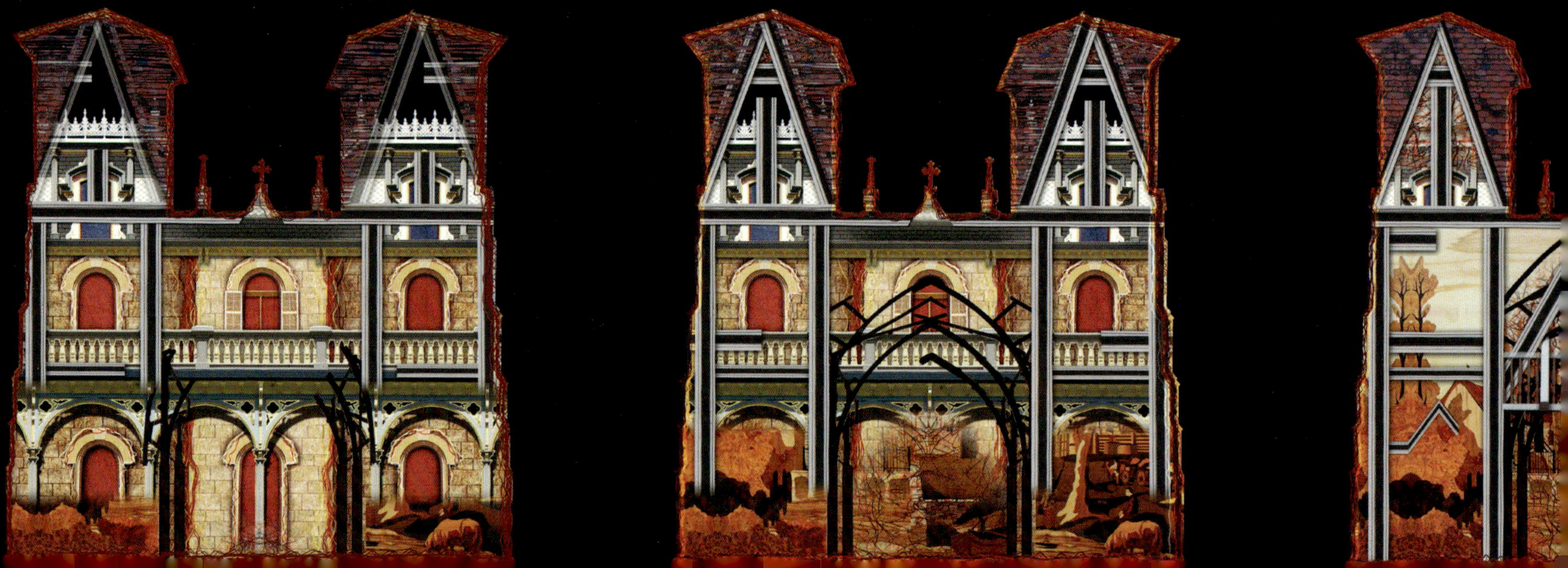

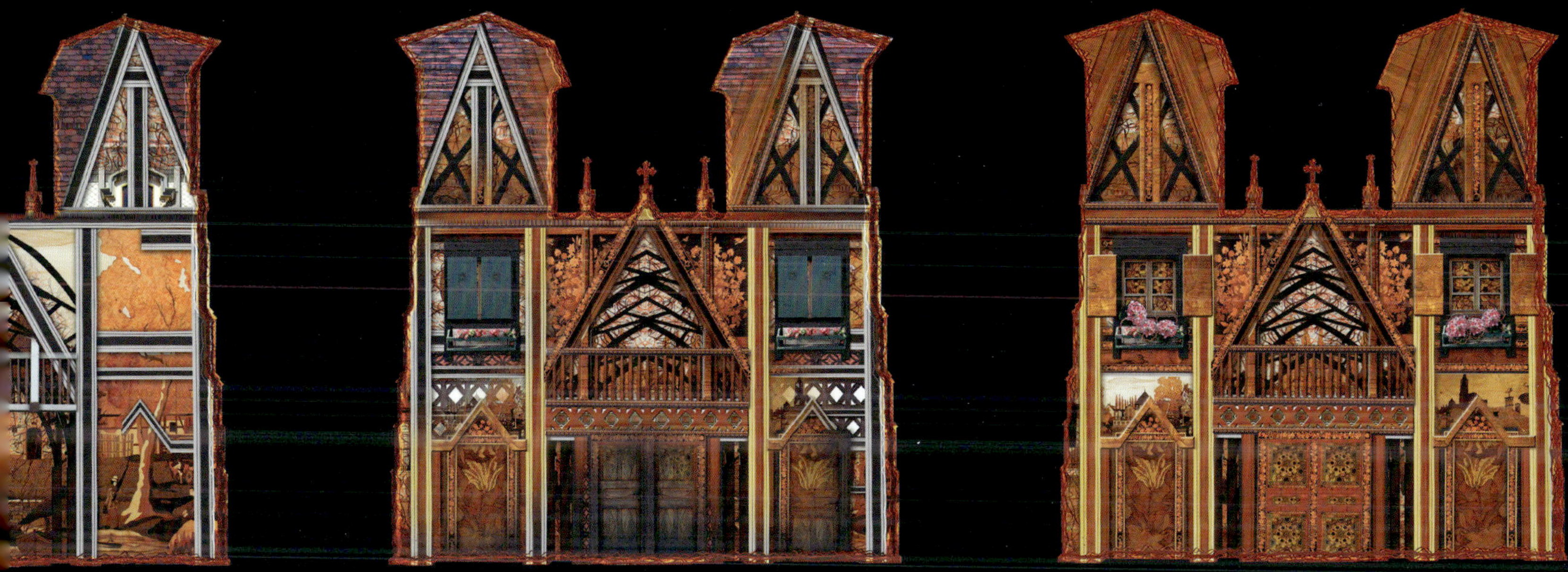

Mercado

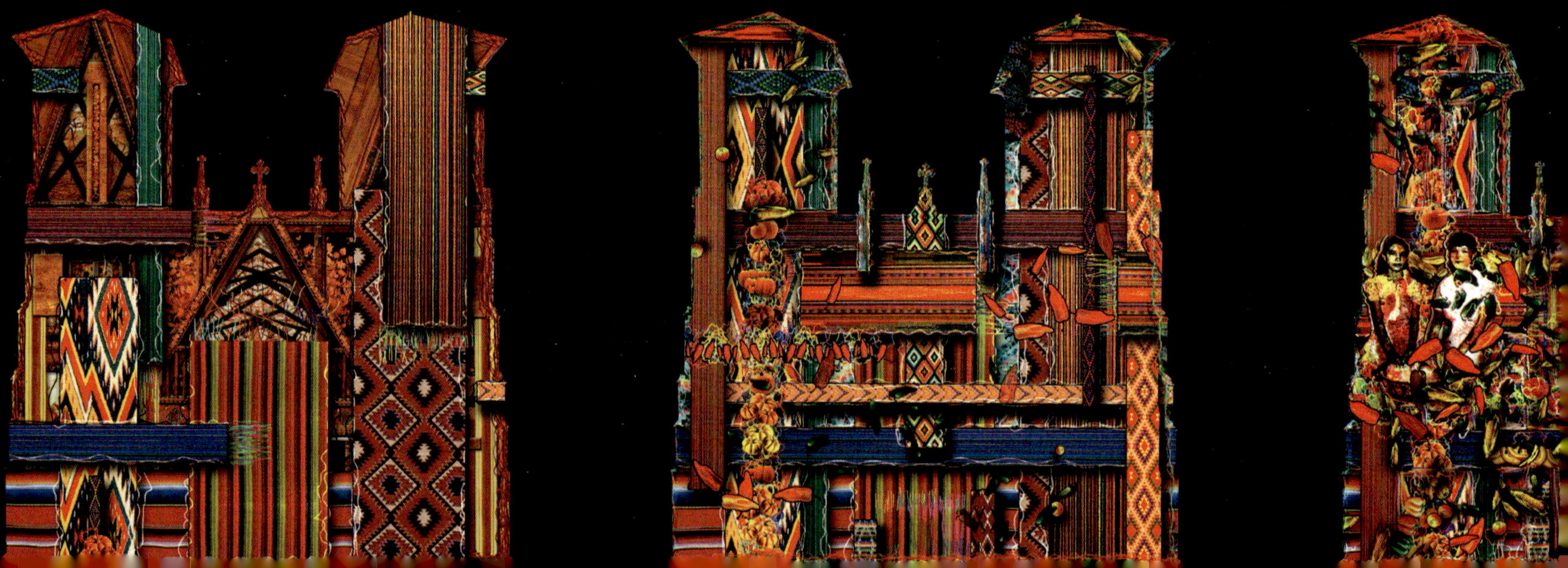

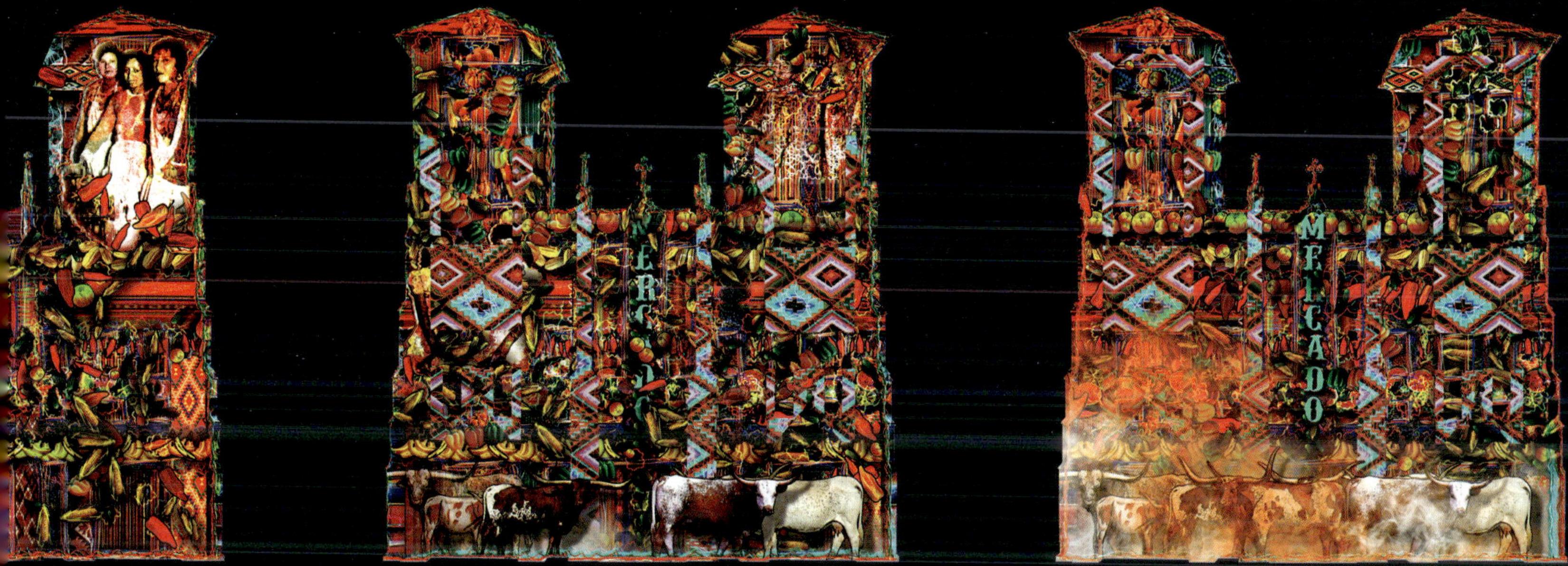

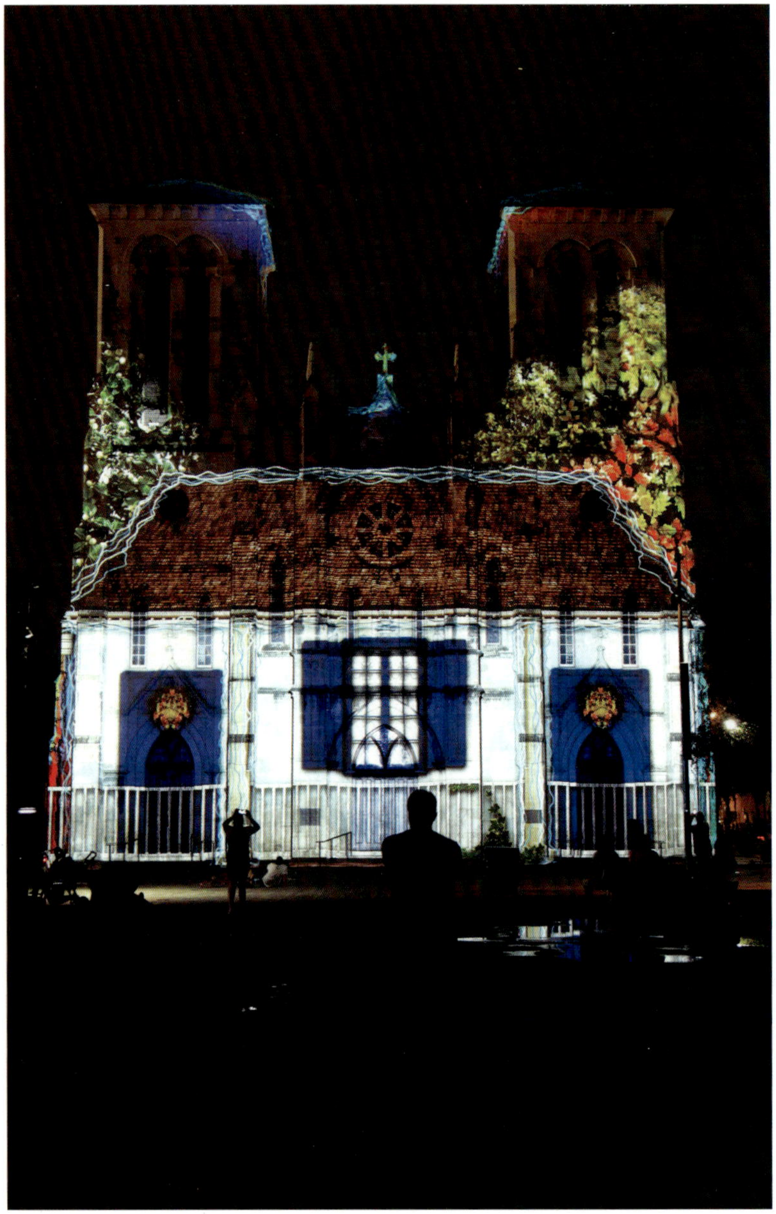

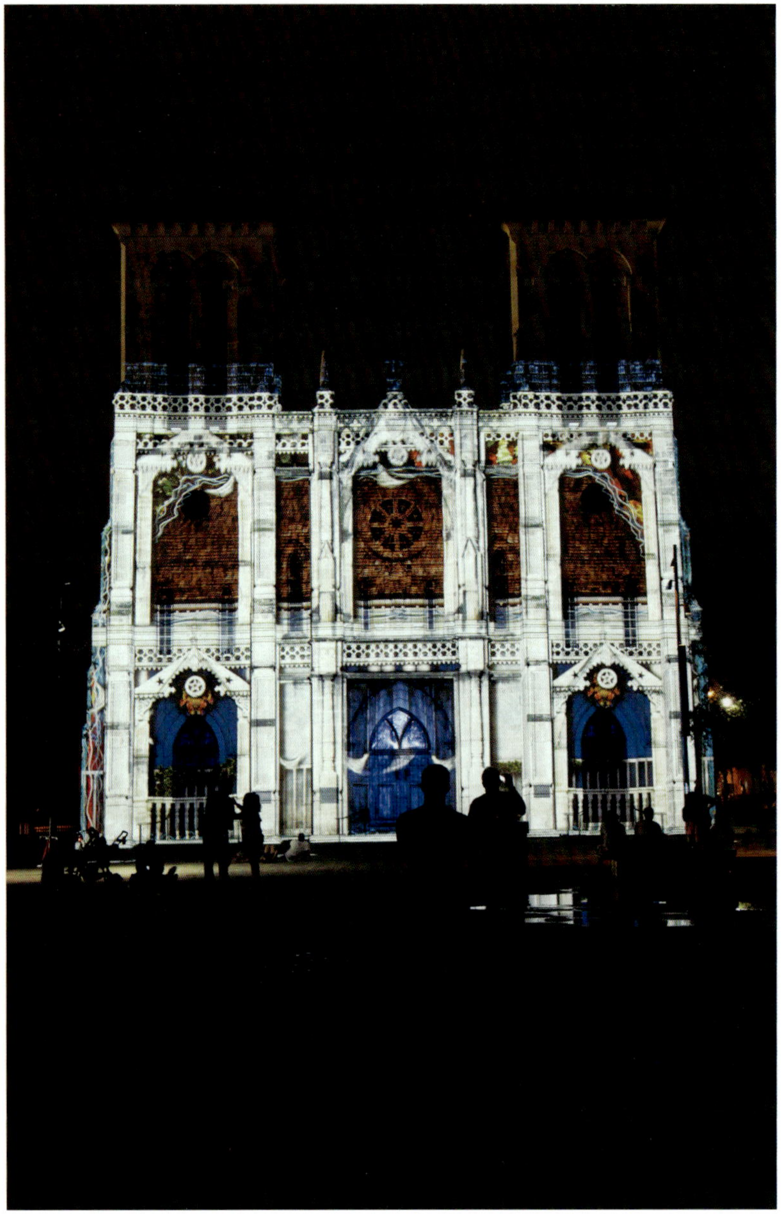

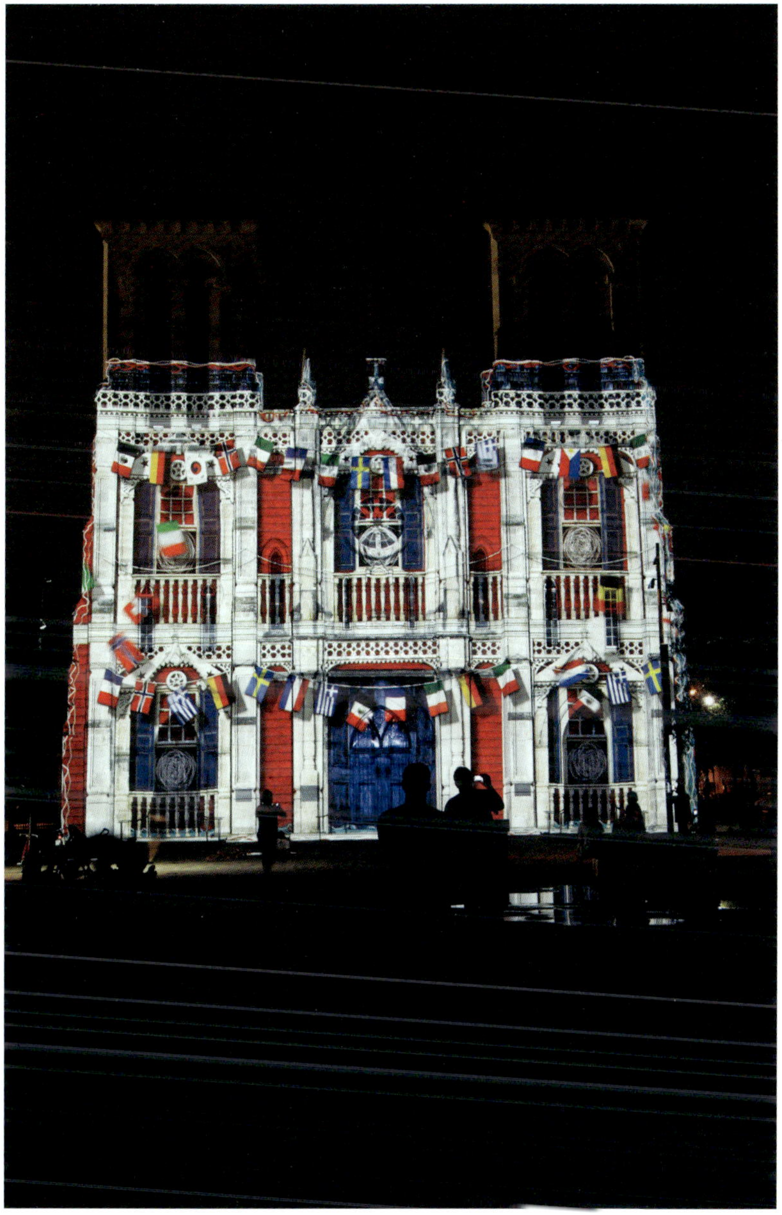

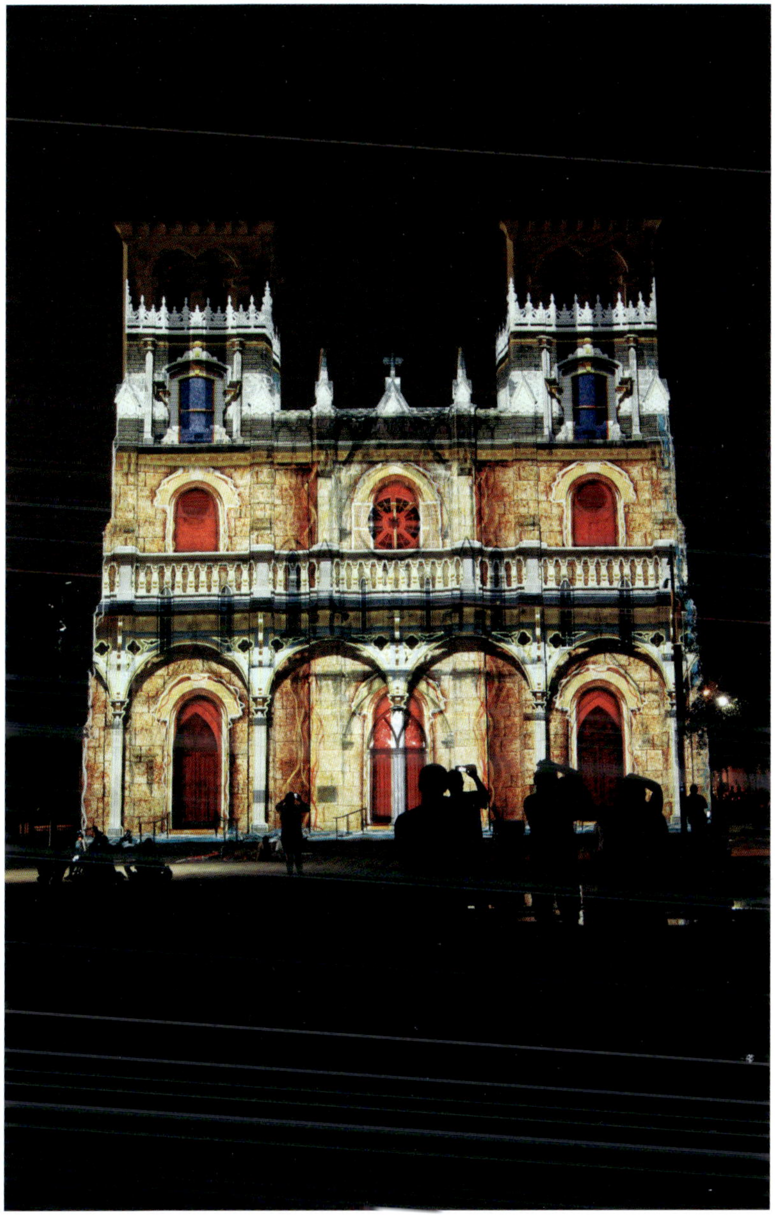

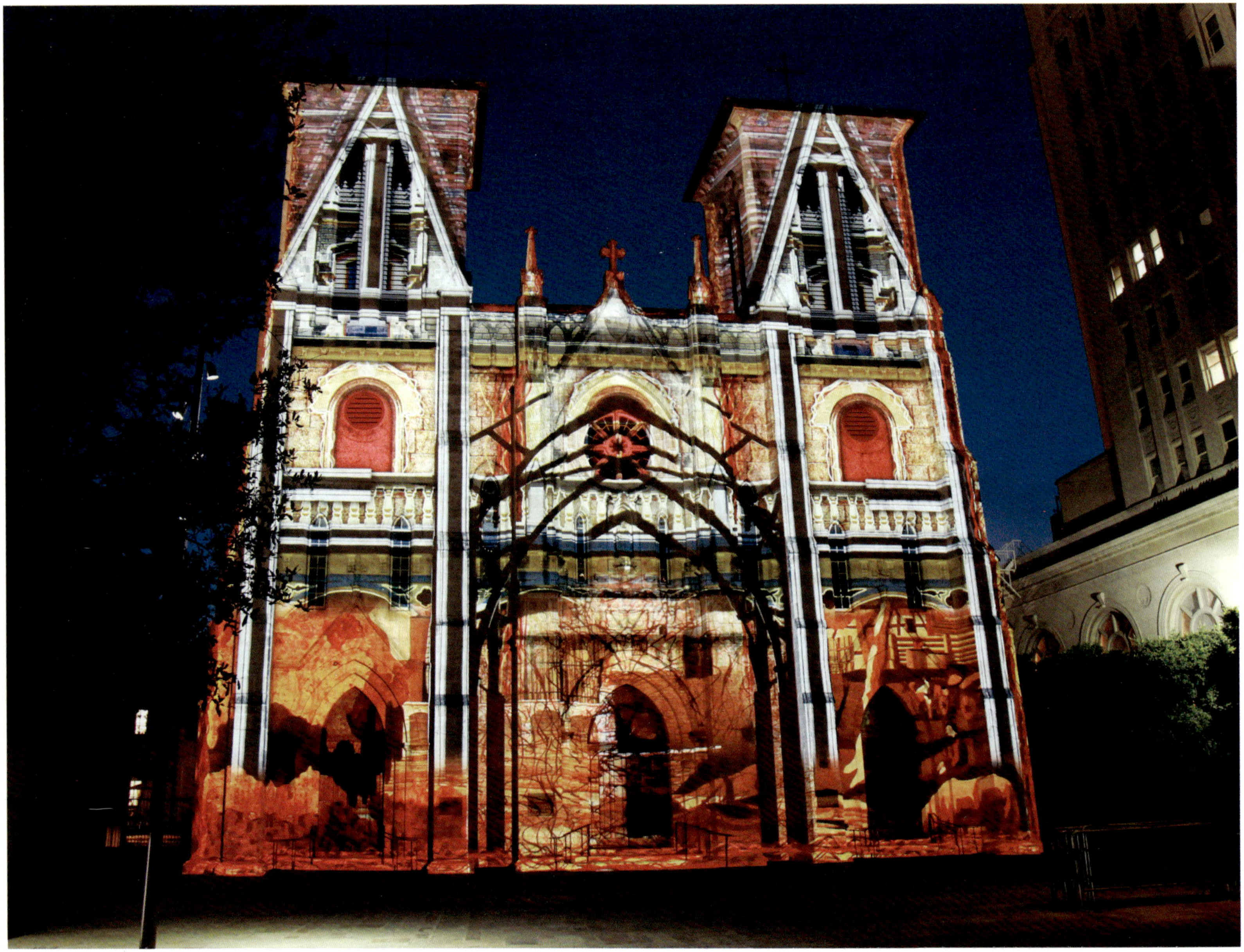

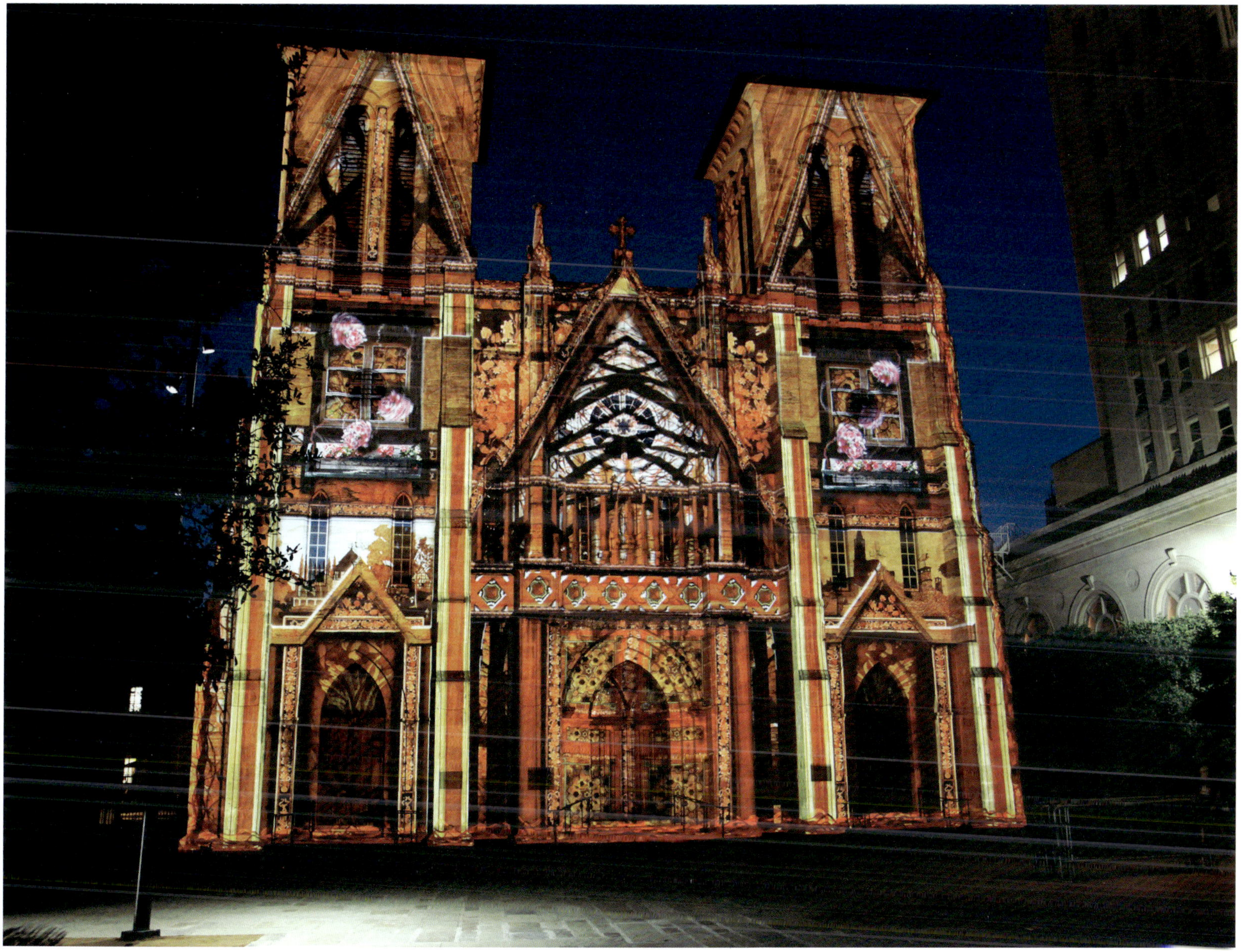

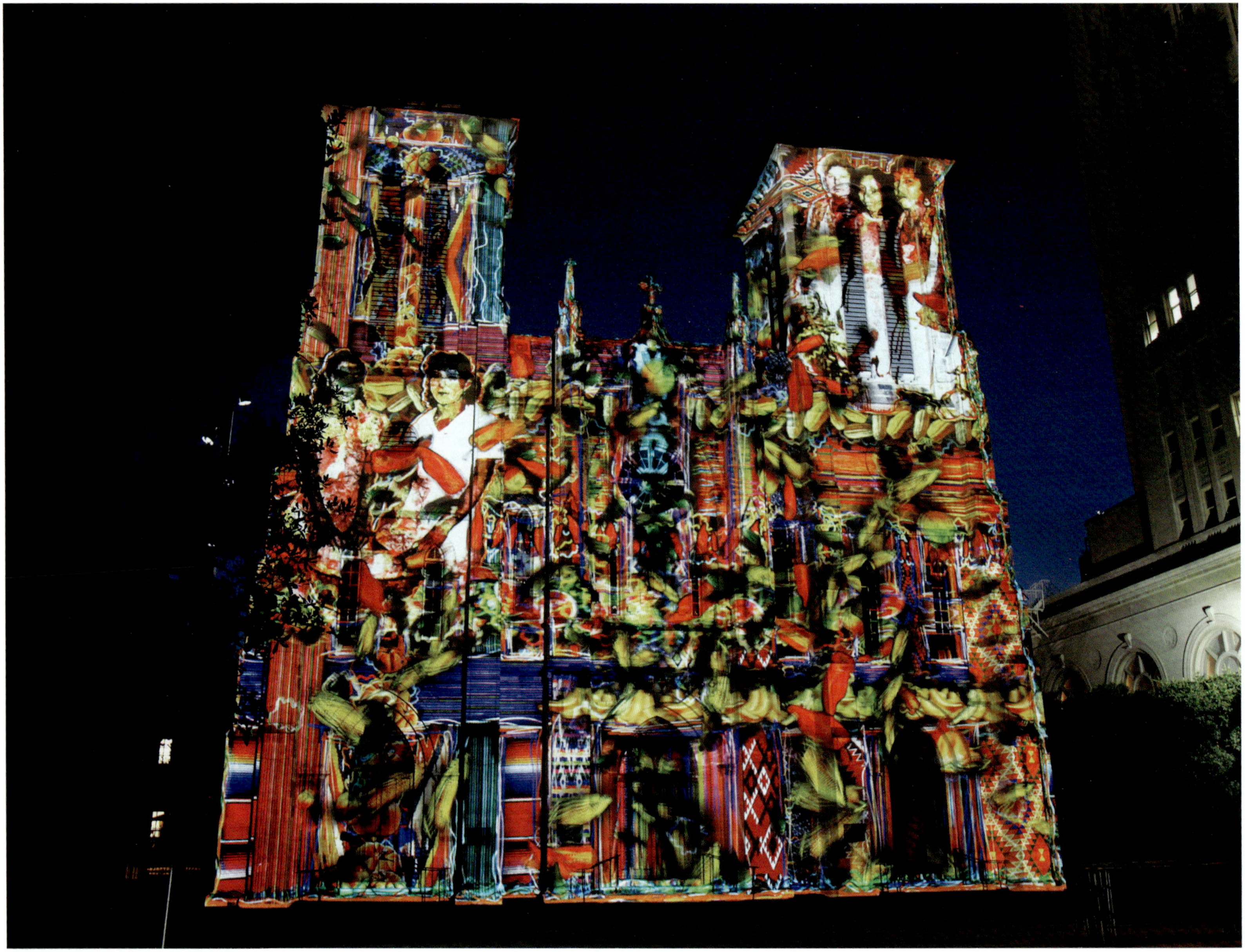

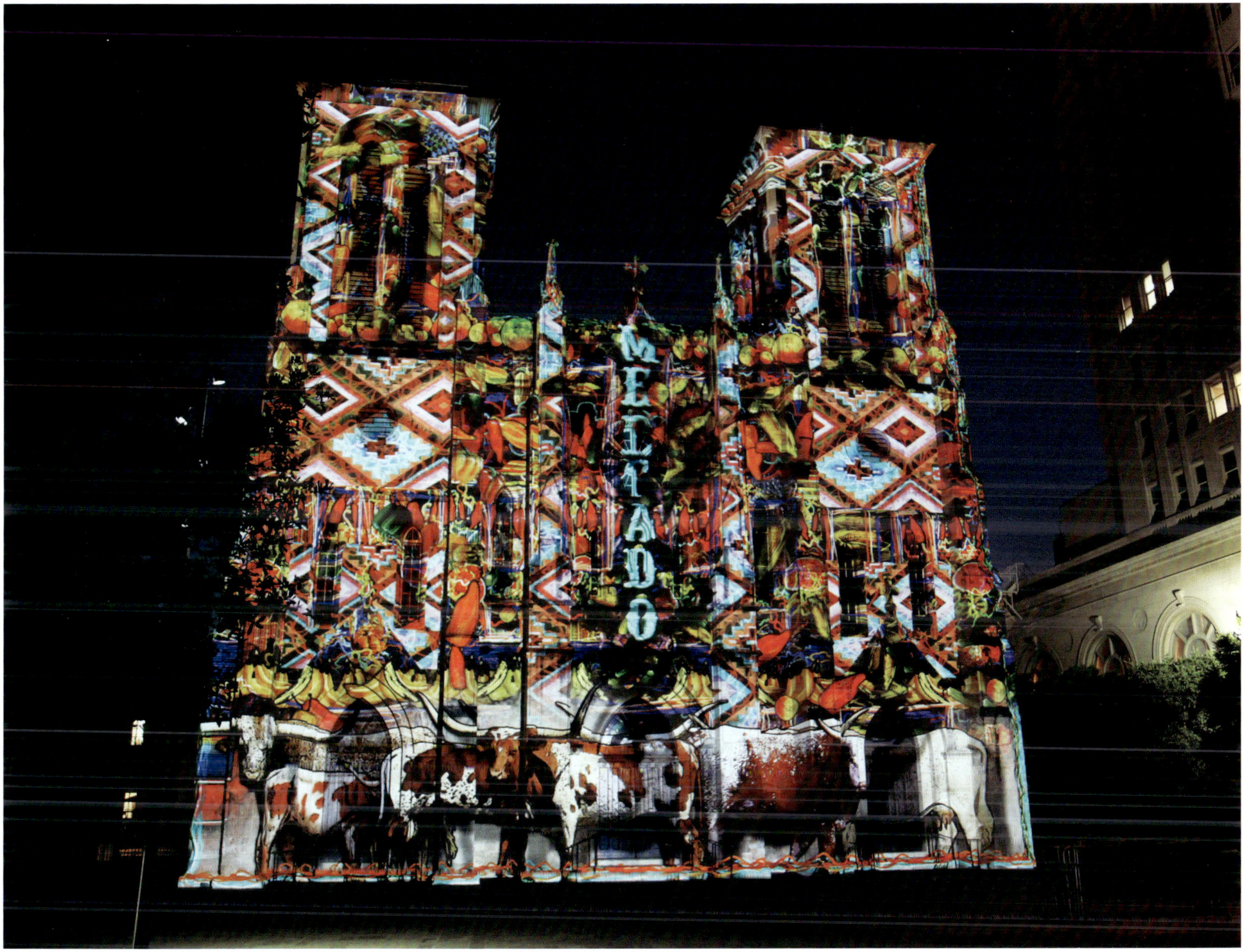
MERCADO

Sequence 8

THE MODERN ERA

OIL

Among the dust of cattle and carriages rises the silver neo gothic façade of San Fernando Cathedral.

As coming from the sub-soils of the city, the monumental steel façade is loaded with decorative silvered elements barrowed from new elegant architecture symbolize the social rise of the city in the last quarter of 19th century.

Discovery of oil in 1901 is major for City development. Pilasters transform into derricks projecting oil jets, spindle top pumps its first gallons of oil, nodding donkeys appear in the windows and spill oily matter.

City is shining as a silver dollar coin.

EMILY MORGAN

Early 20th Century welcomes the first railroad station in San Antonio. Train is delivering and transporting people, cattle and oil tanks.

New buildings show up in the City. The famous Emily Morgan Hotel was built in the twenties as a Medical Arts Building.

A great number of neo gothic constructions grow in the City.

Civilized era is on its way.

Trains steam across Main Plaza.

Population increases.

SOCIETY

The city grows richer, the Cathedral wears an elegant neo gothic costume made out of rose stone decorated with multiple Art Deco effigies and decorations.

Beautiful women, from all origins represent the cheerful, cosmopolitan and political society in San Antonio the suffragettes appear in the first quarter of 20th Century.

NOTE

19th century ends with ambitious achievements. The economy is doing well, San Antonio builds more and more beautiful Gothic Revival buildings which flourish until the 1929 great crisis. Texas discovers the resources of oil in 1901 and business is prosperous. The current Cathedral is built until 1873 under direction of François Giraud, French architect, in the neo gothic style quite well represented in San Antonio architecture. The second tower will be built in 1902. The railroad gets to San Antonio in 1877, connections with the East in 1878 and 1881. Oil makes things go faster, in 1902 the first railroad station is built, Sunset Station. *Train stations are real palaces.*
Paintings by Robert Henri and John Singer Sargent from SA Museum of Art.
Music by native Texan Scott Joplin and Afro American Symphony by William Grant Still, first black composer of a symphonic piece in the U.S.

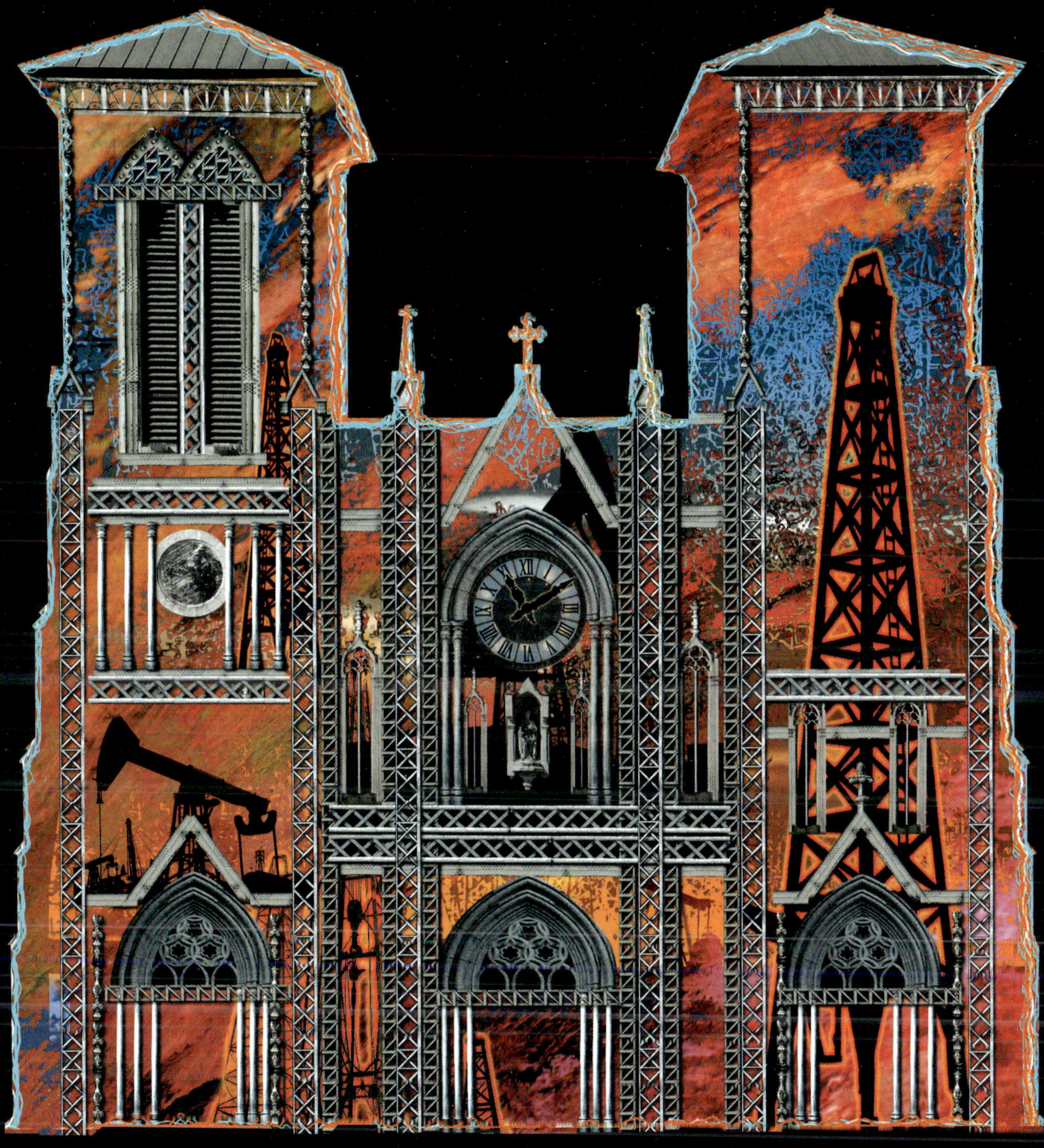

Oil

Oil

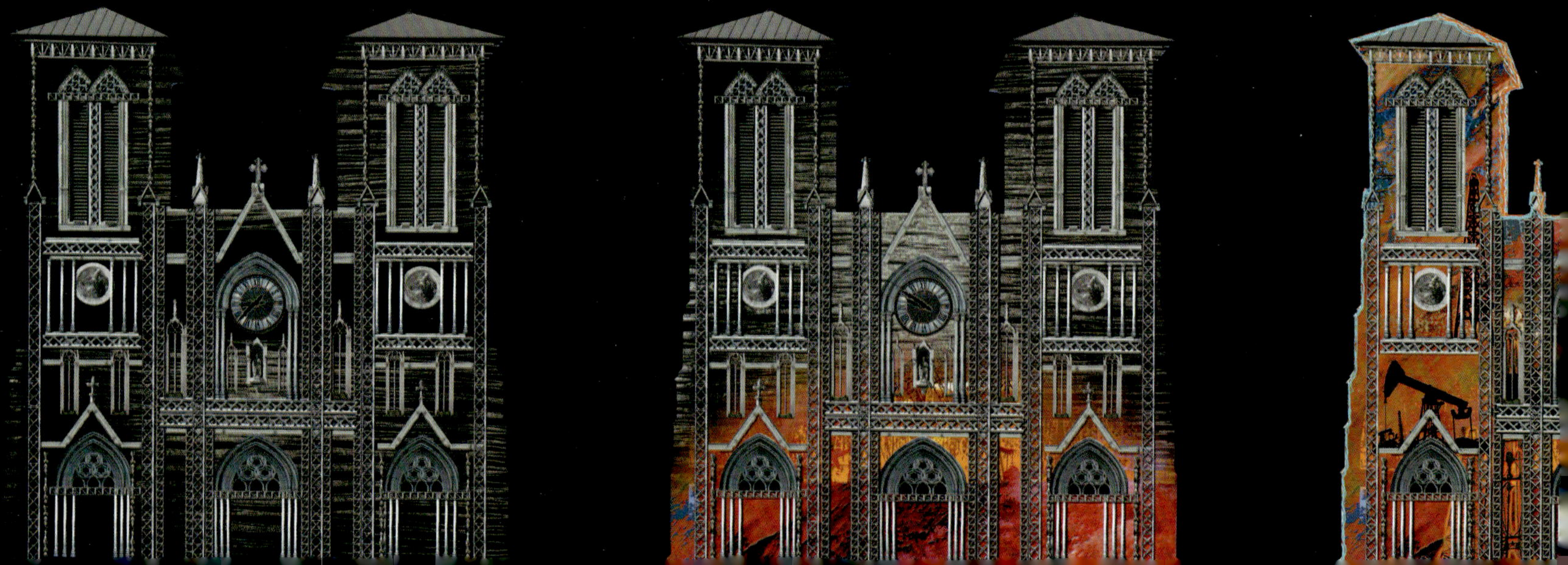

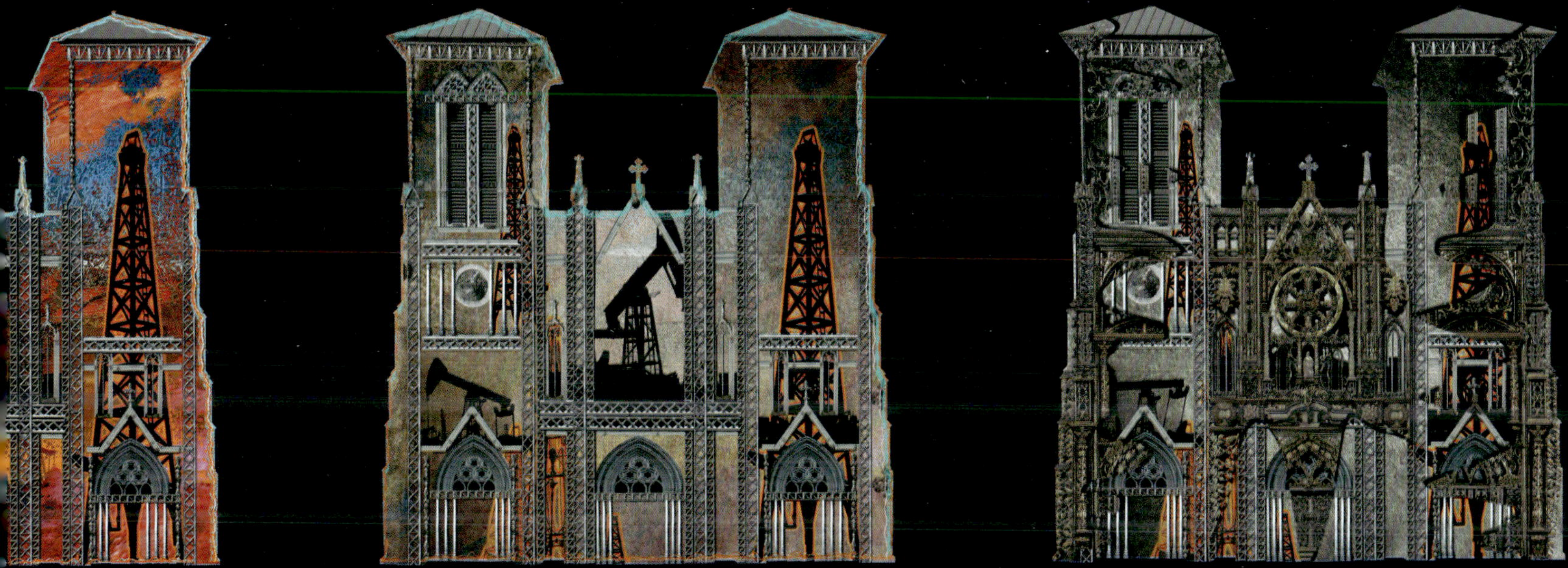

Silver

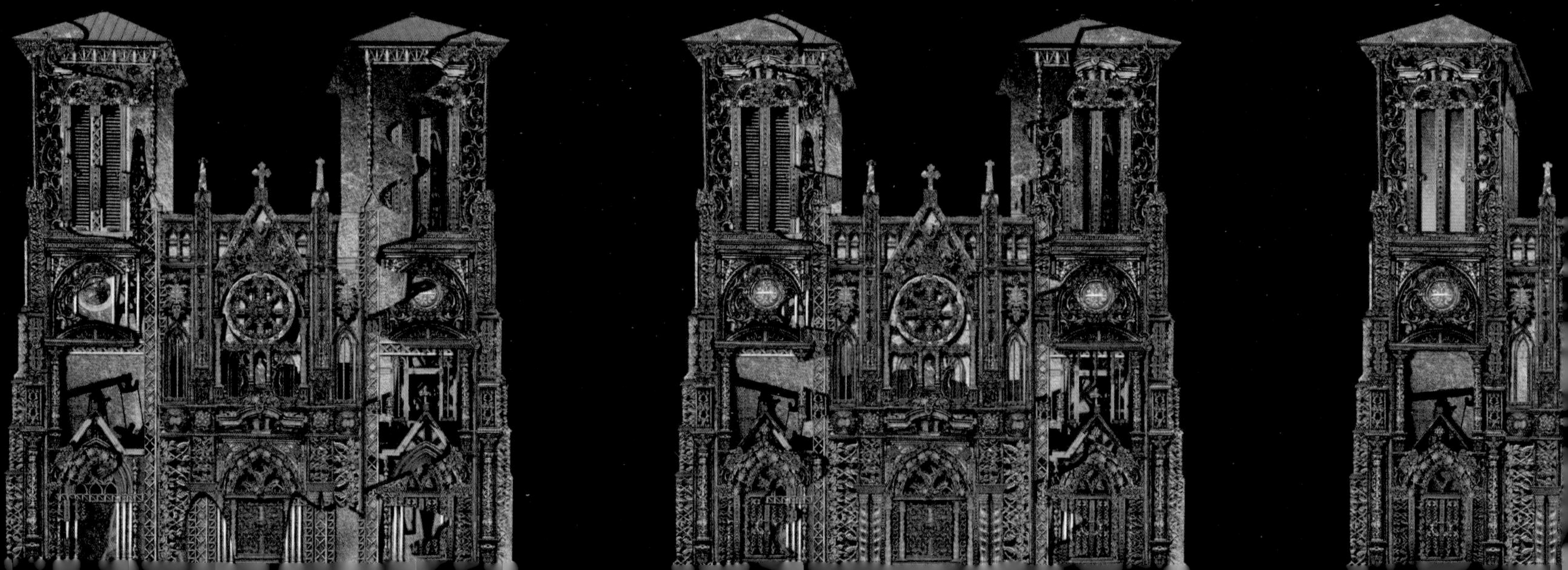

Emily Morgan

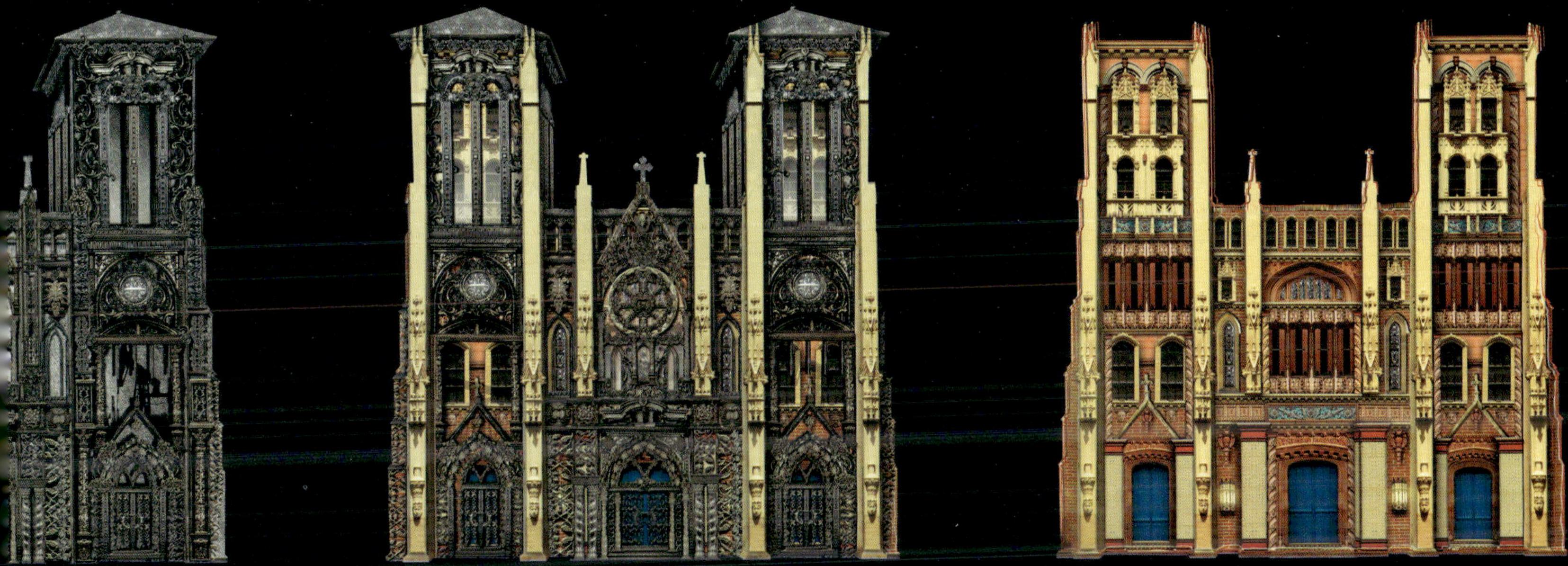

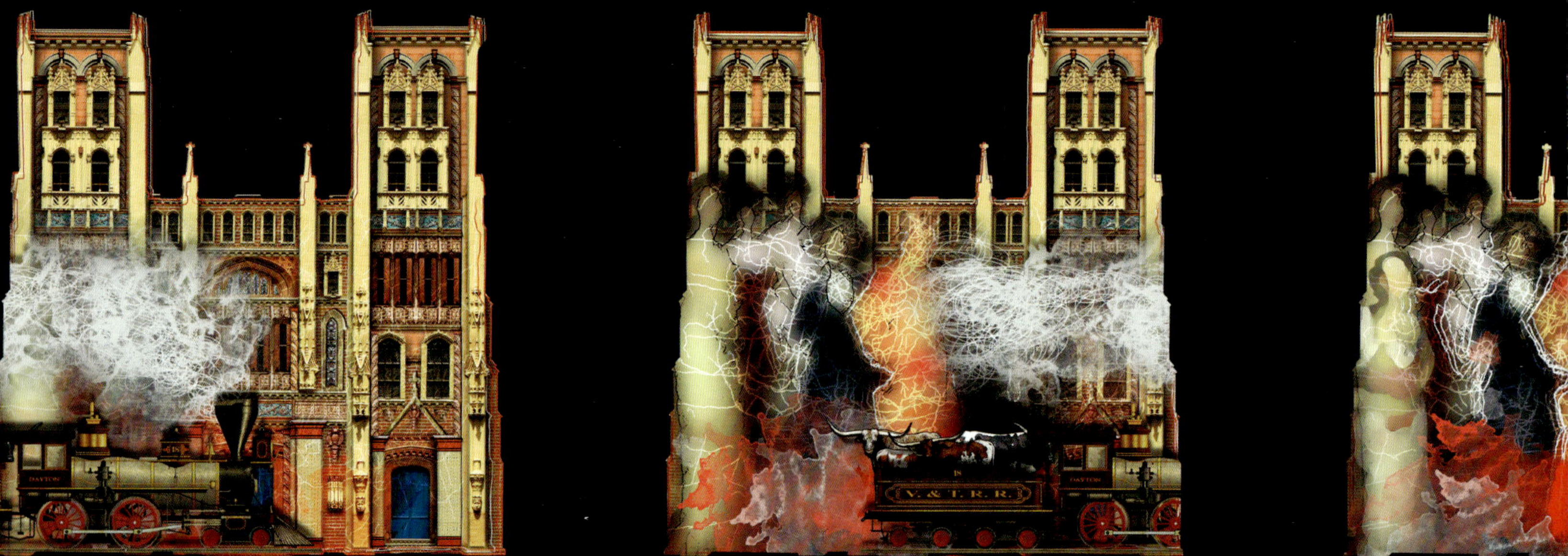
V. & T. R. R.

Society

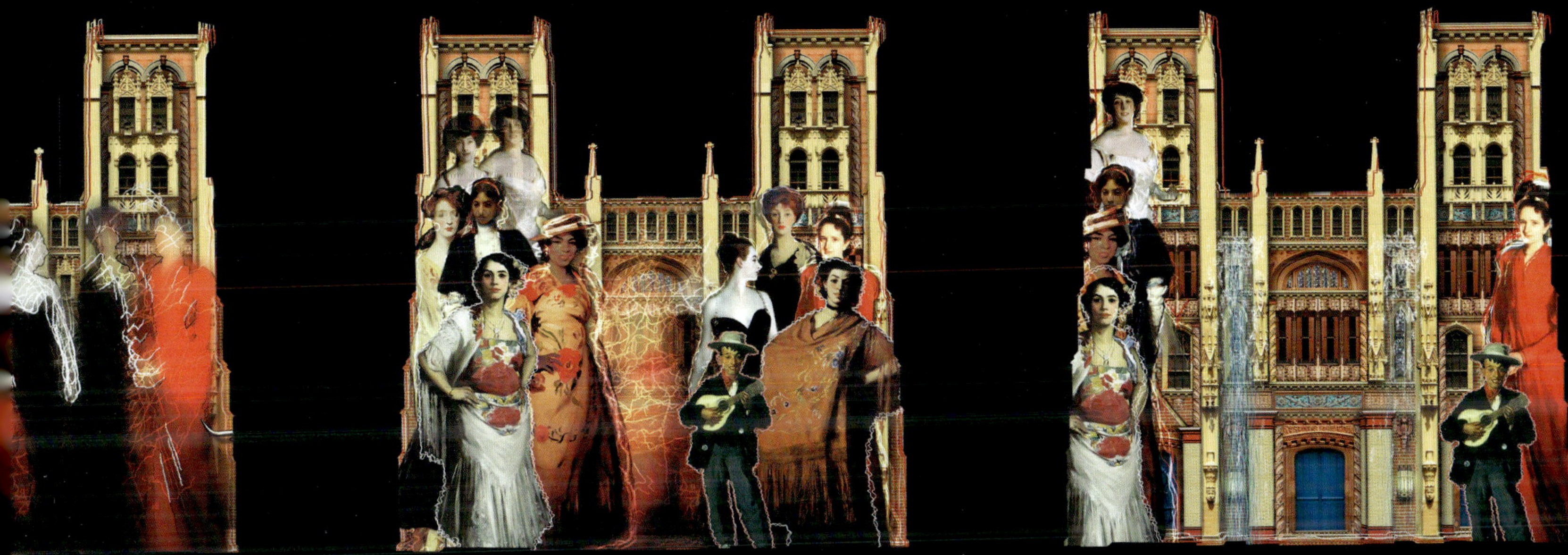

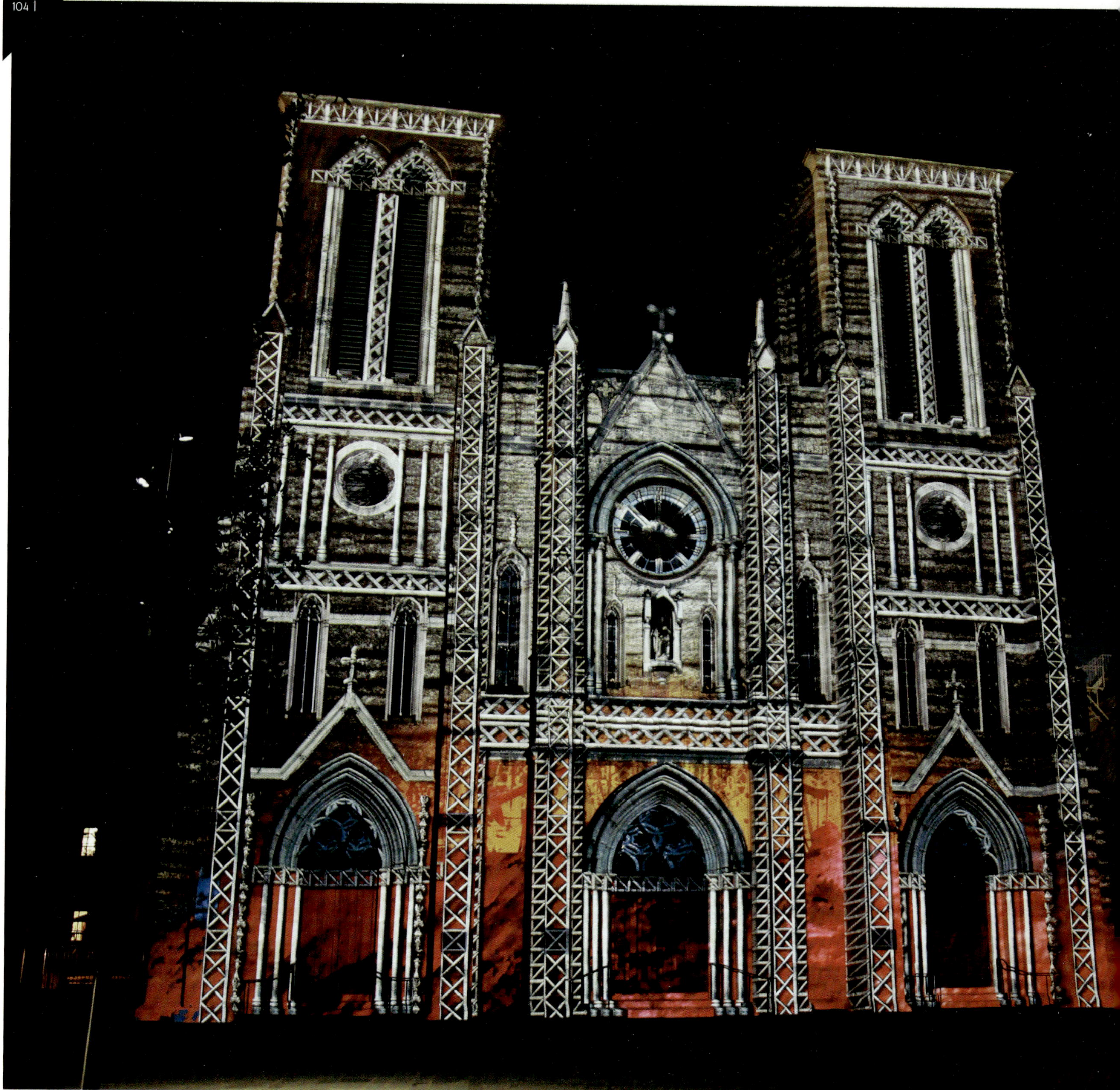

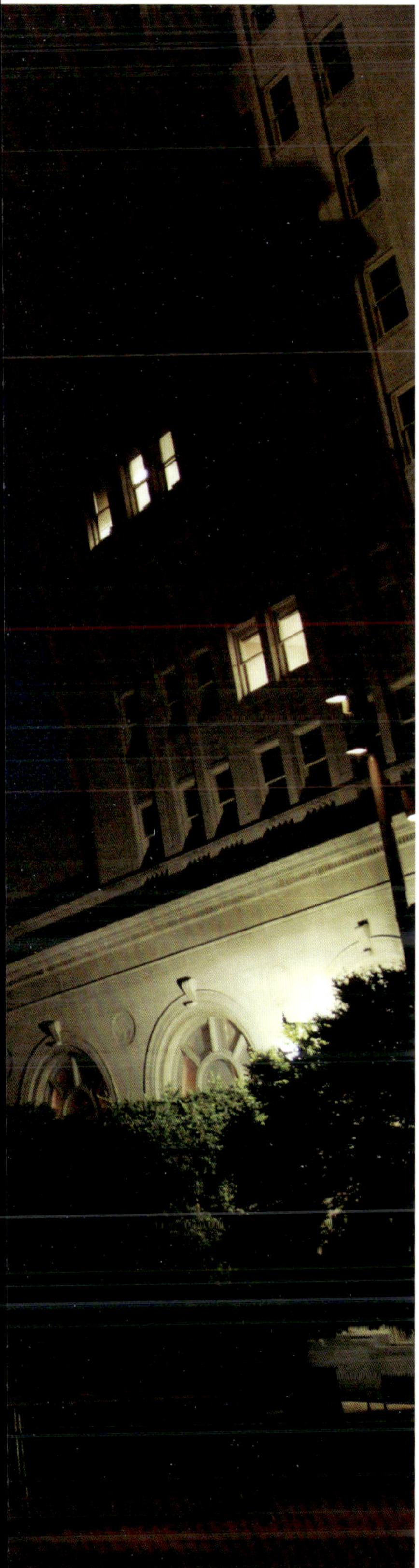

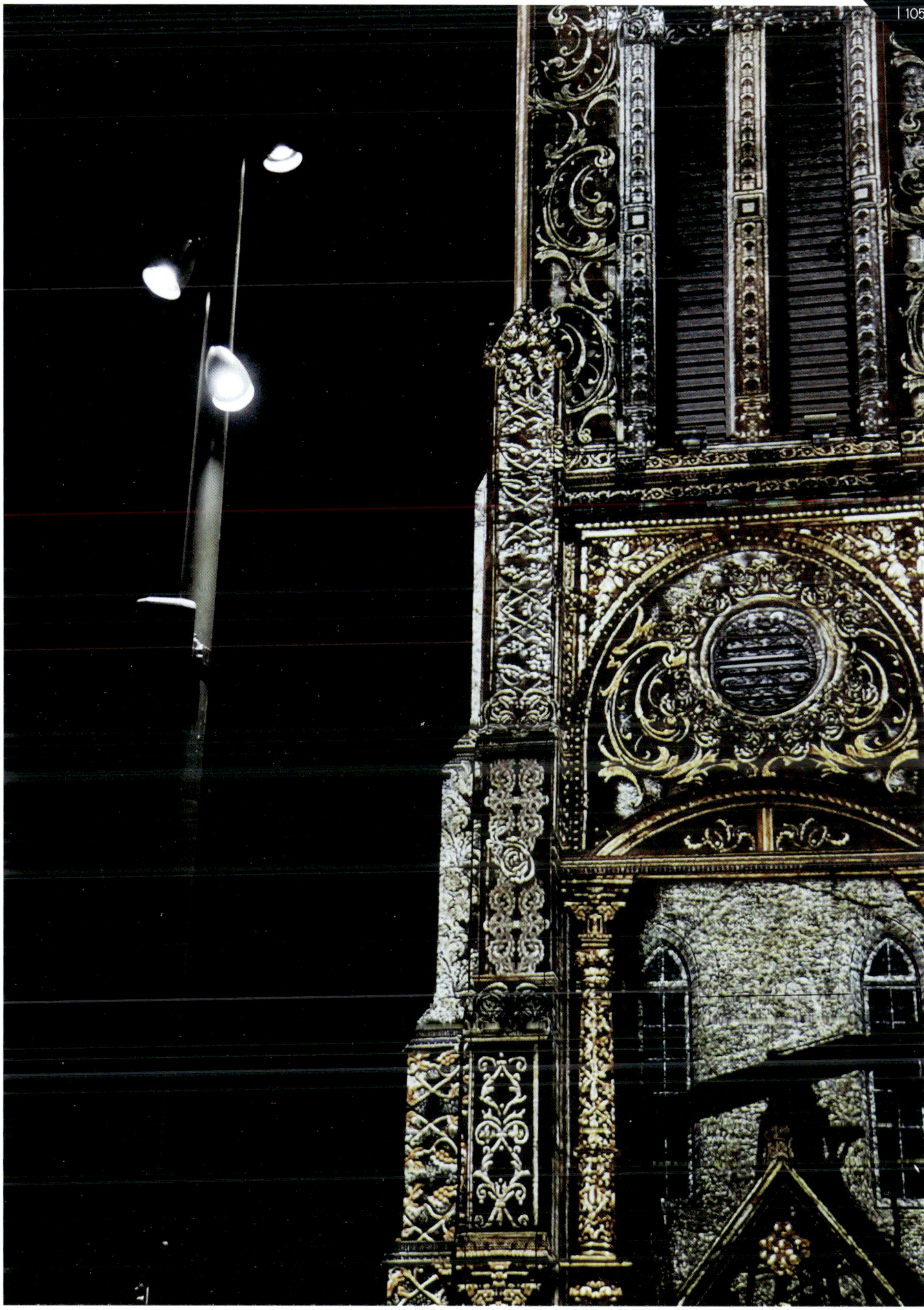

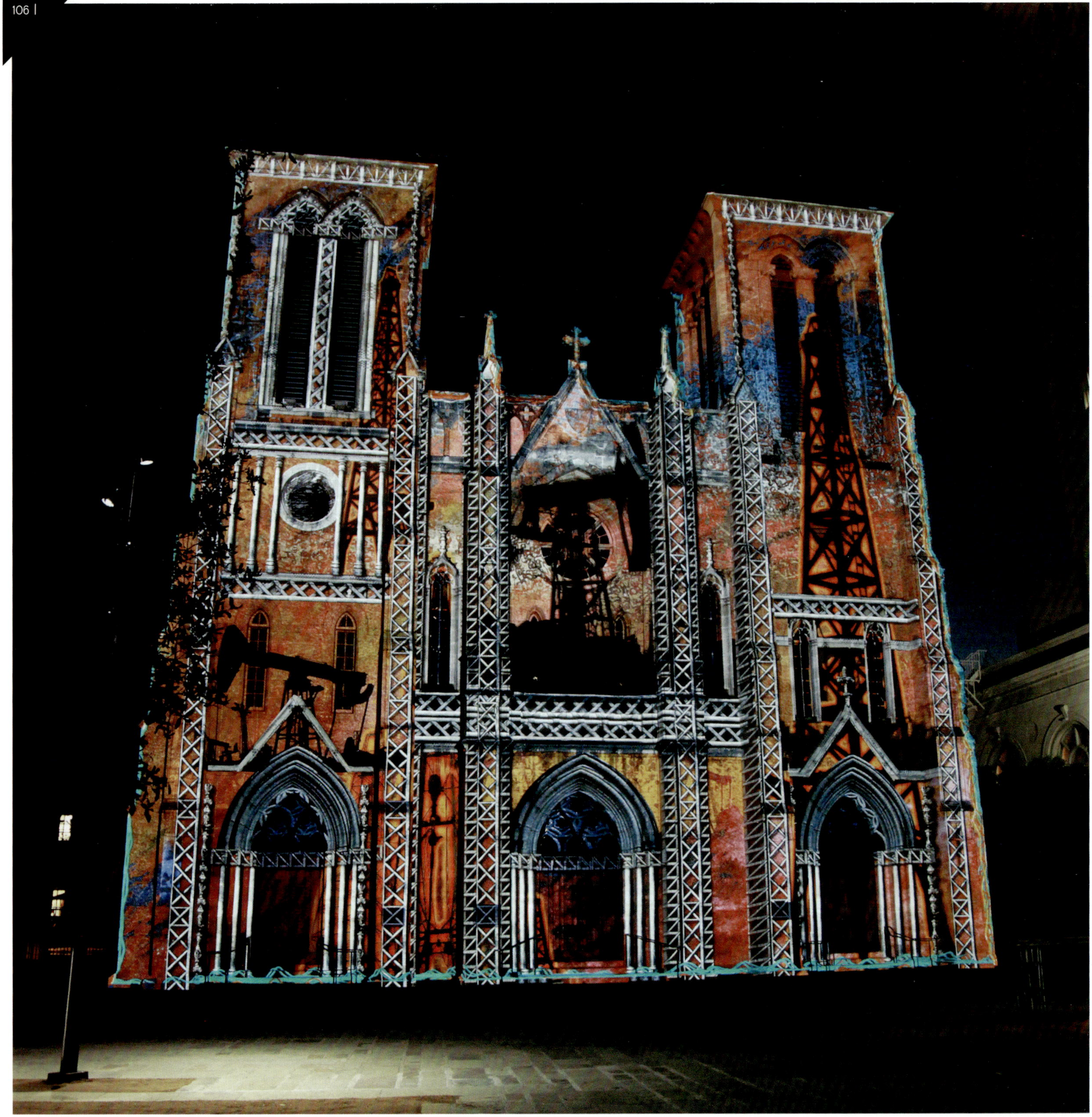

- SAN ANTONIO THE SAGA -

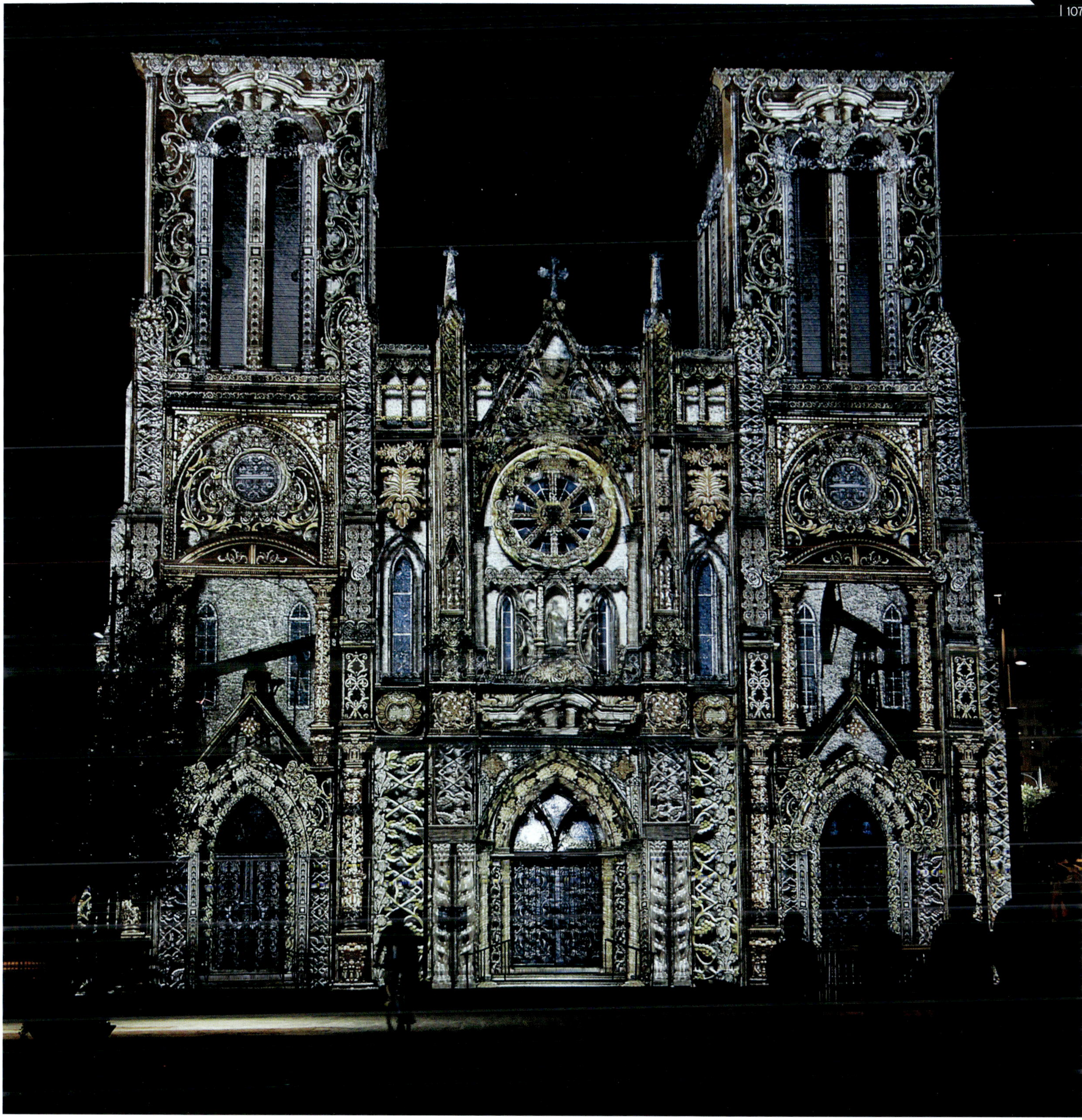

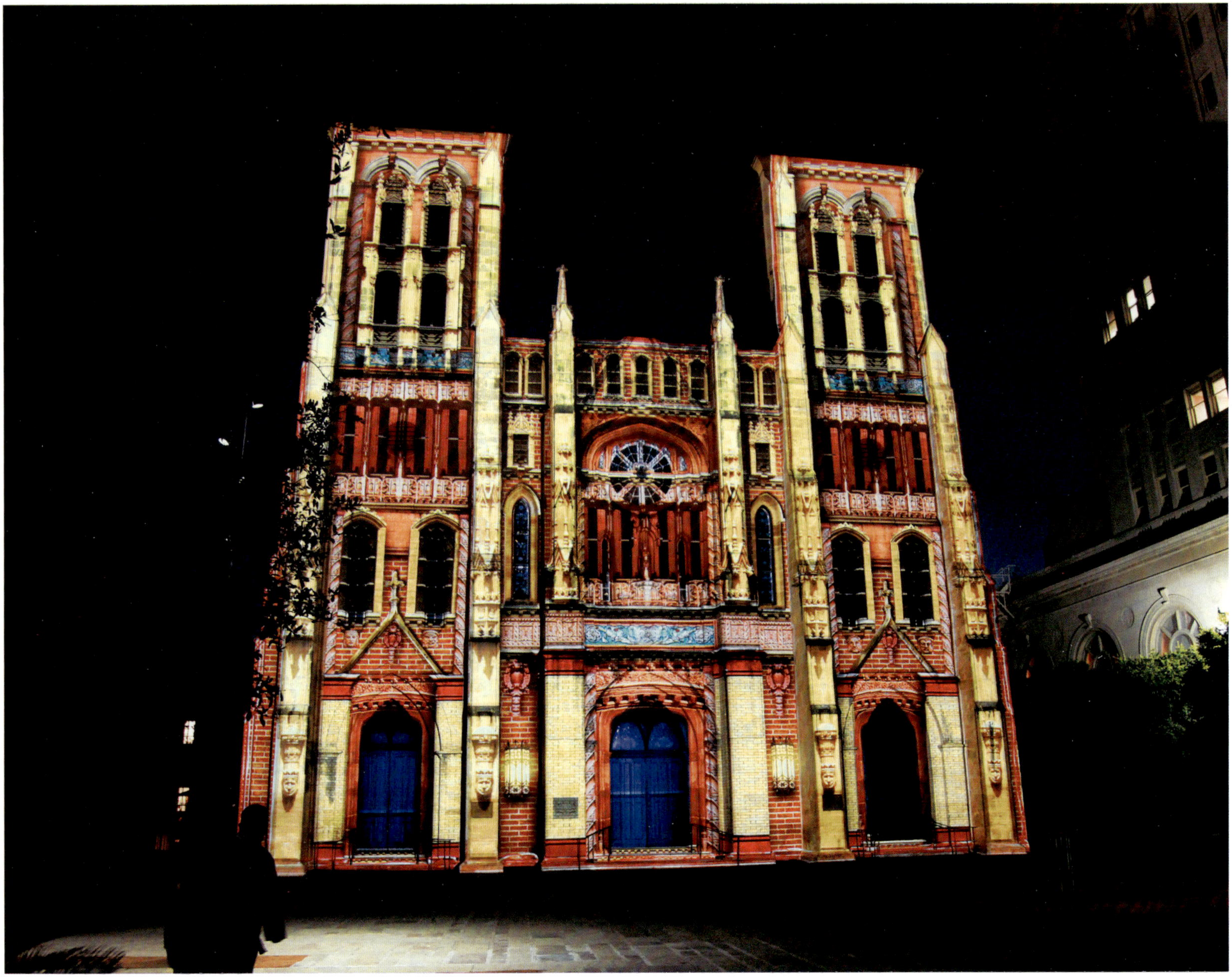

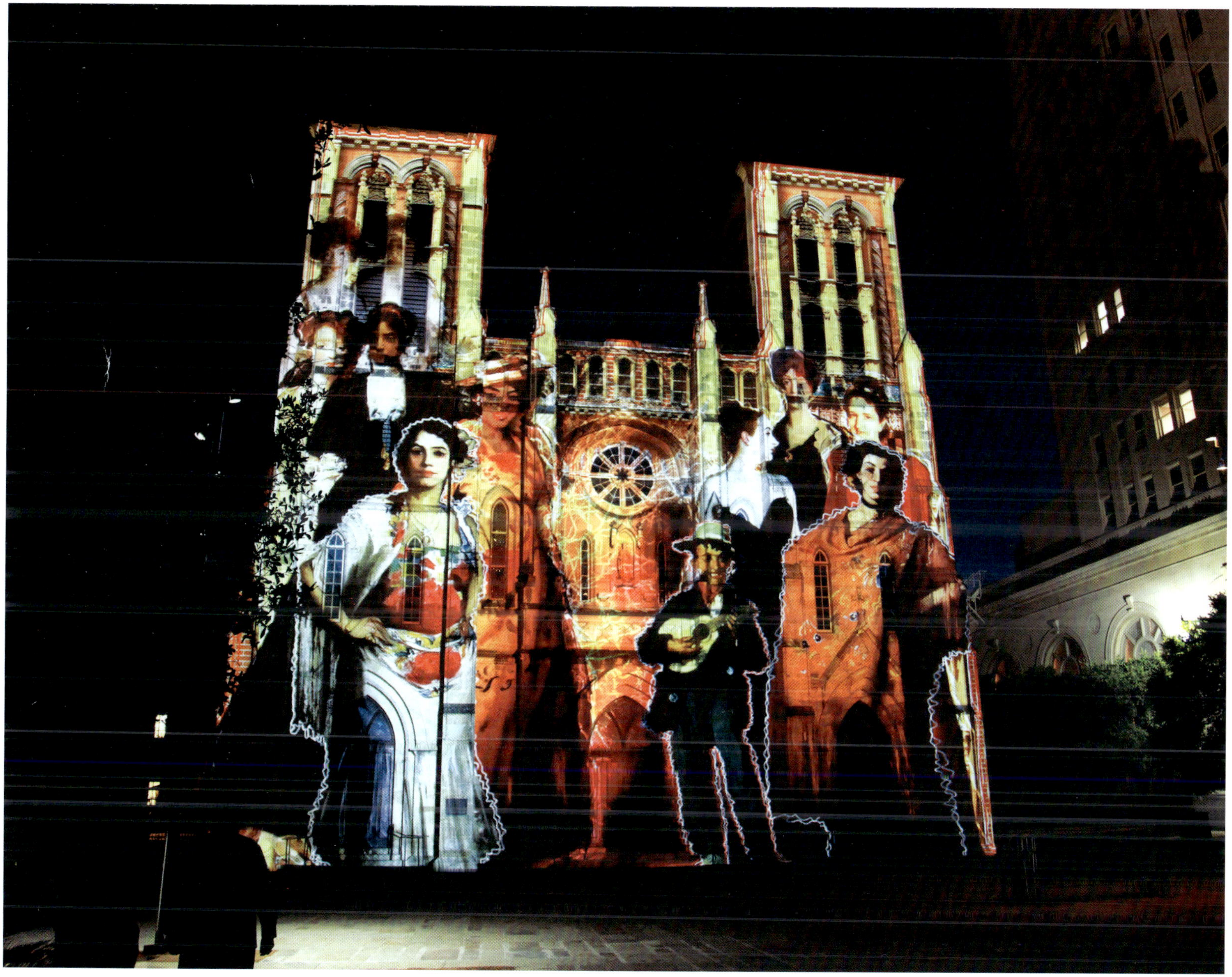

Sequence 9

THE RIVER

THE FLOOD AND THE DAM

The water on the Cathedral sides has remained on the façade through time and shows its freedom in 1921, during the great flood that led to the construction of the dam and to the diversion of the river bed, thus creating the perfect landscape to developing the *River Walk*.

A violent waterfall appears on the Cathedral dressed as the Emily Morgan Hotel, involving vibrating contours of a flooding catastrophe.

The river flow rises on the façade and water spills from the windows.

CITY OF LIGHT

A heavy stone harrow shaped, creates the dam and falls on the river obstructing the flood and reducing the river flow.

San Antonio River prepares for becoming the River Walk. Towers, buildings and hotels design the new landscape around the main attraction of the City.

Construction grows along the river with the revival of this new protected area. The *Hemisfair* tower appears in the City as a symbol of modernity. Enlightened with neon, the vision of the City gradually covers the whole façade showing signage and old logos.

The river flows among San Antonio architecture.

WILD FLOWERS OF TEXAS

Along with the evening neon lights and a Honky Tonk Blues, the wild flowers of Texas come alive.

Blue Bonnets, *Esperanzas* and Indian Paint brush bring in a floral ballet and the elements of San Antonio today: Main Plaza and its *Shade Structures* , new buildings, parking lots, Sebastian sculpture and the river, always the river.

International flags complete the composition.

Music by *Flaco* Jimenez melts with *Tejano* songs.

PEOPLE

Inside Texas *Lonestar* appears the smiling face of a young boy with a Texan hat. His smile is followed by a great number of happy faces from all over Texas and the world, popping in and out of San Fernando frontage as a joyful visiting population.

Among the people appears famous characters giving their blessing to the Plaza: John Paul II, Martin Luther King, Archbishop Flores, Cesar Chavez, Selena... and local figures as Archbishop Gustavo, Father David, *Flaco* Jimenez, Tony Parker, Bill, Gini, Jane, Emilio, parishioners of Concepción mission and the artist. Music plays to the tunes of *Flaco*, Esteban, *Tish*...

FLAGS

Like fireworks, flags fly from all over the world on the façade among a whirling of confettis and balloons.

International flags turn into the 50 flags of the United States of America.

RIVER

A blue curtain of water closes.

The river ends the fiesta.

The piece is done.

NOTE

The 1925 flood brings modifications of the river course.
Catastrophe leads to the construction of an important dam, the Olmos dam.
The river Horseshoe *curve, causing the flood, is diverted and a new branch linking the two sides of the buckle is built. Thus the flood runs much slower.*
The river becomes a big deal during1929 crisis, the City council and private companies join to fight pessimism and the idea of the River Walk becomes reality.
Since the fifties the City is joyful, cosmopolitan and playful, with many attractions and fame. Hemisfair *in 1968, music, art fairs, Mexican traditions, basketball and the* Spurs *make San Antonio a most attractive international destination.*

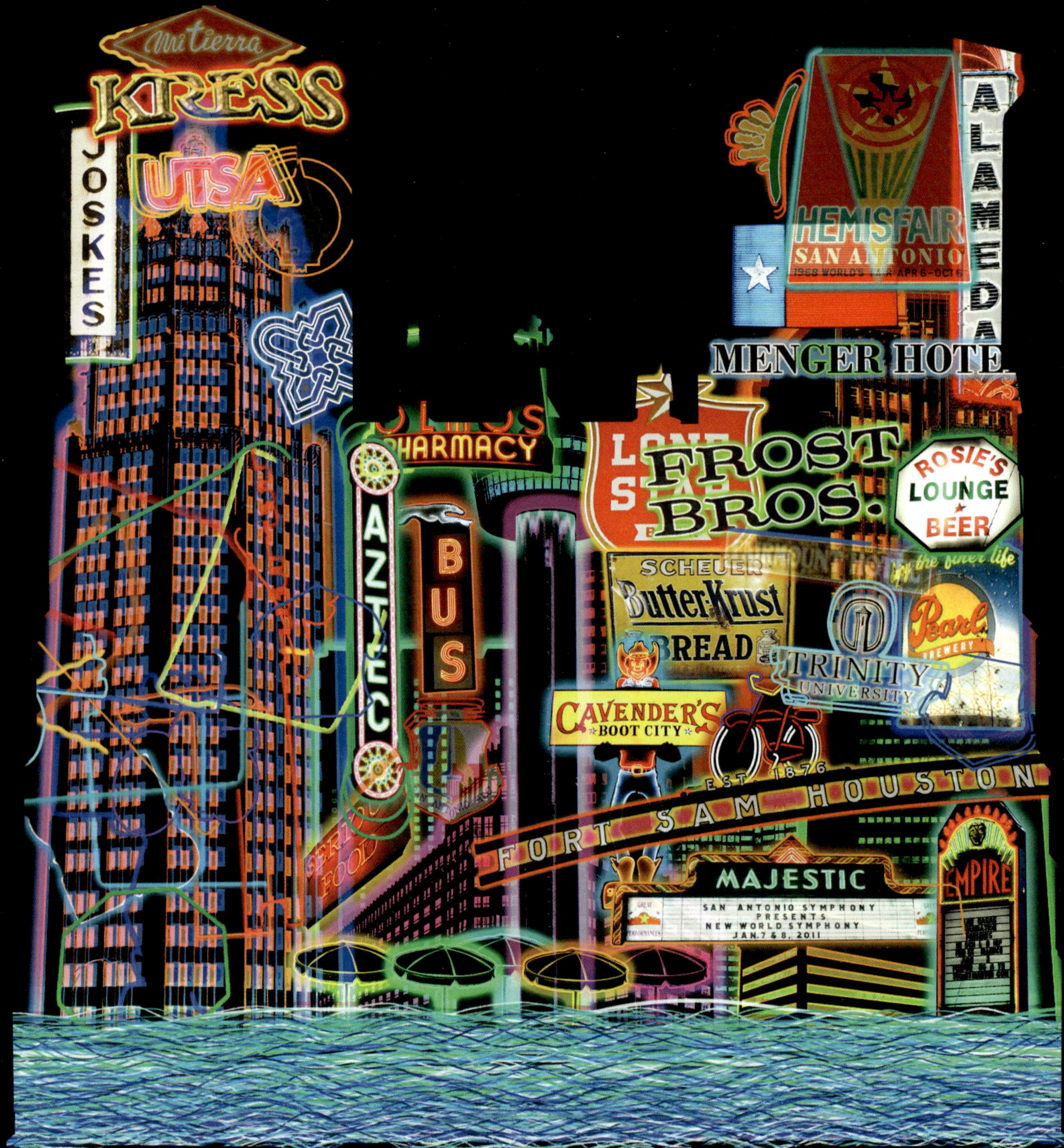

City of Light

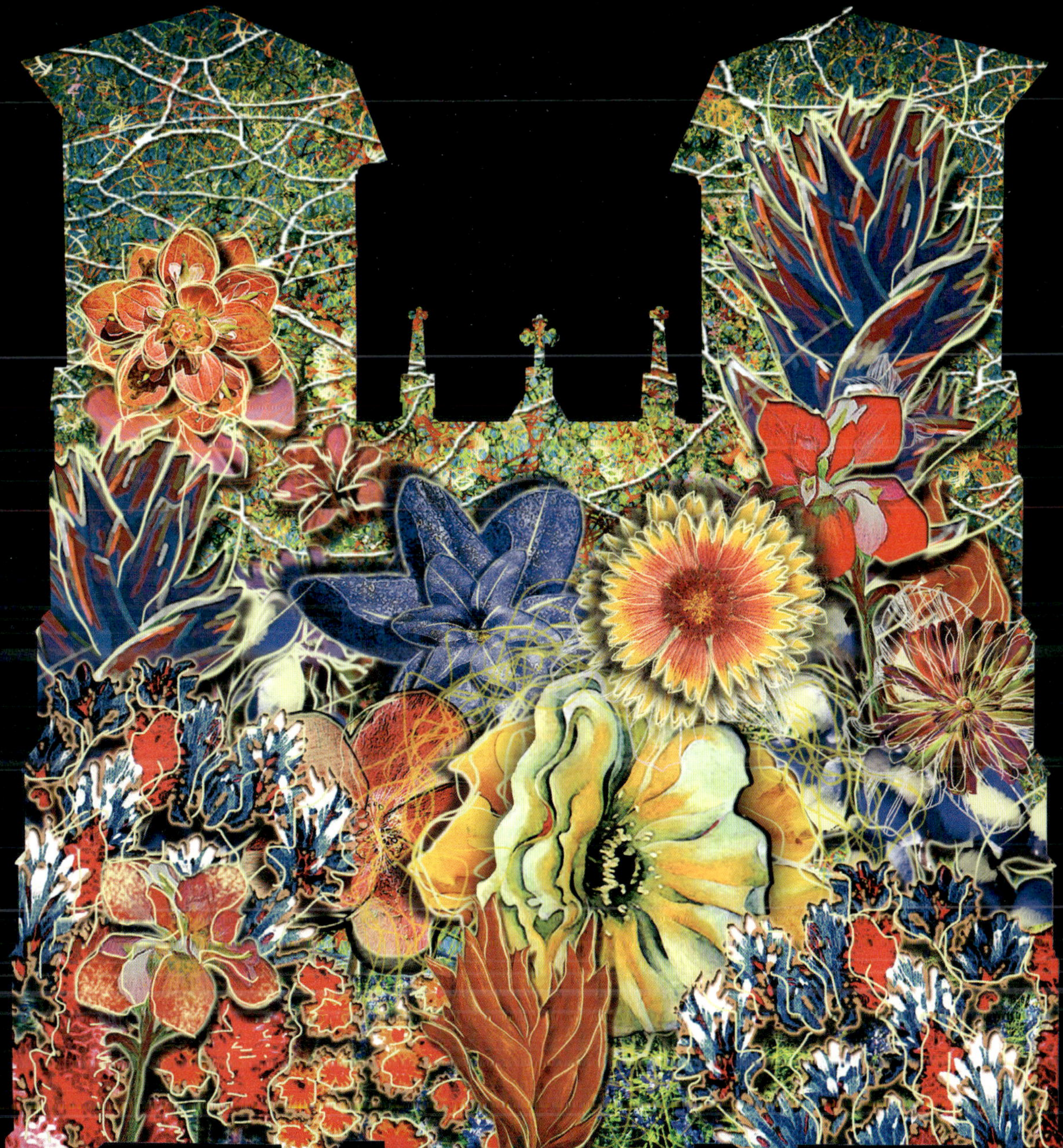

Wild flowers of Texas

The Flood and the Dam

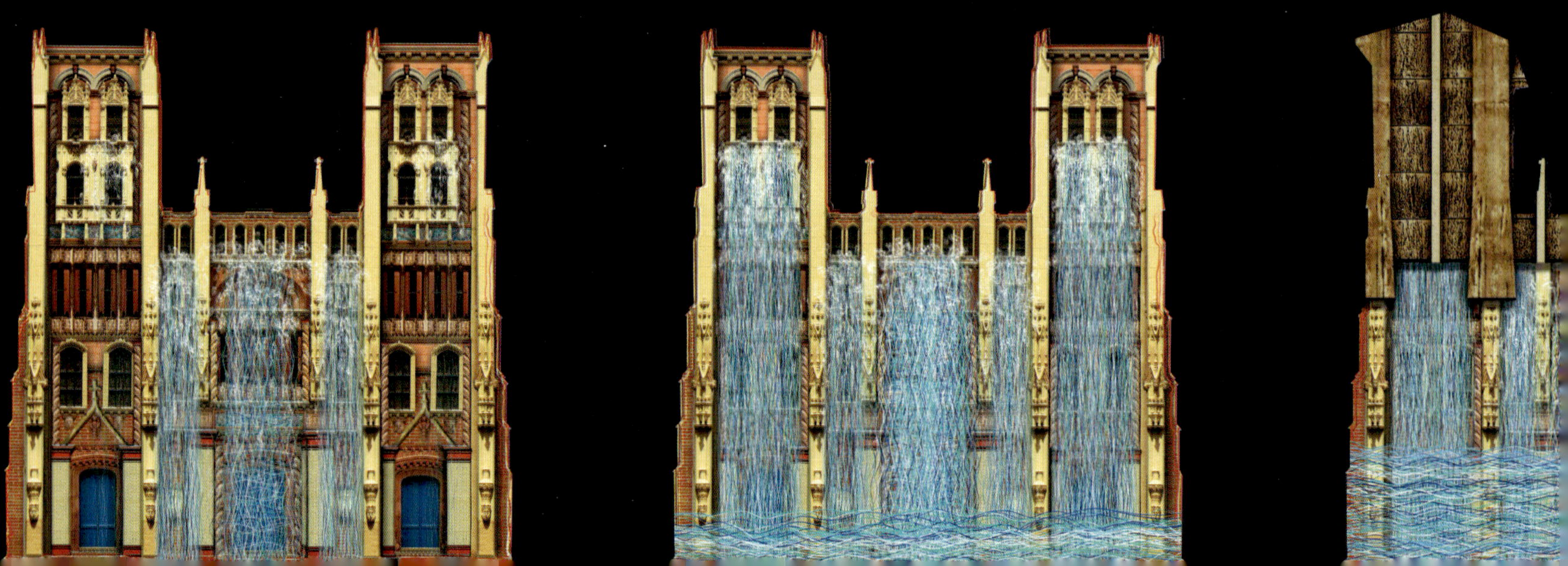

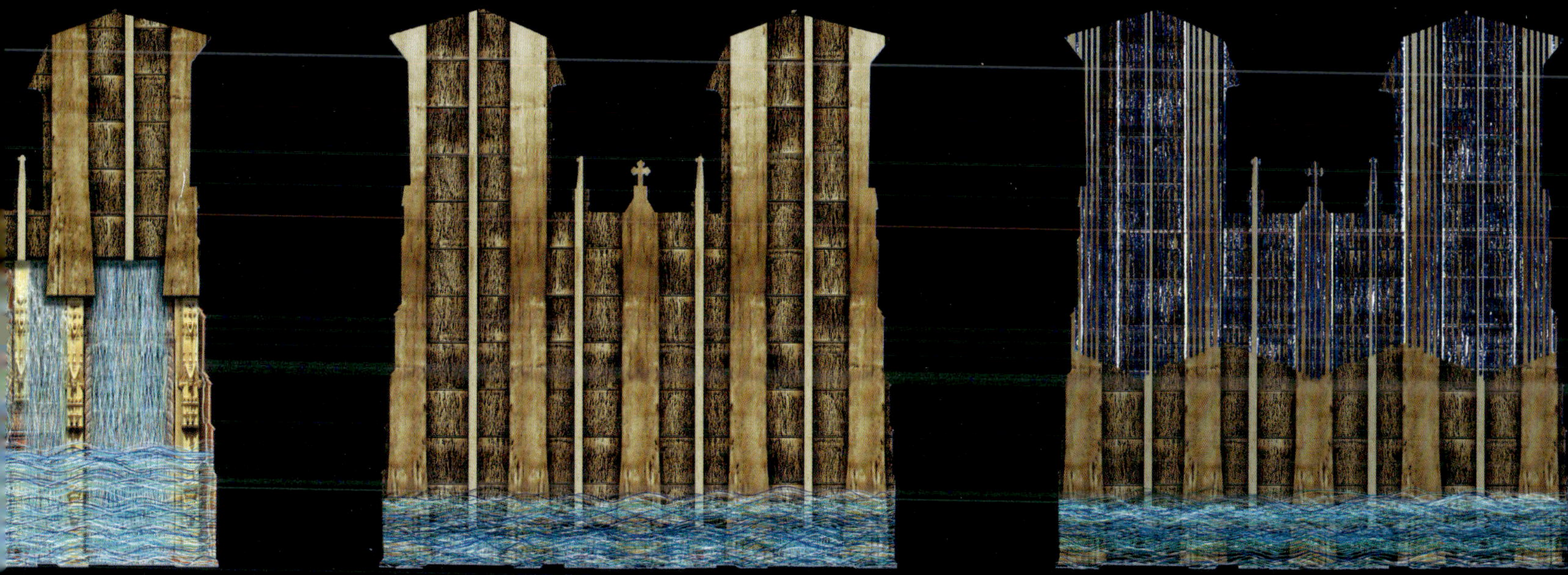

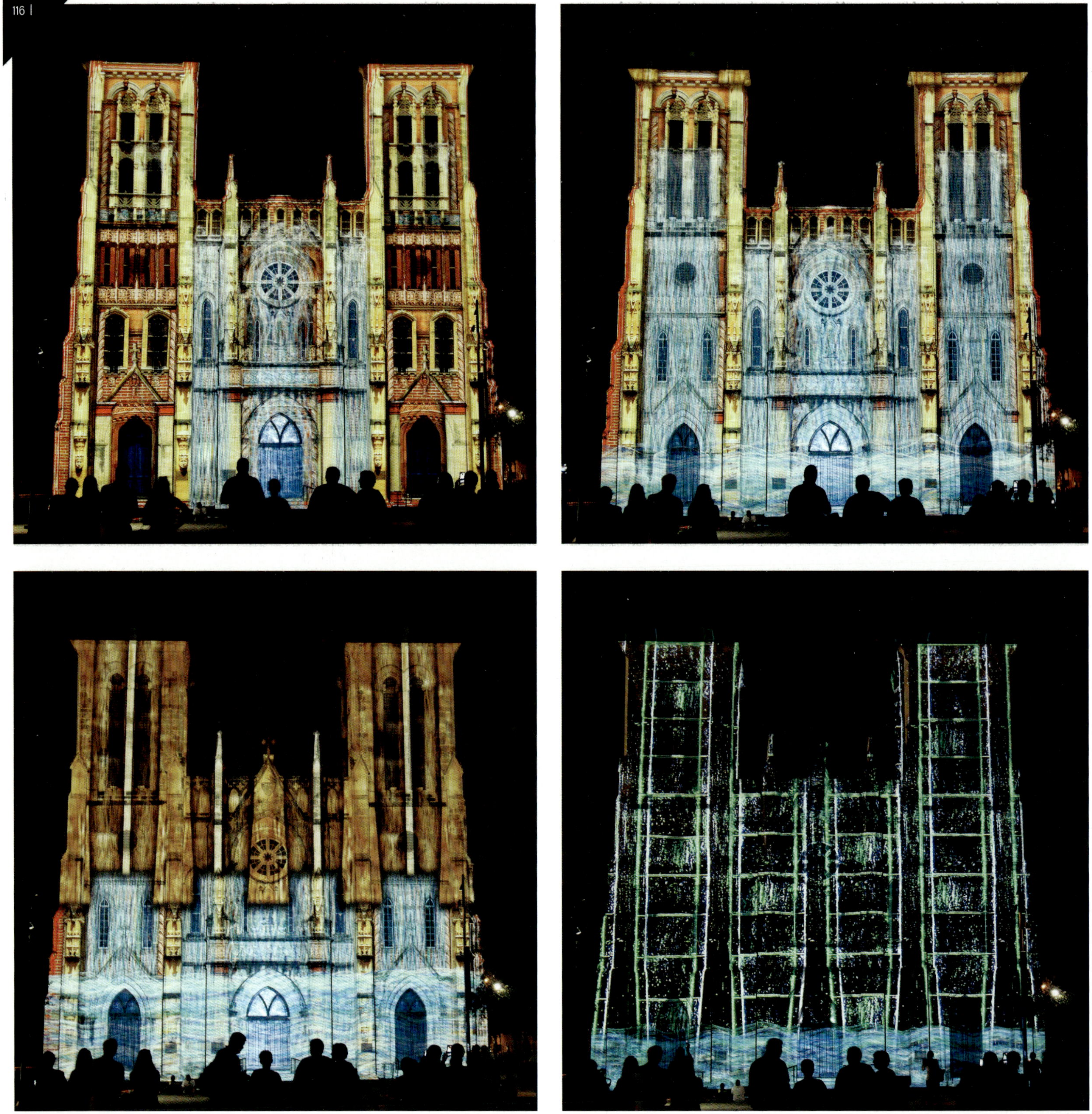

- SAN ANTONIO THE SAGA -

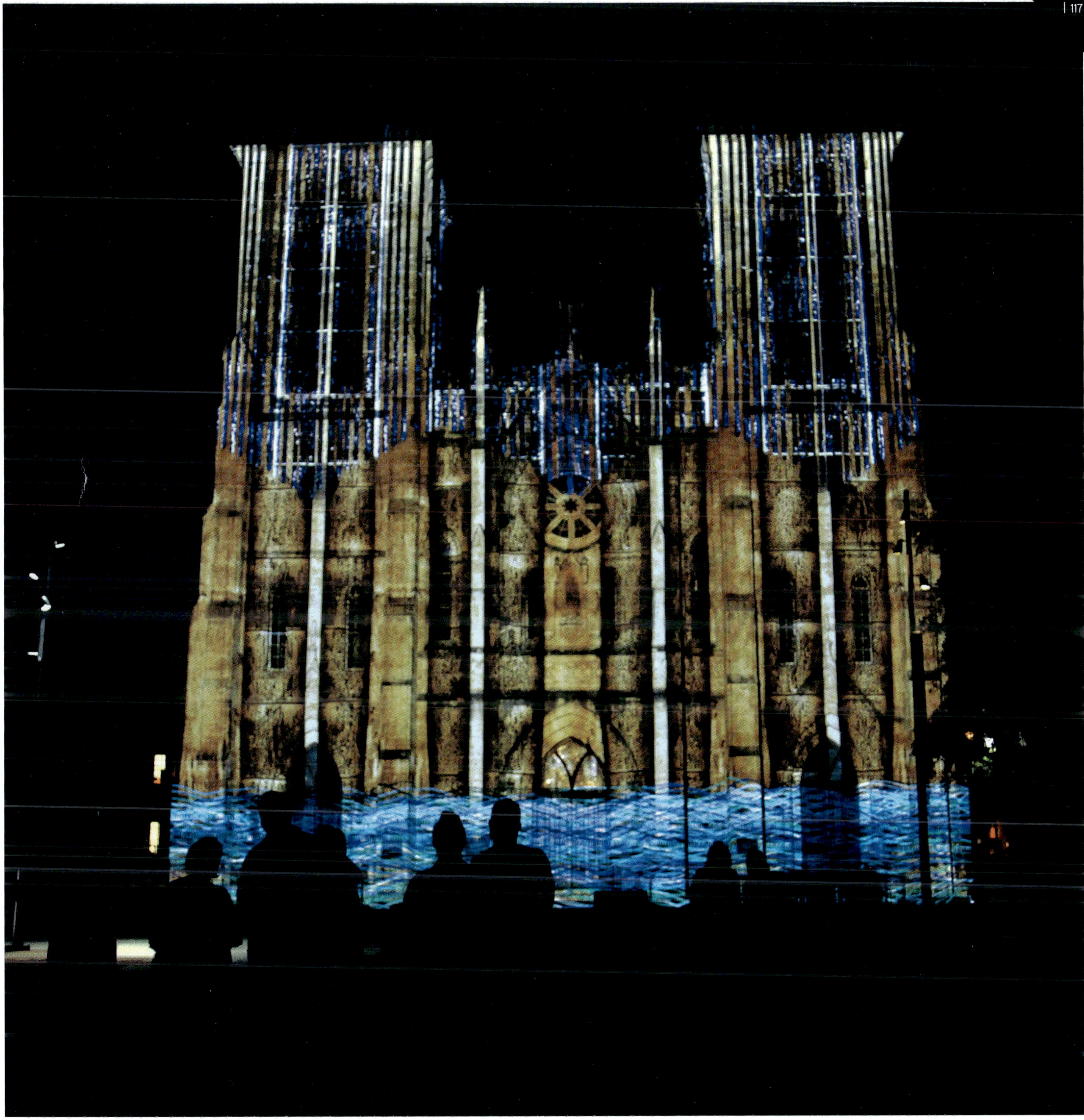

City of Light

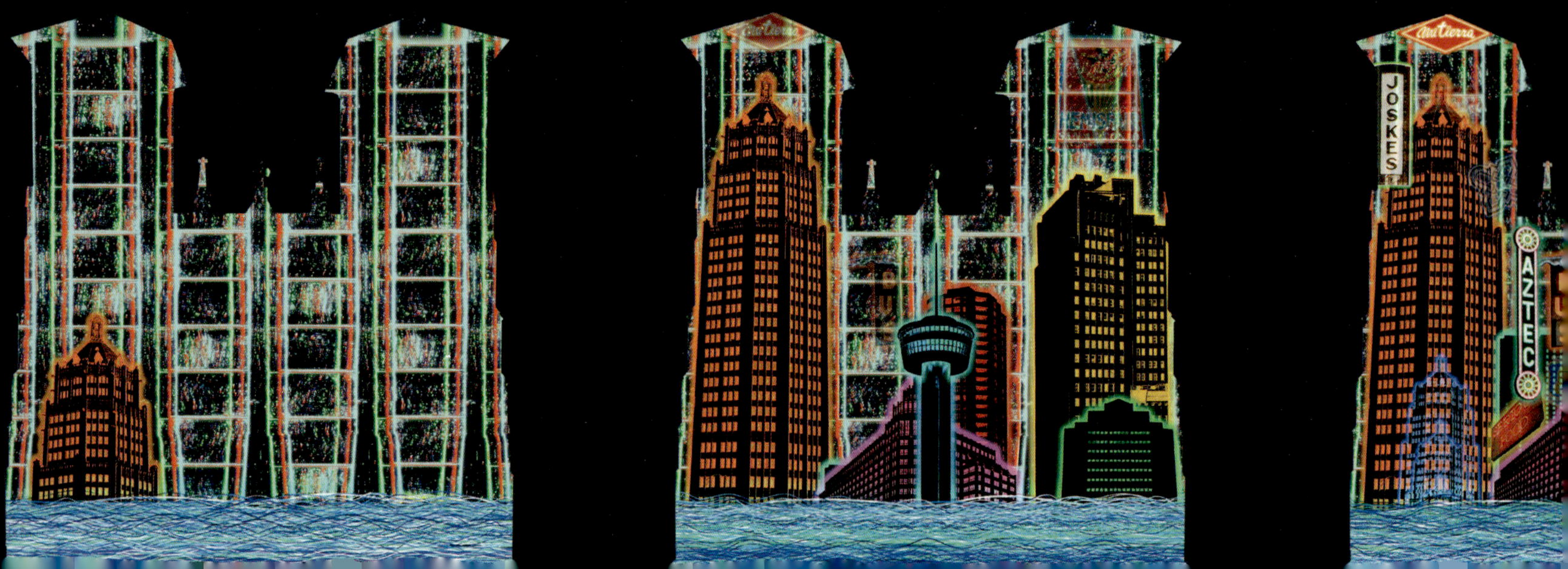

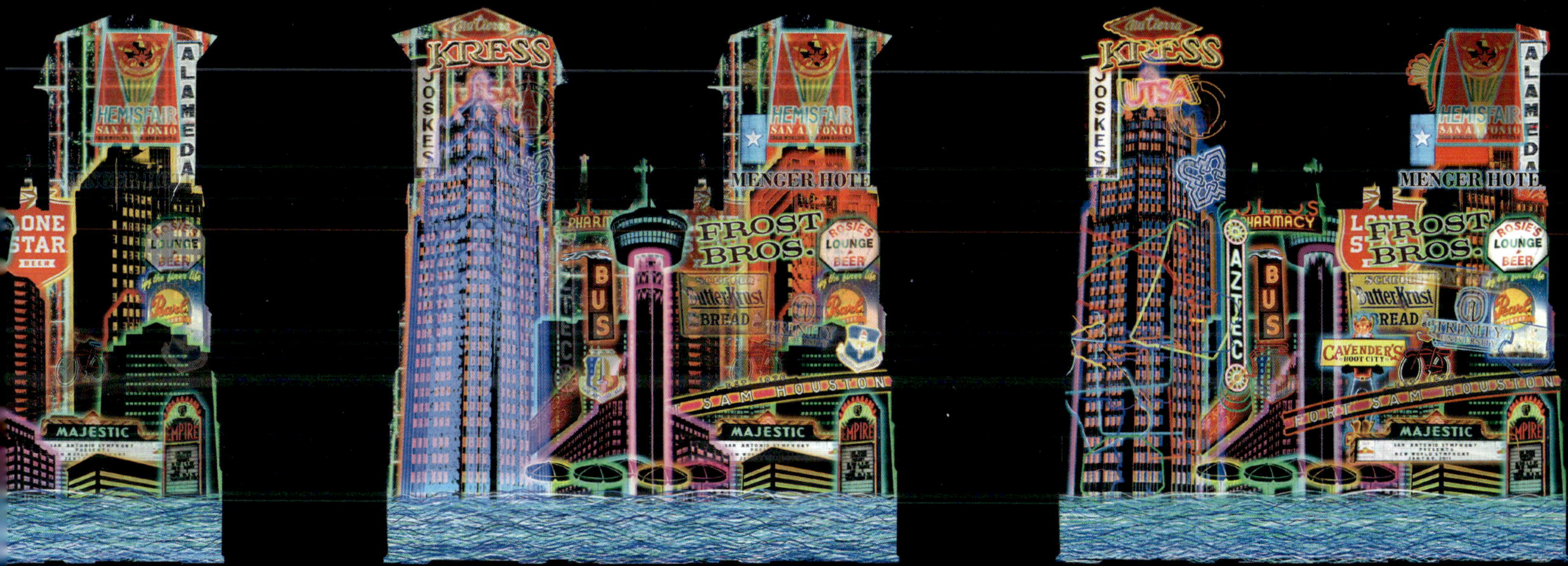
KRESS
JOSKES
UTSA
HEMISFAIR
SAN ANTONIO
ALAMEDA
MENGER HOTEL
PHARMACY
AZTEC
BUS
FROST BROS.
ROSIE'S LOUNGE BEER
Butter Krust BREAD
TRINITY
CAVENDER'S
FORT SAM HOUSTON
MAJESTIC
EMPIRE
ONE STAR

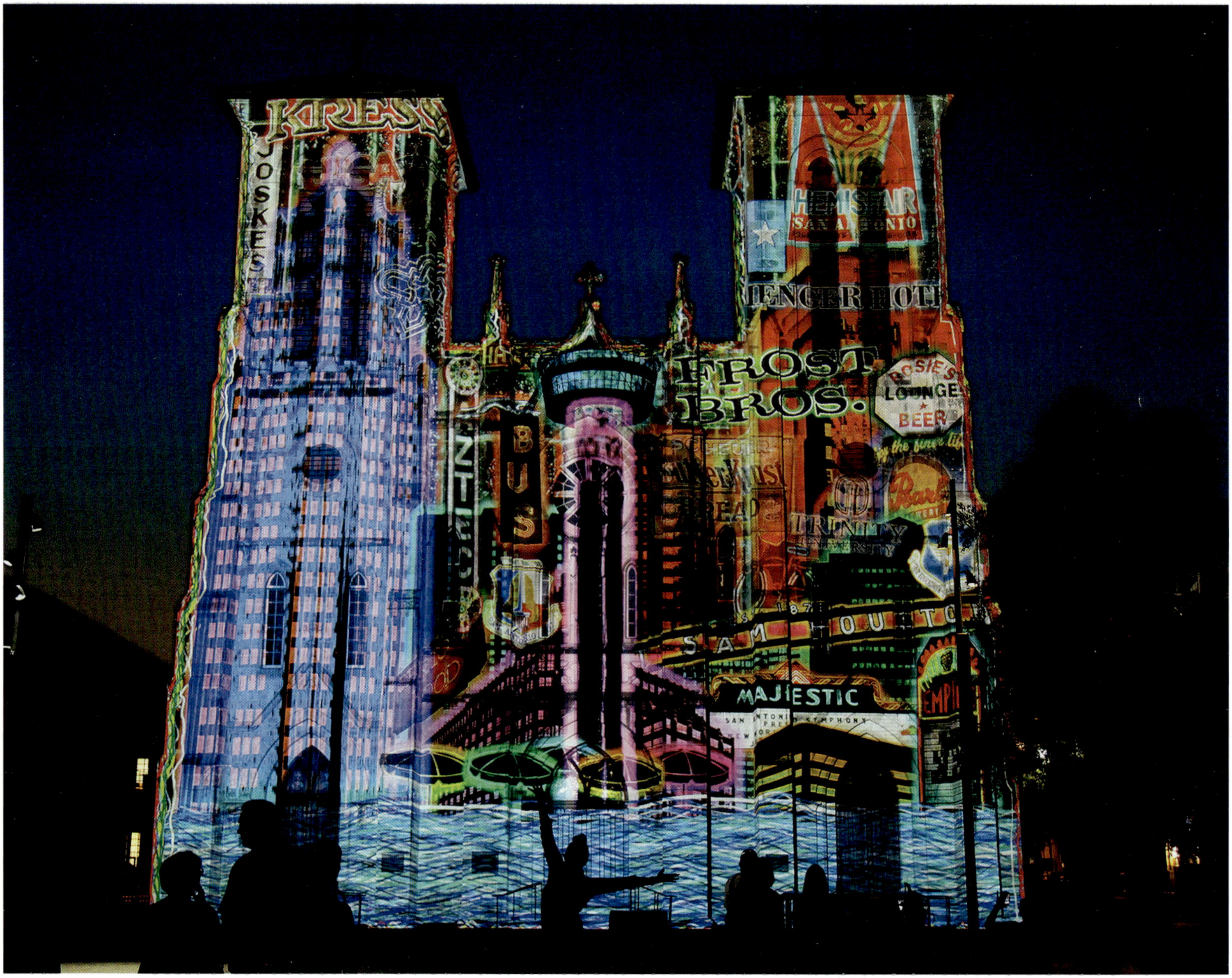
KRESS
JOSKES
FROST
BROS.
ROSIE'S
LOUNGE
BEER
BUS
MAJESTIC

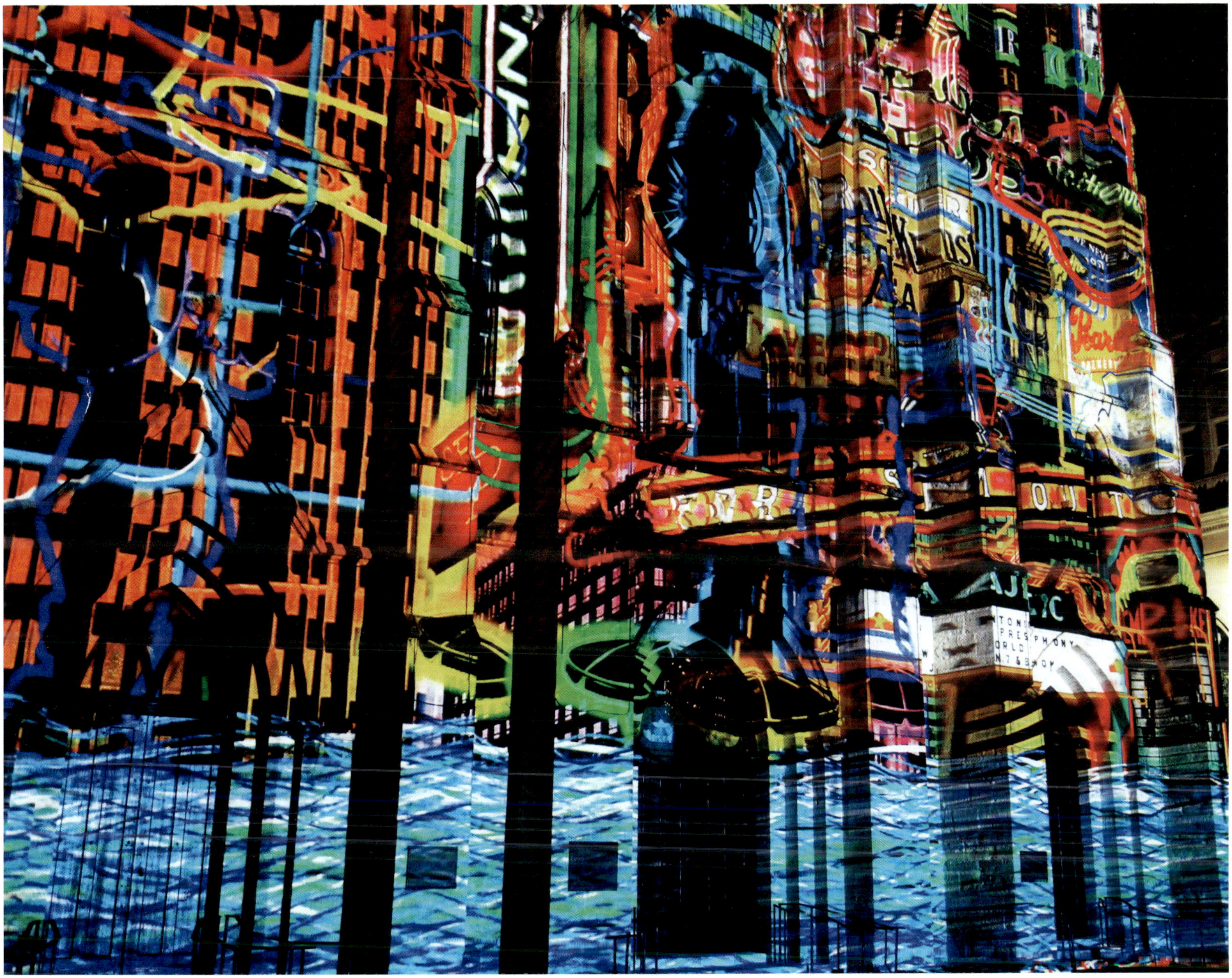

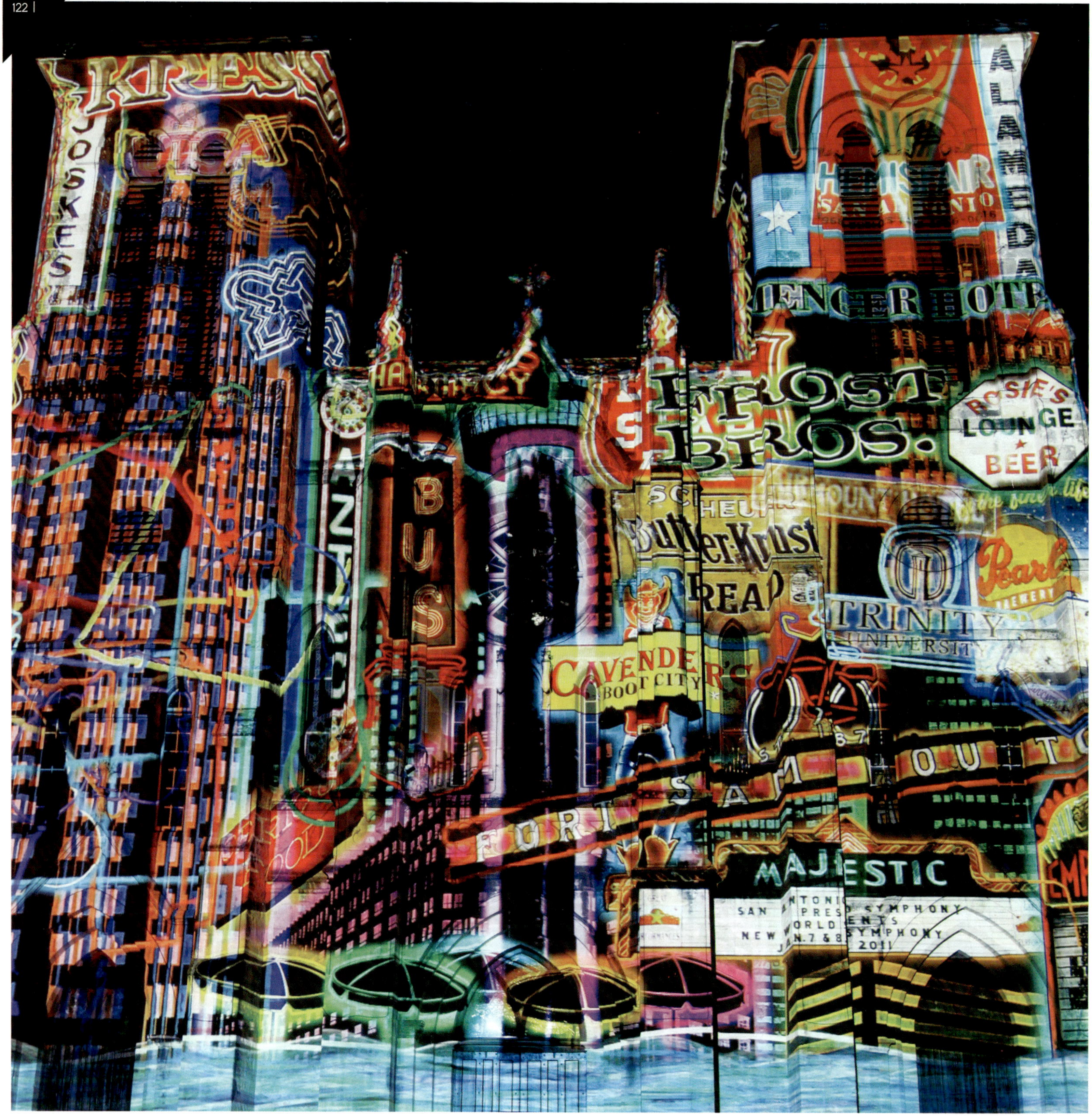
JOSKES
ALAMEDA
FROST BROS.
ROSIE'S LOUNGE BEER
BUS
Butter-Krust
TRINITY UNIVERSITY
CAVENDER'S BOOT CITY
MAJESTIC

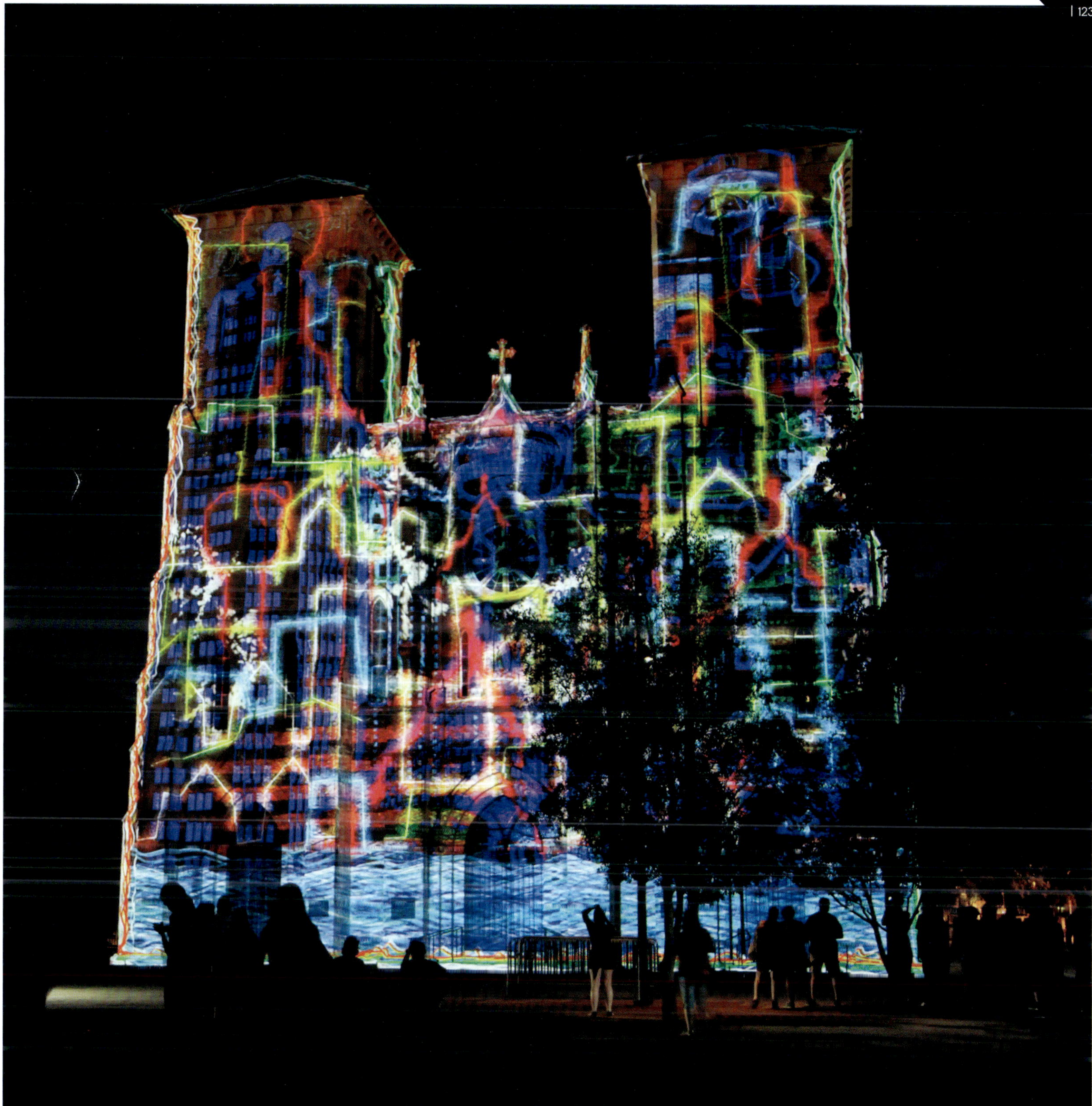

Wild flowers of Texas

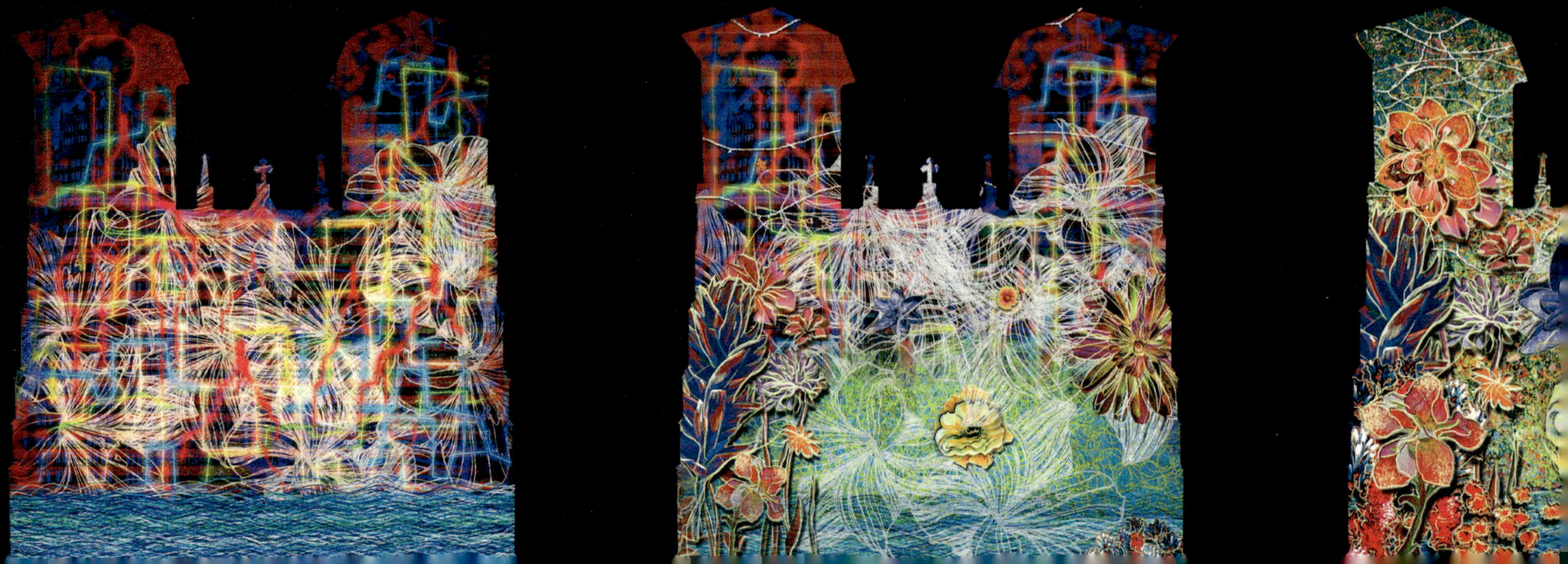

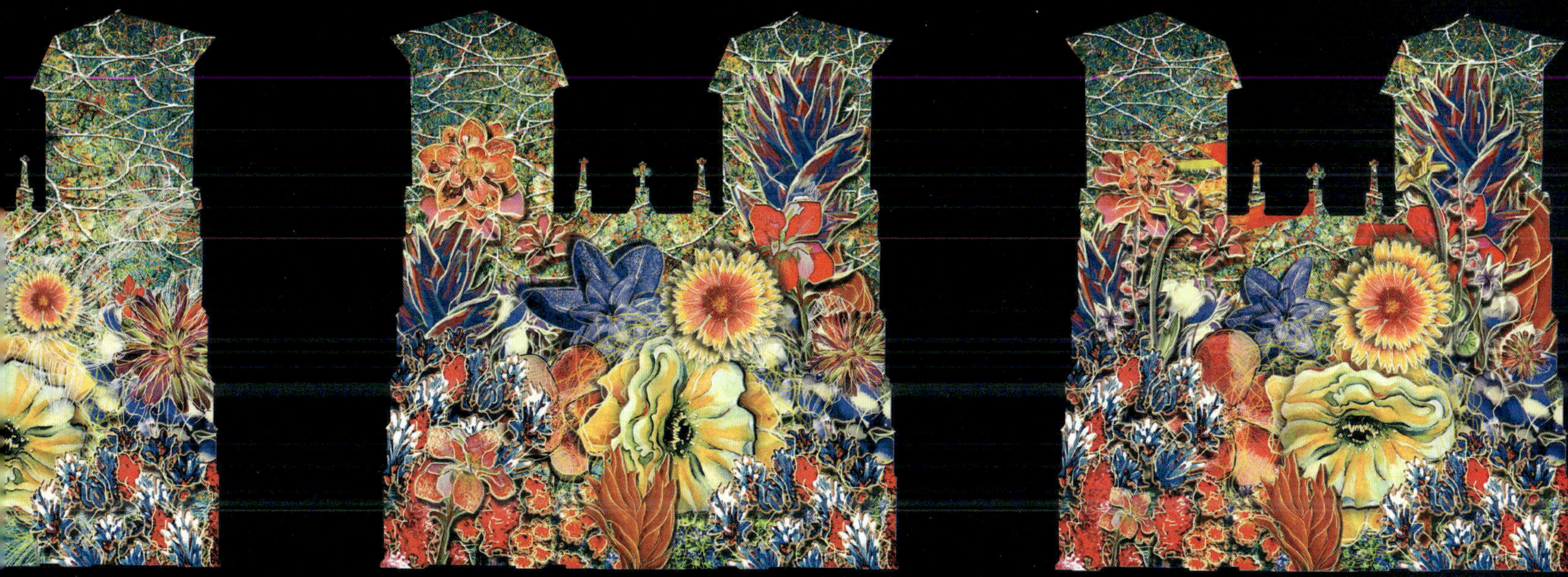

Main Plaza

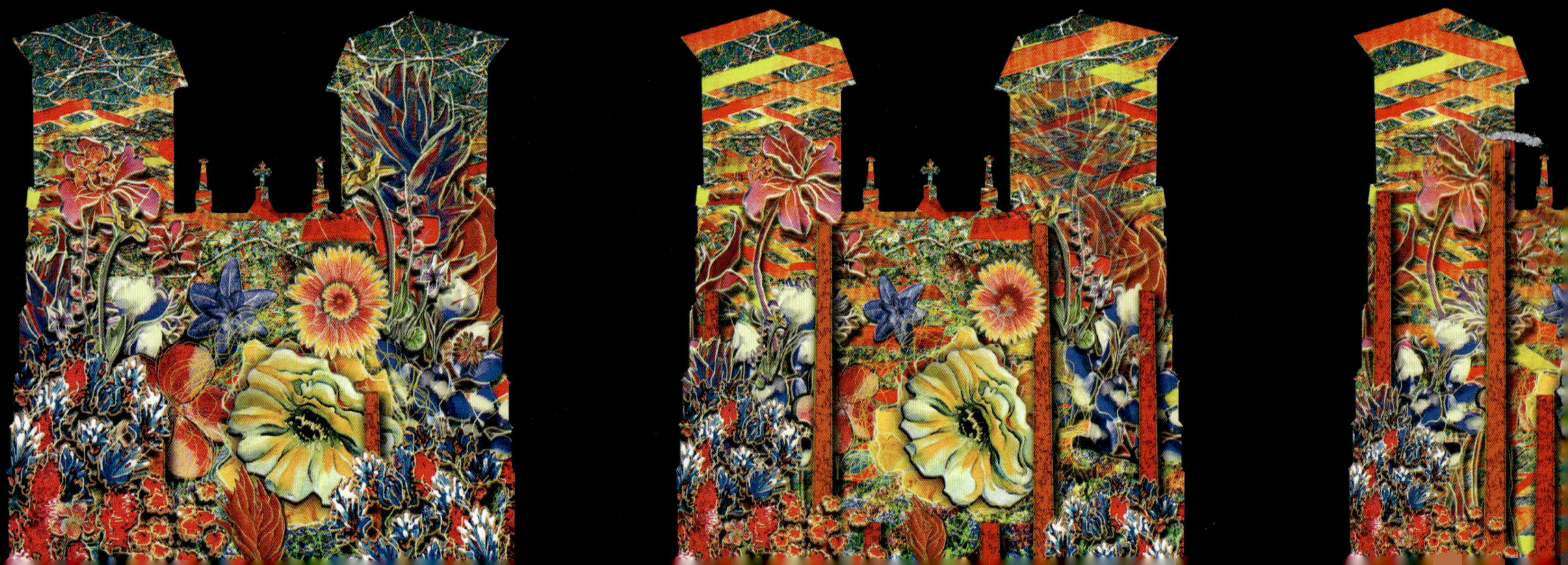

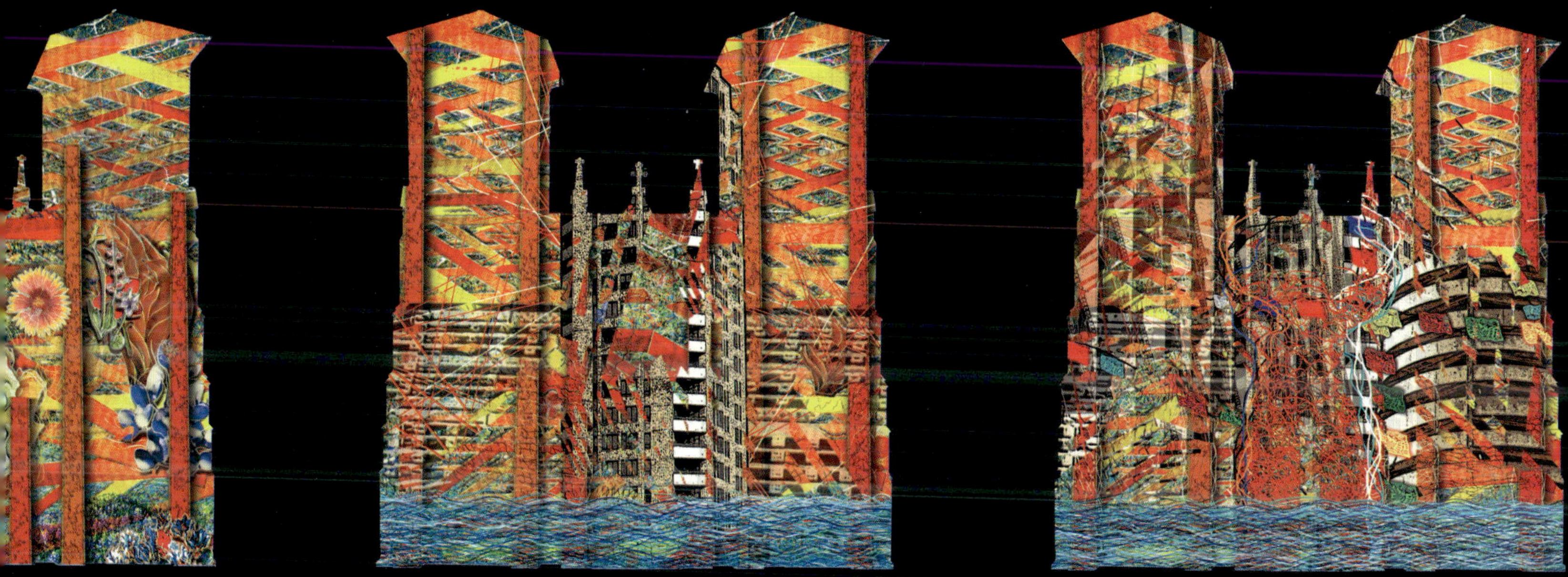

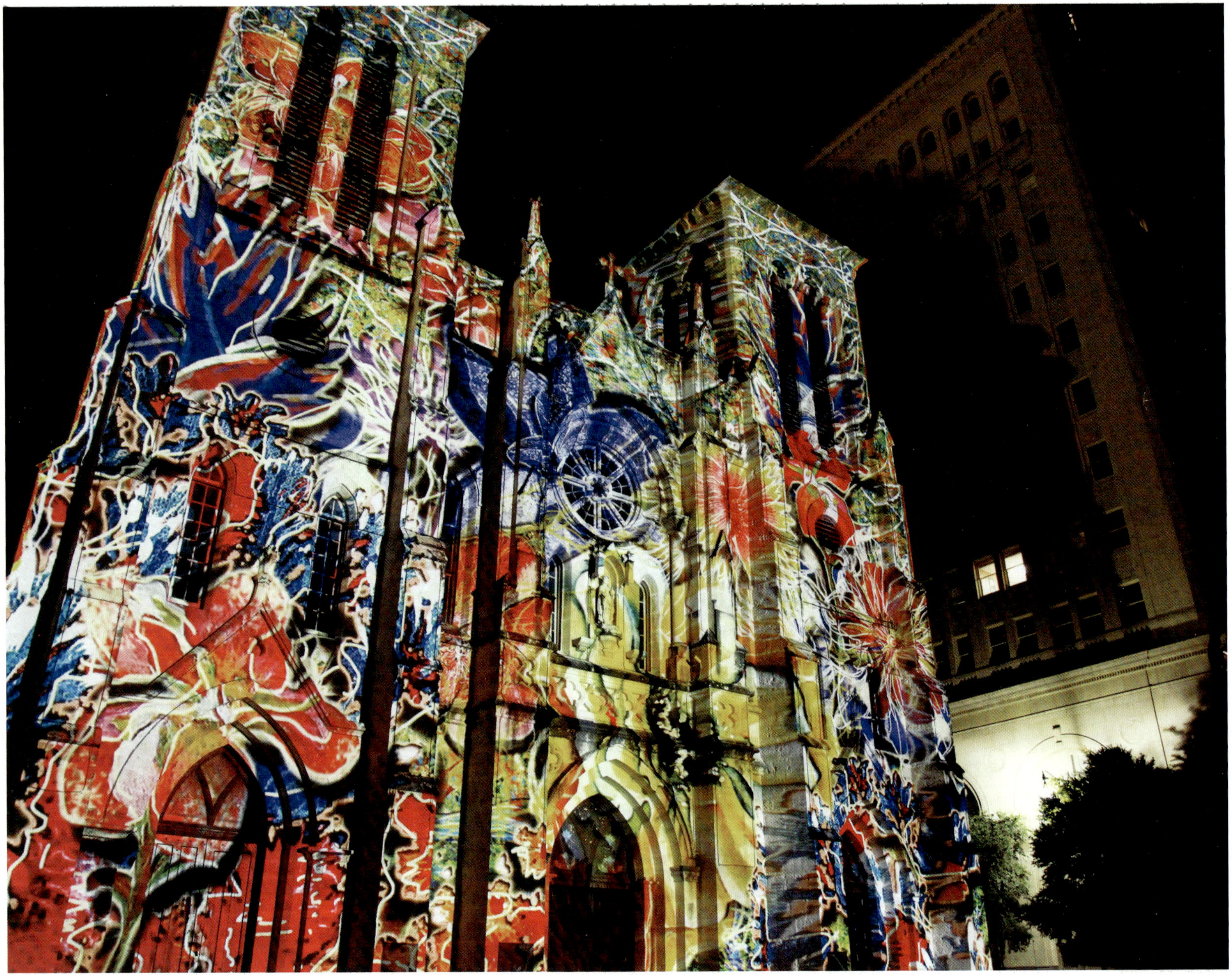

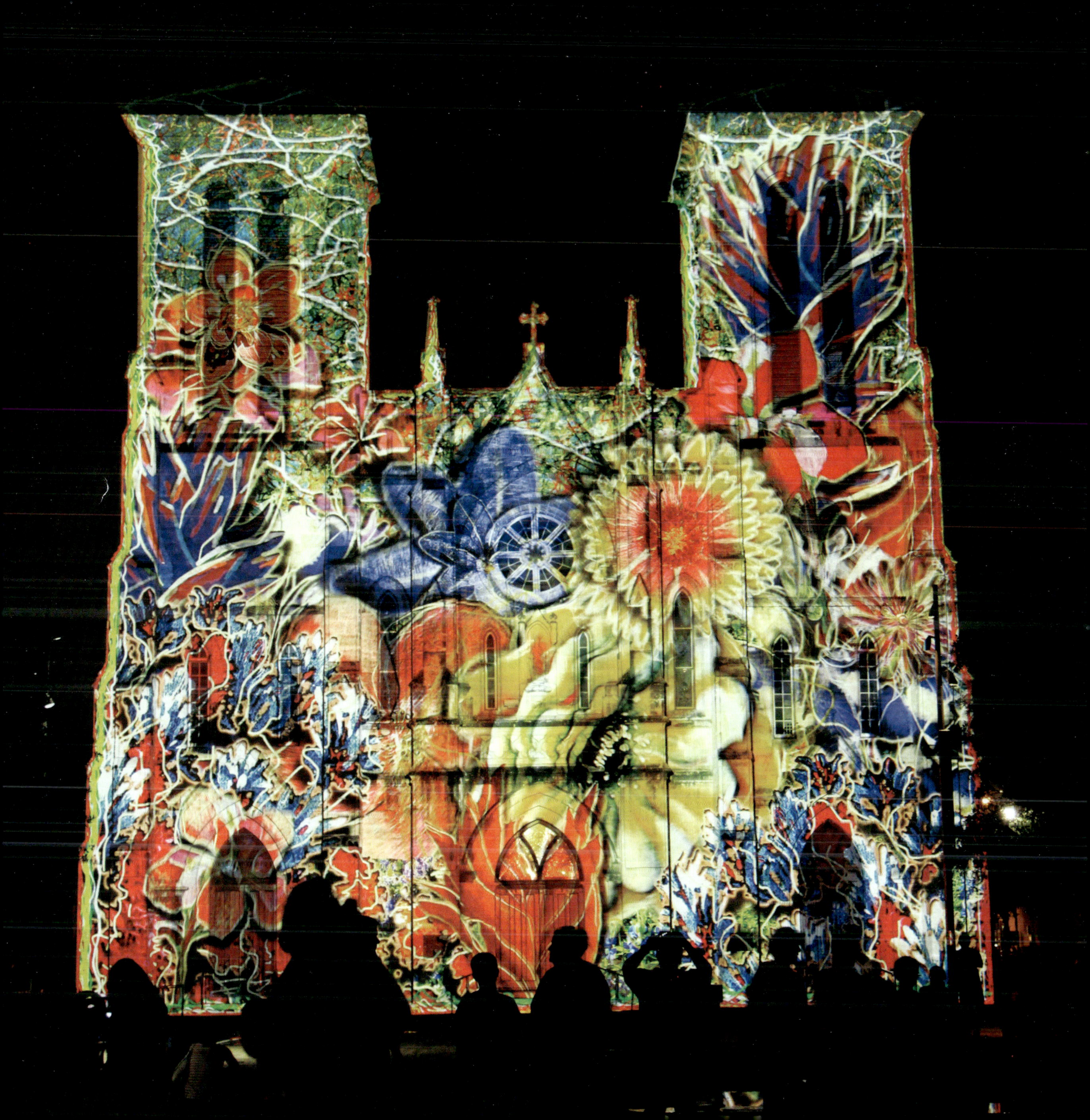

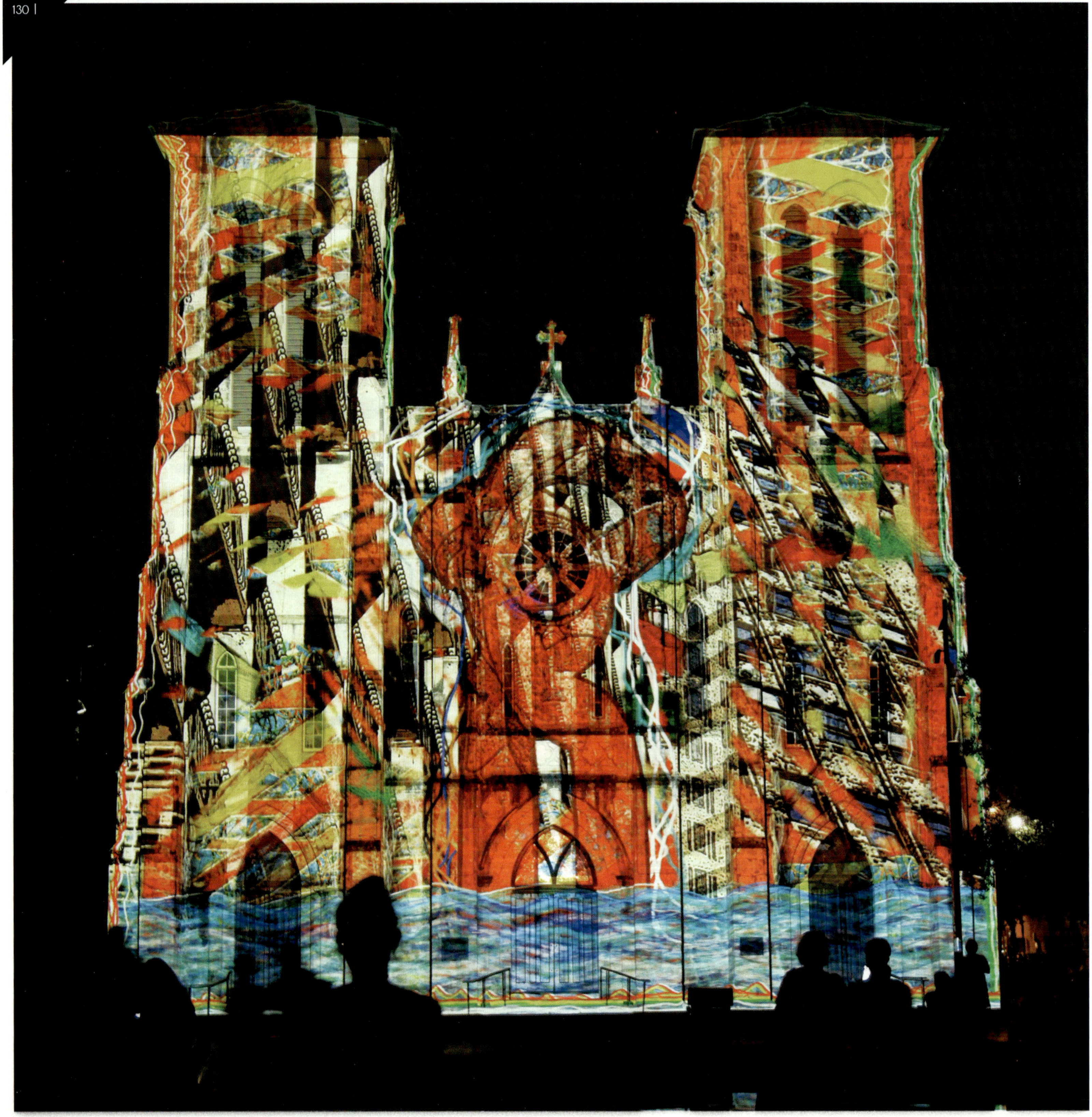

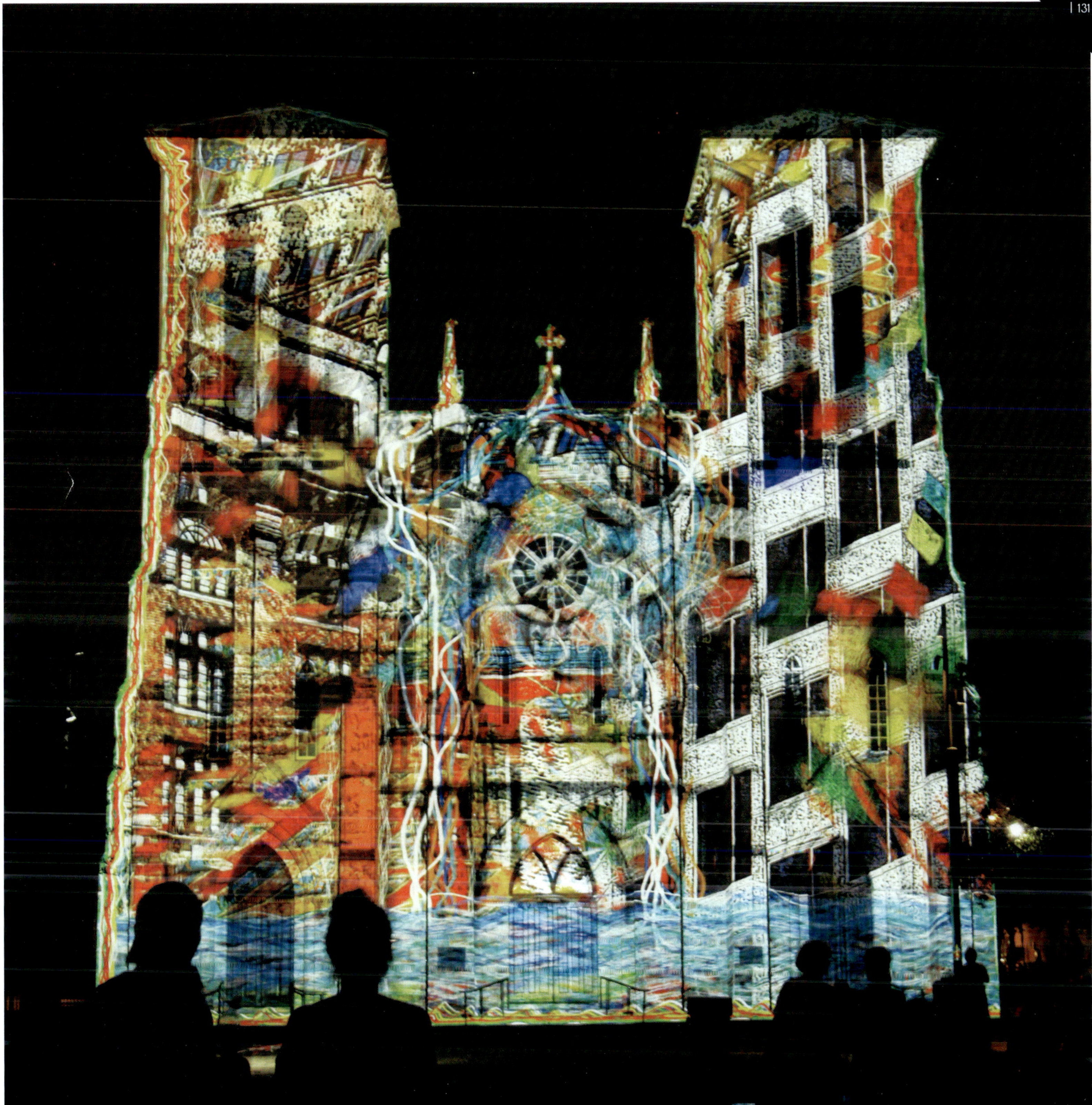

People

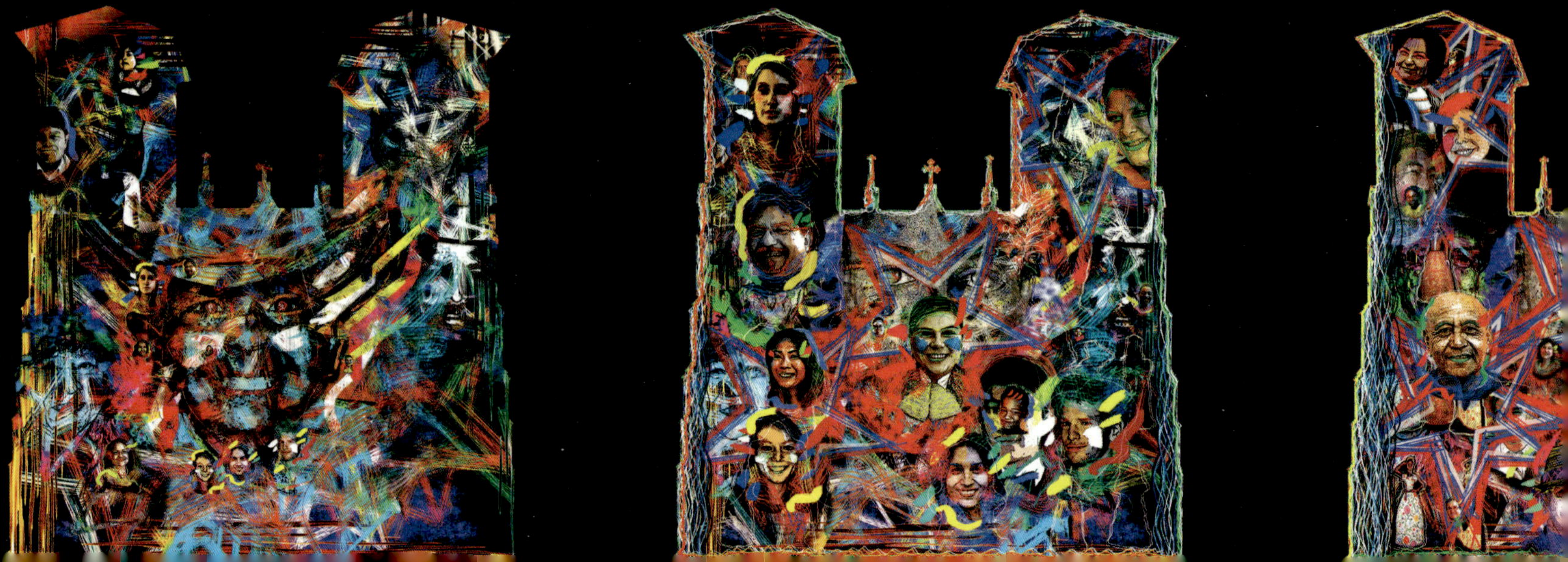

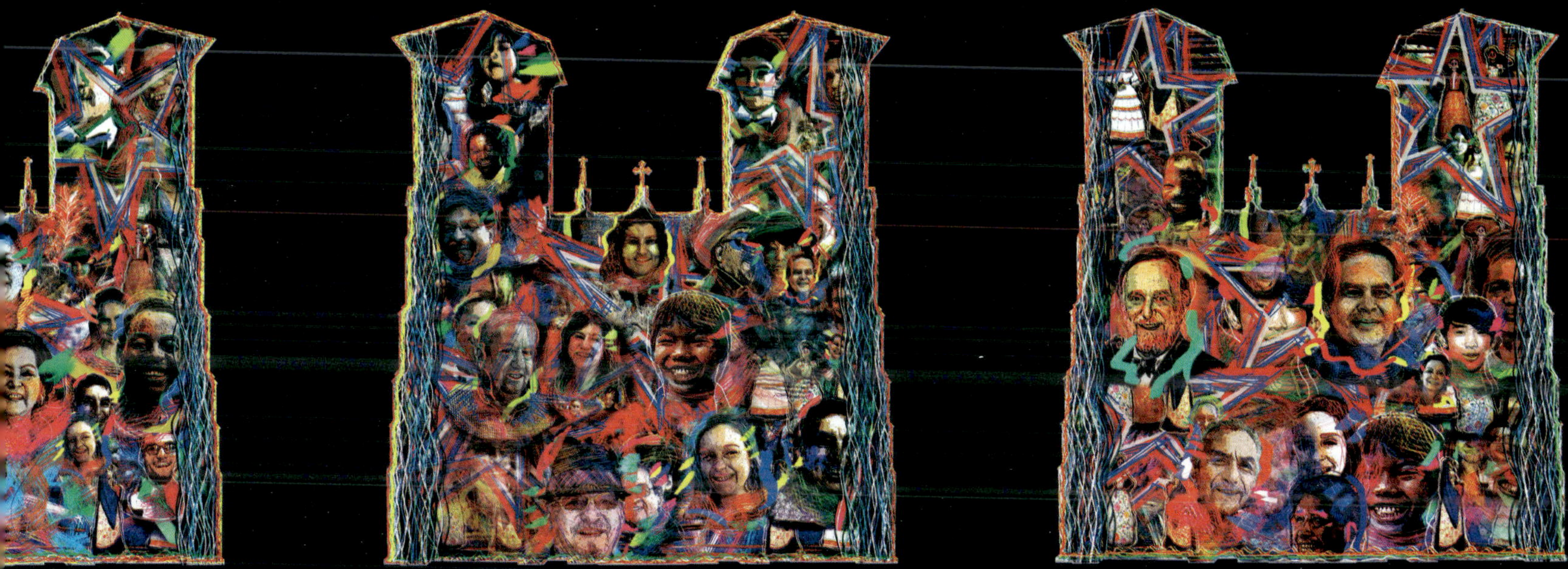

People

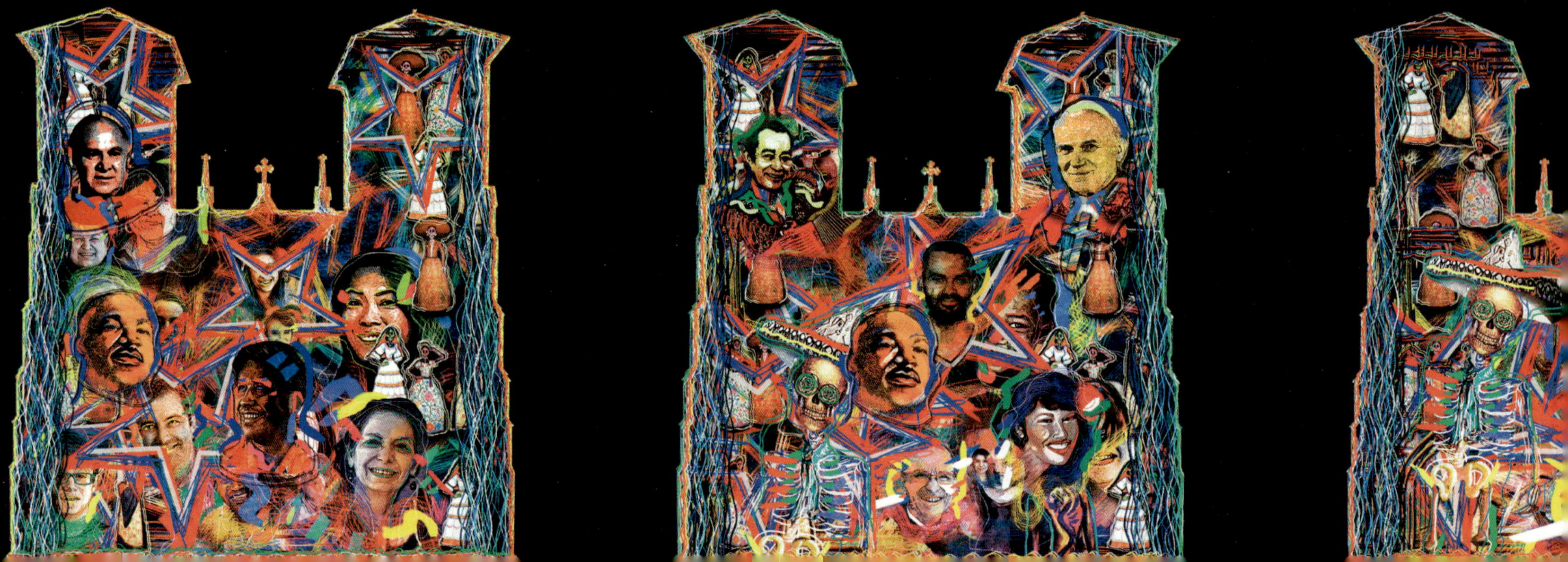

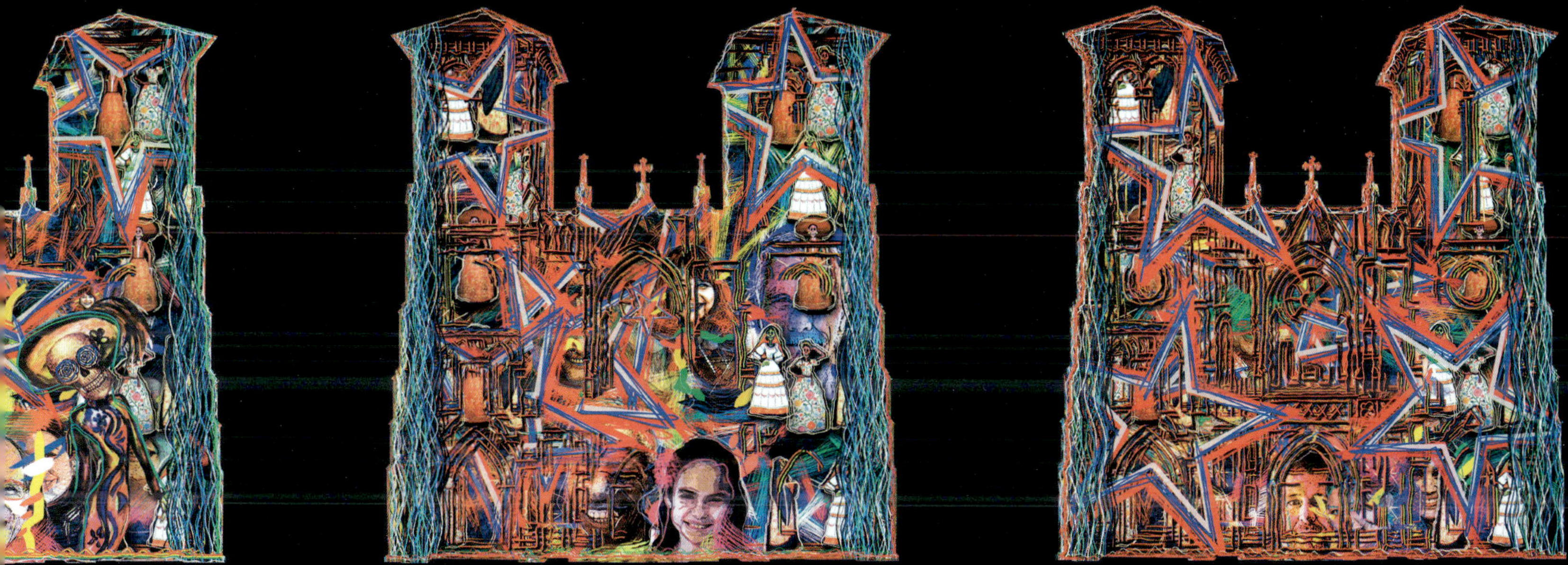

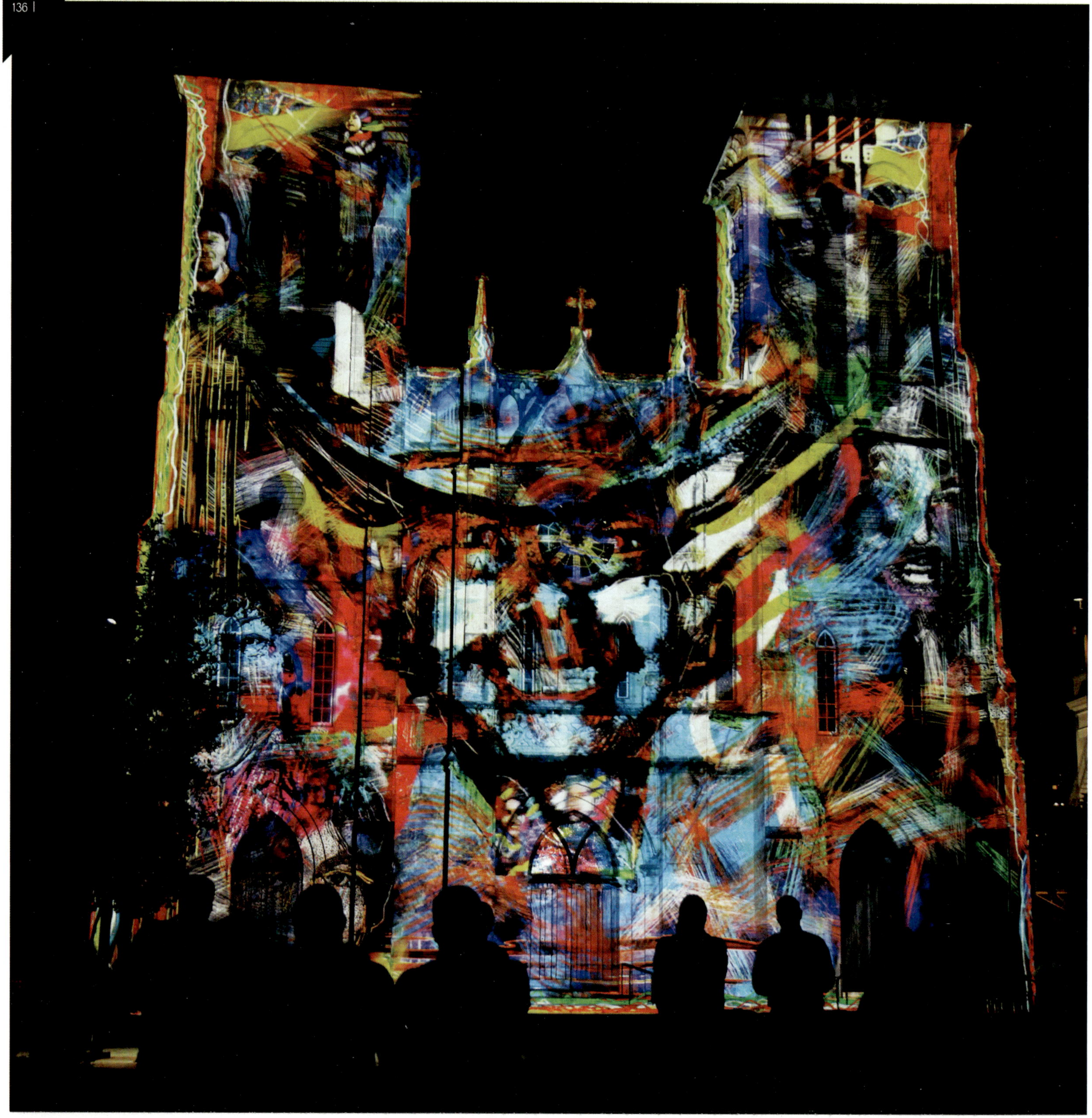

– SAN ANTONIO THE SAGA –

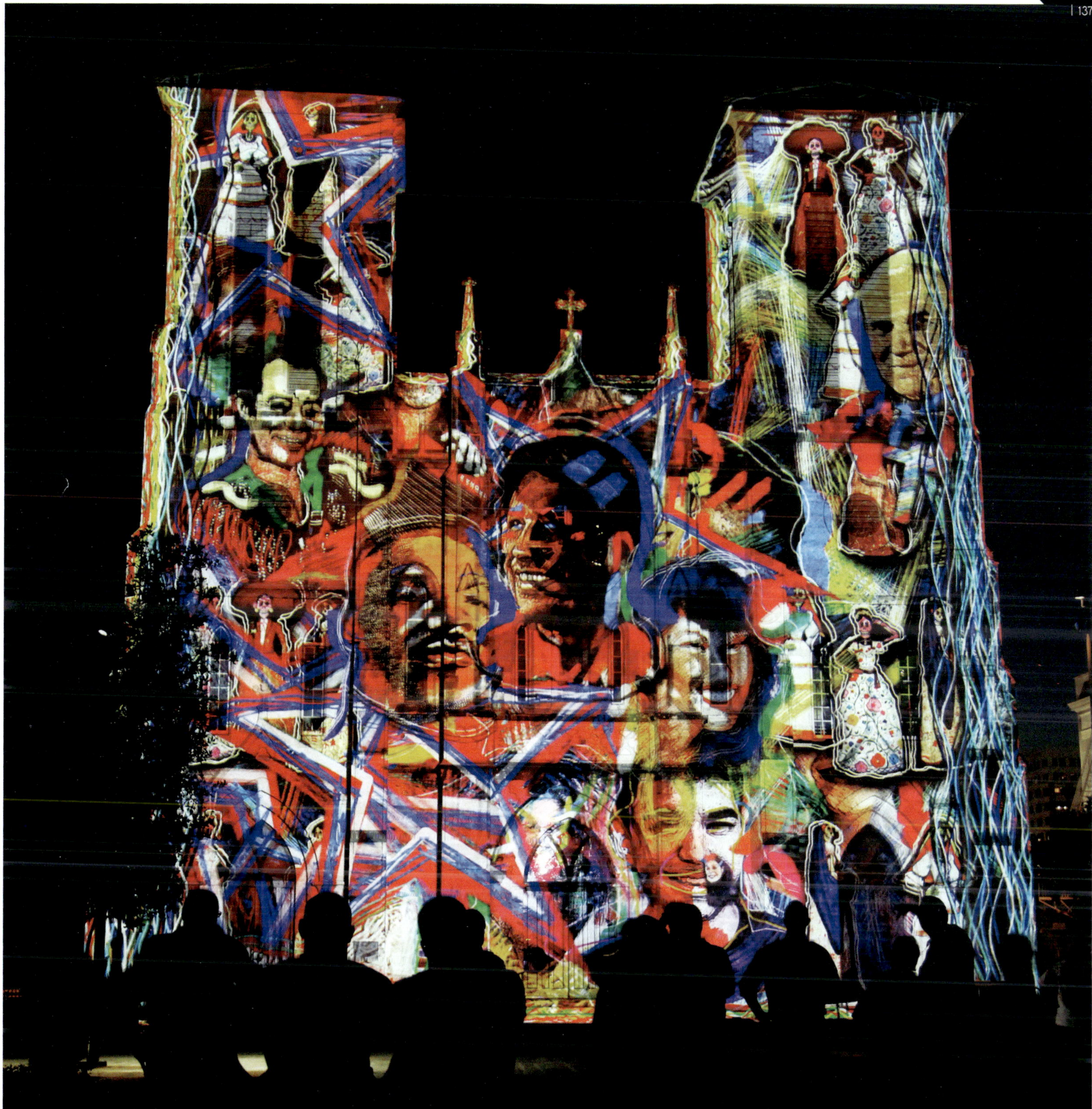

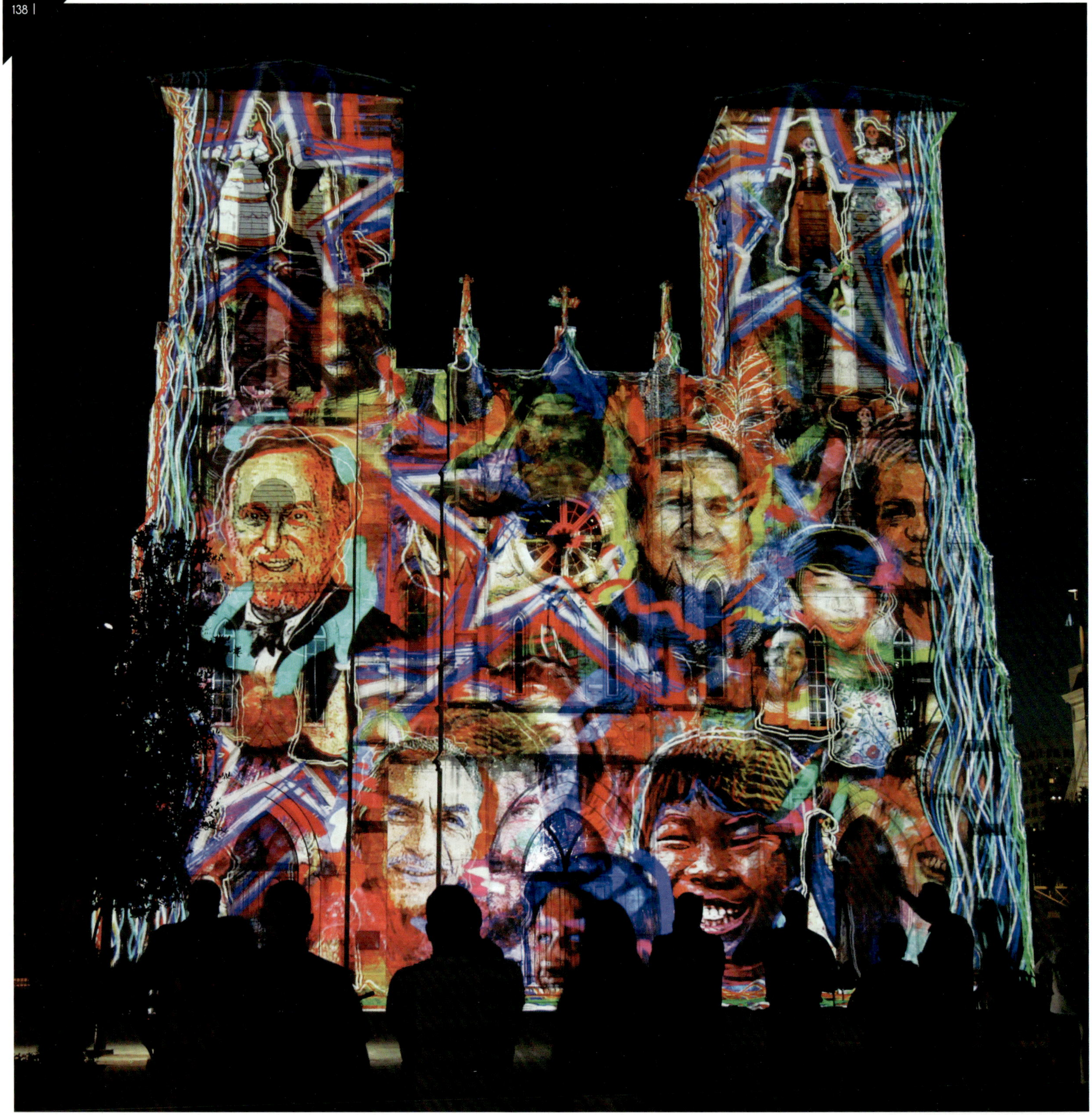

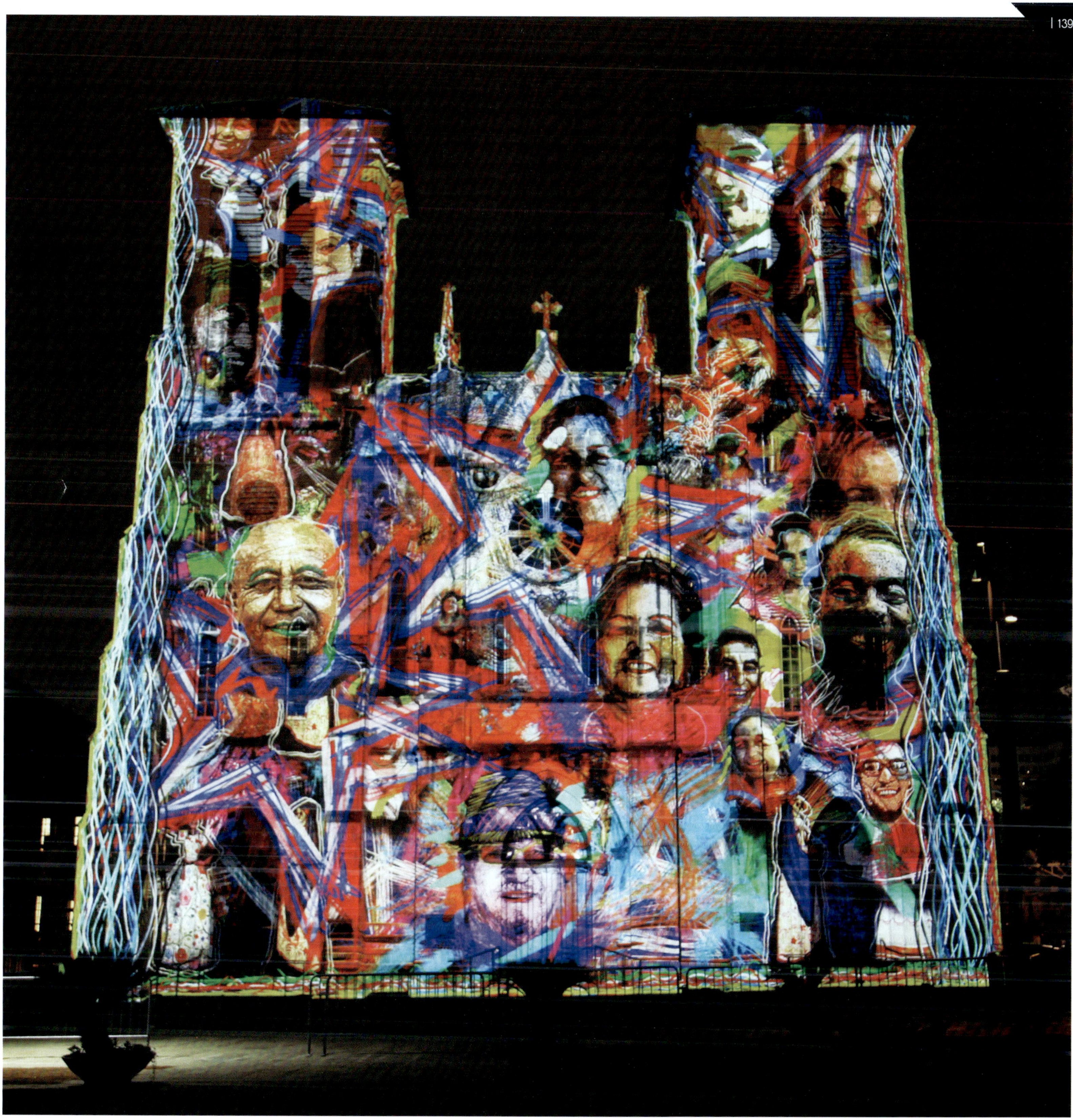

Flags

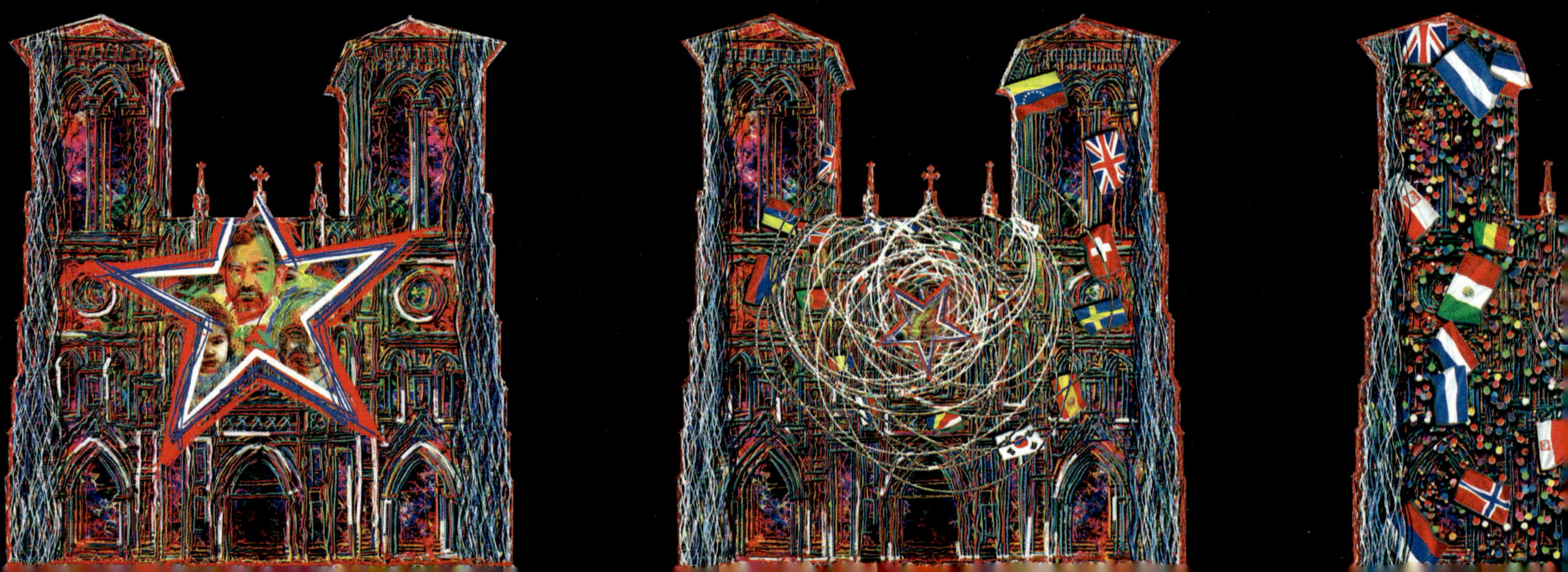

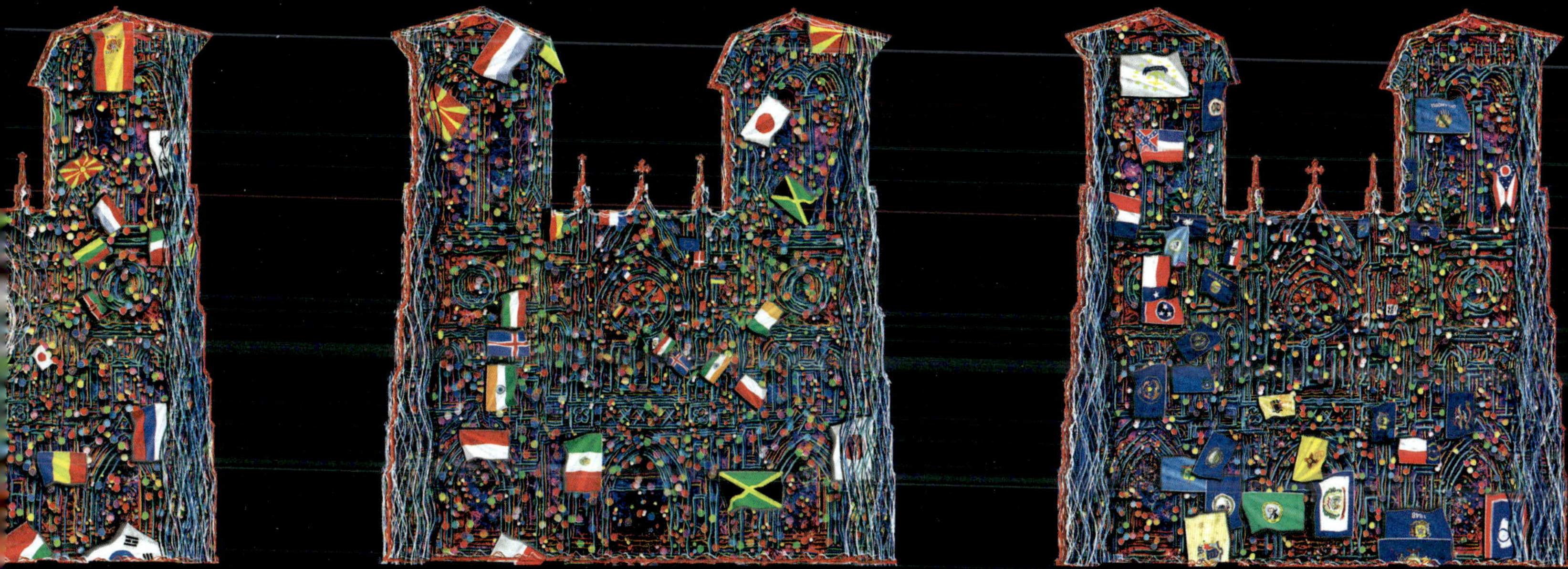

Flags

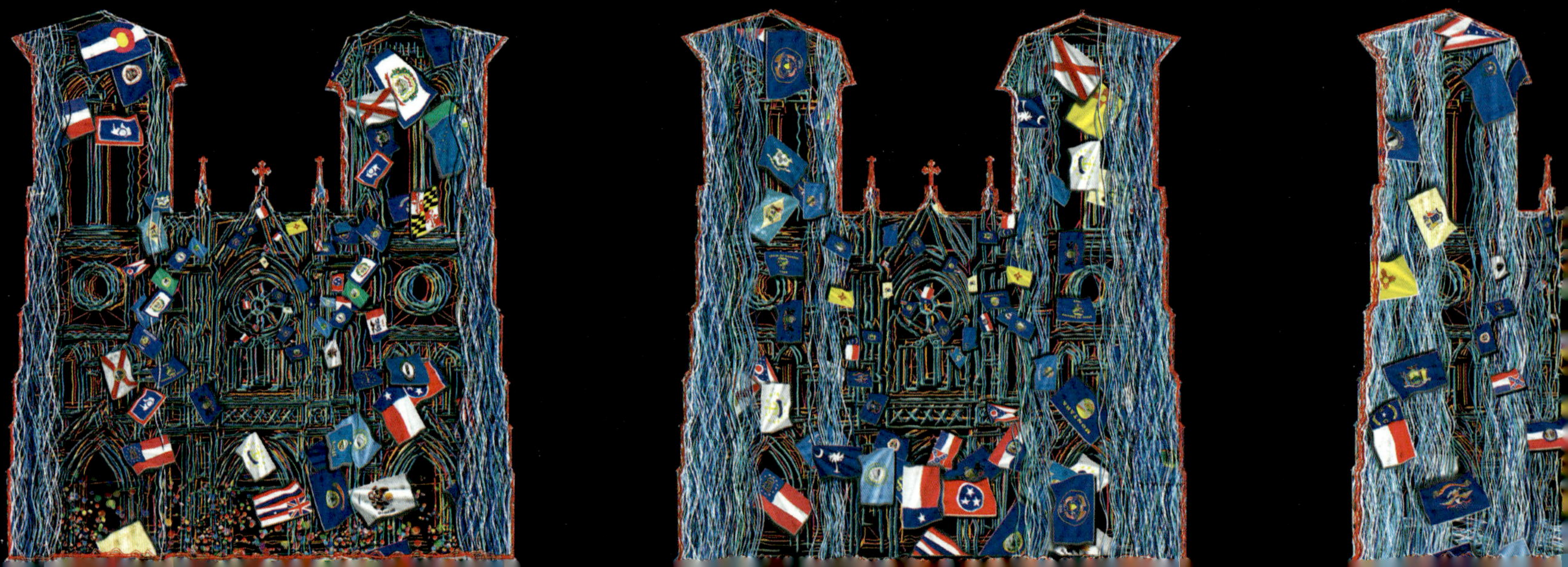

River

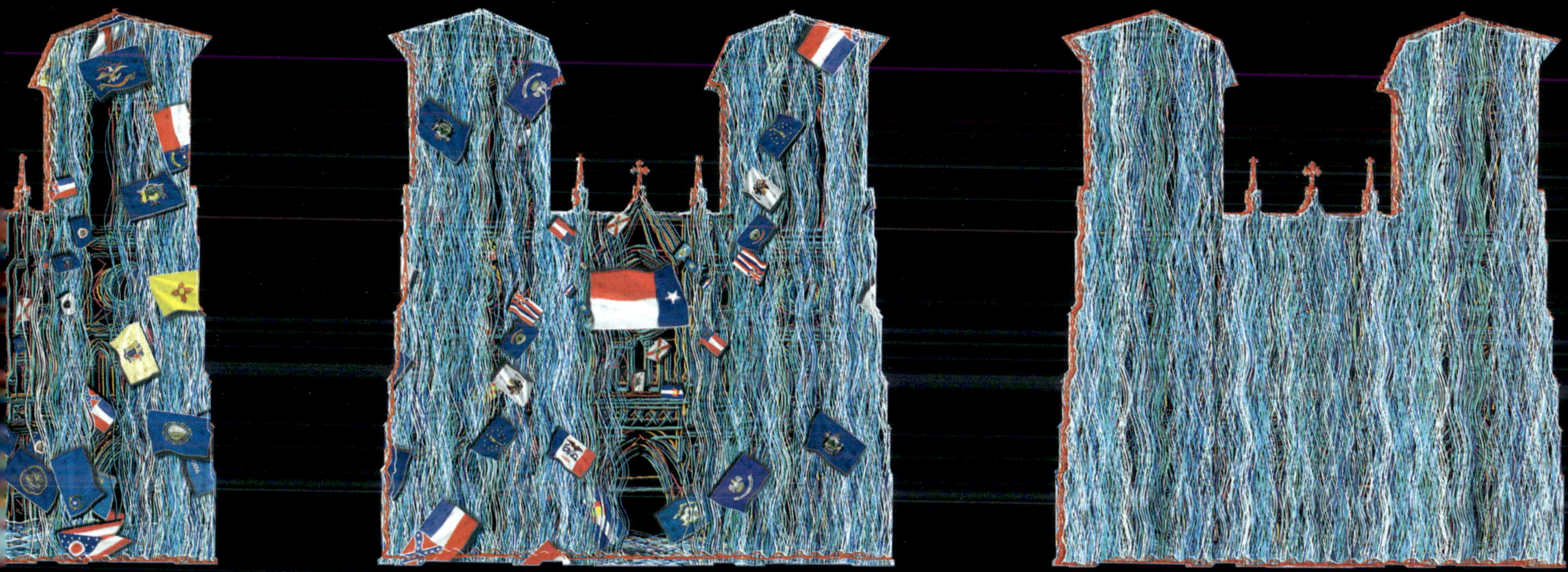

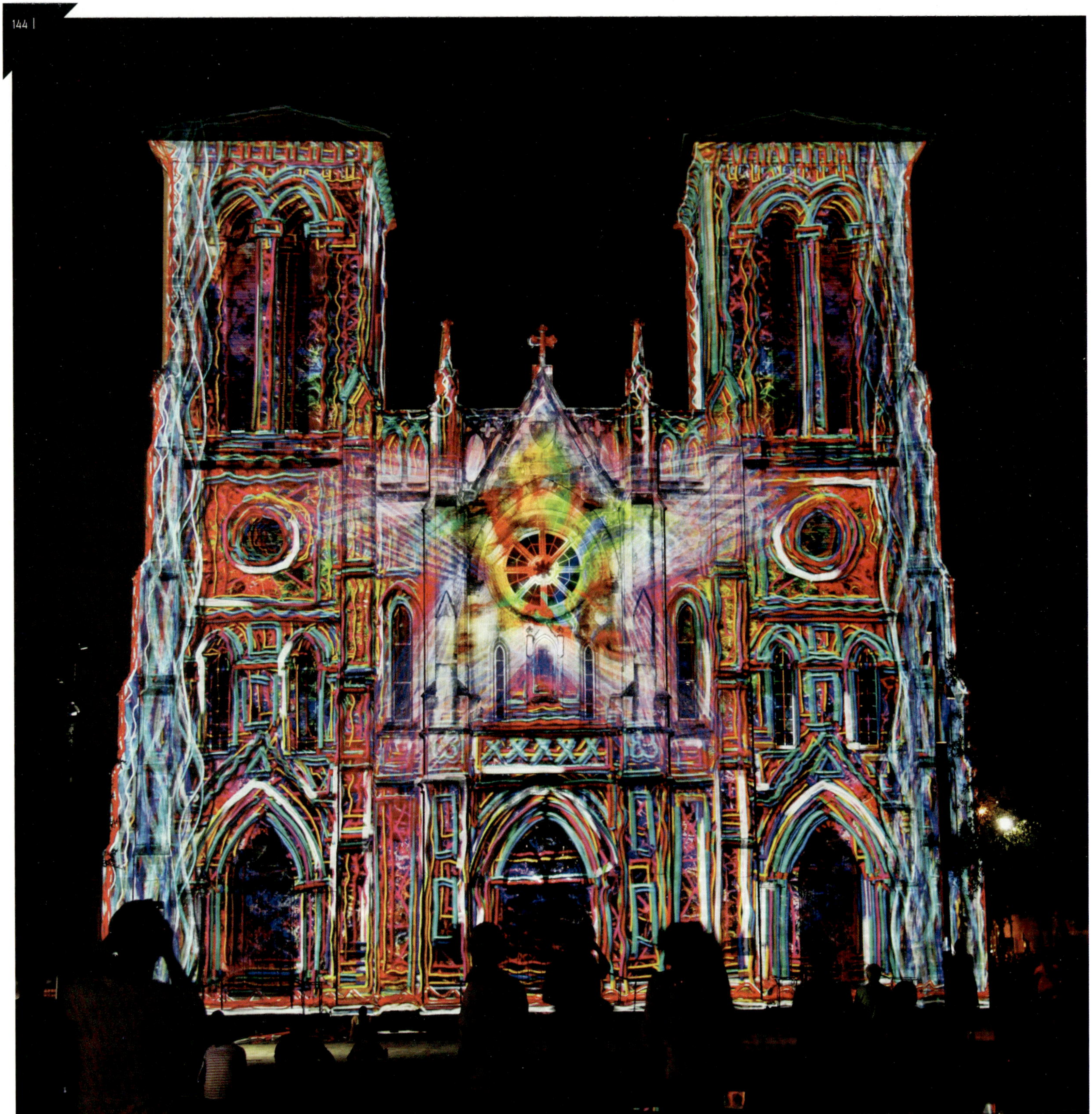

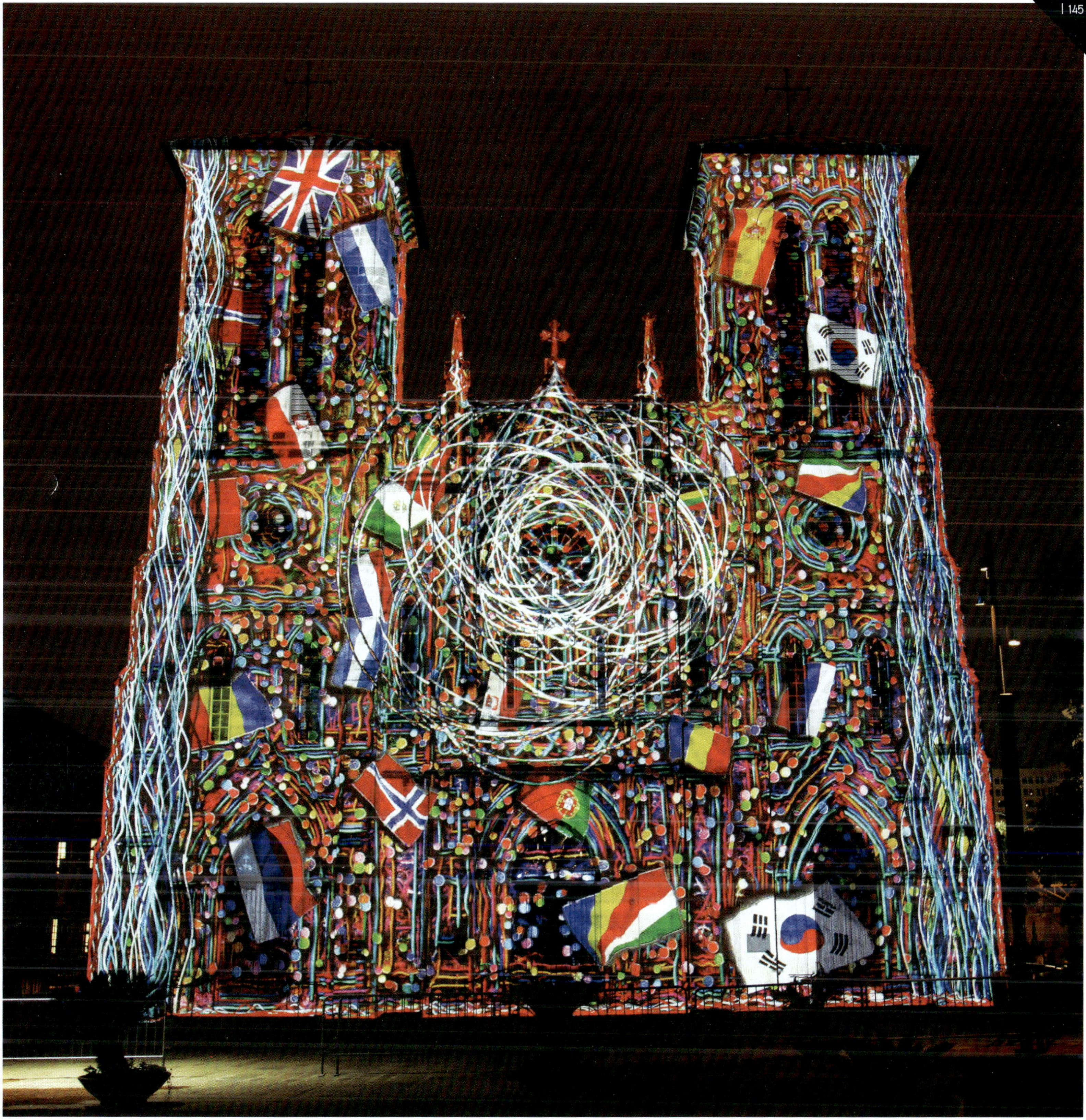

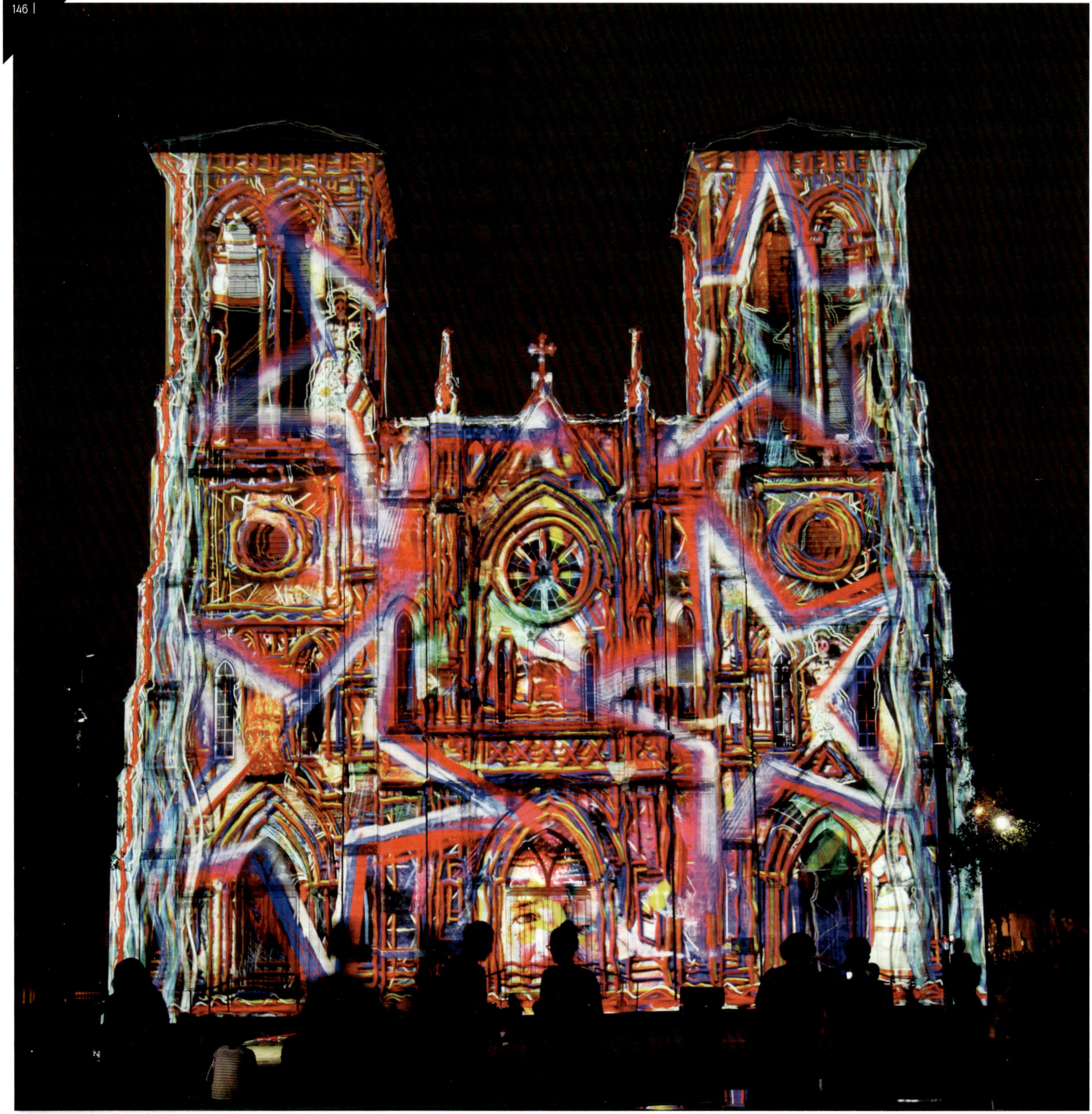

- SAN ANTONIO THE SAGA -

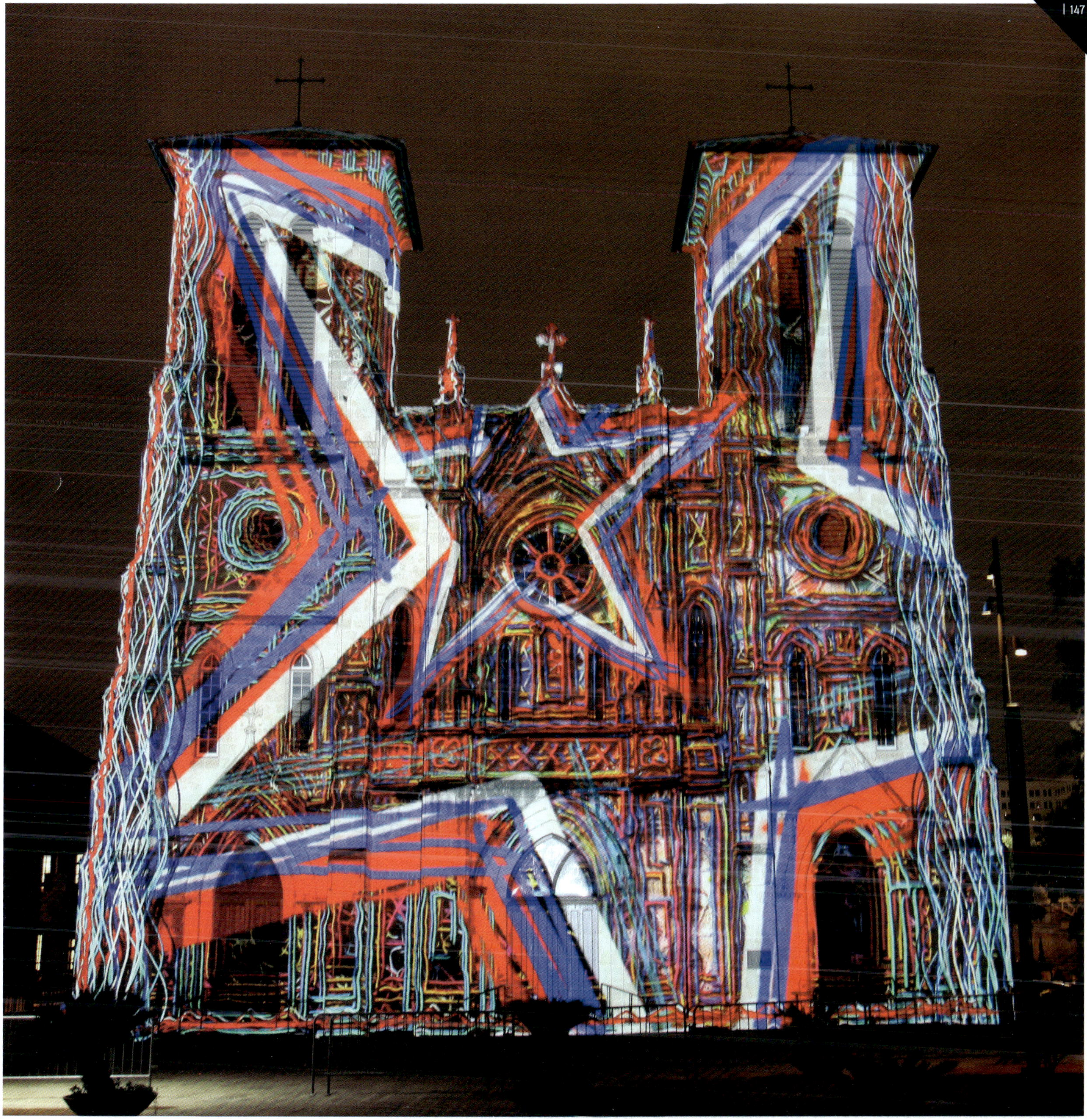

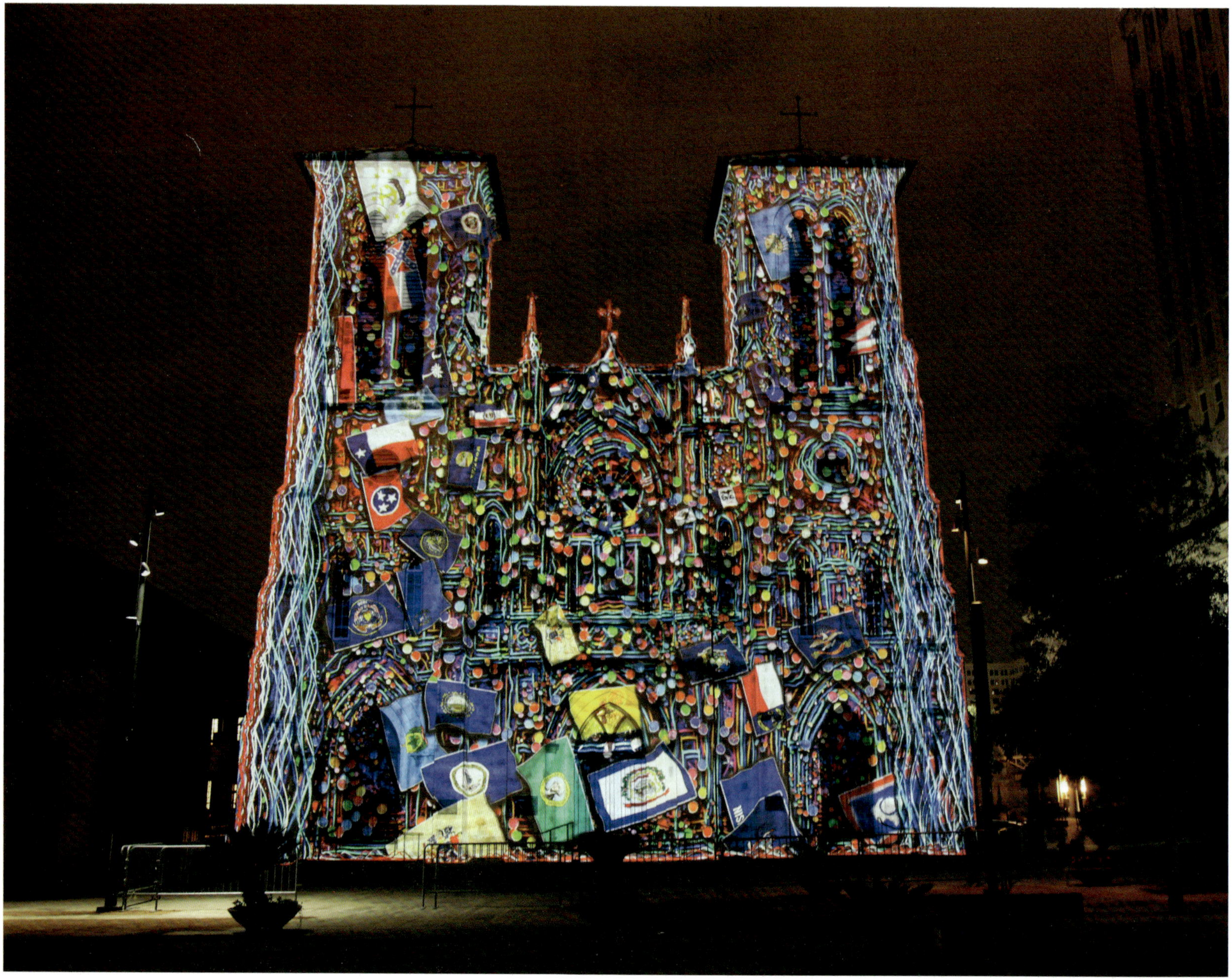

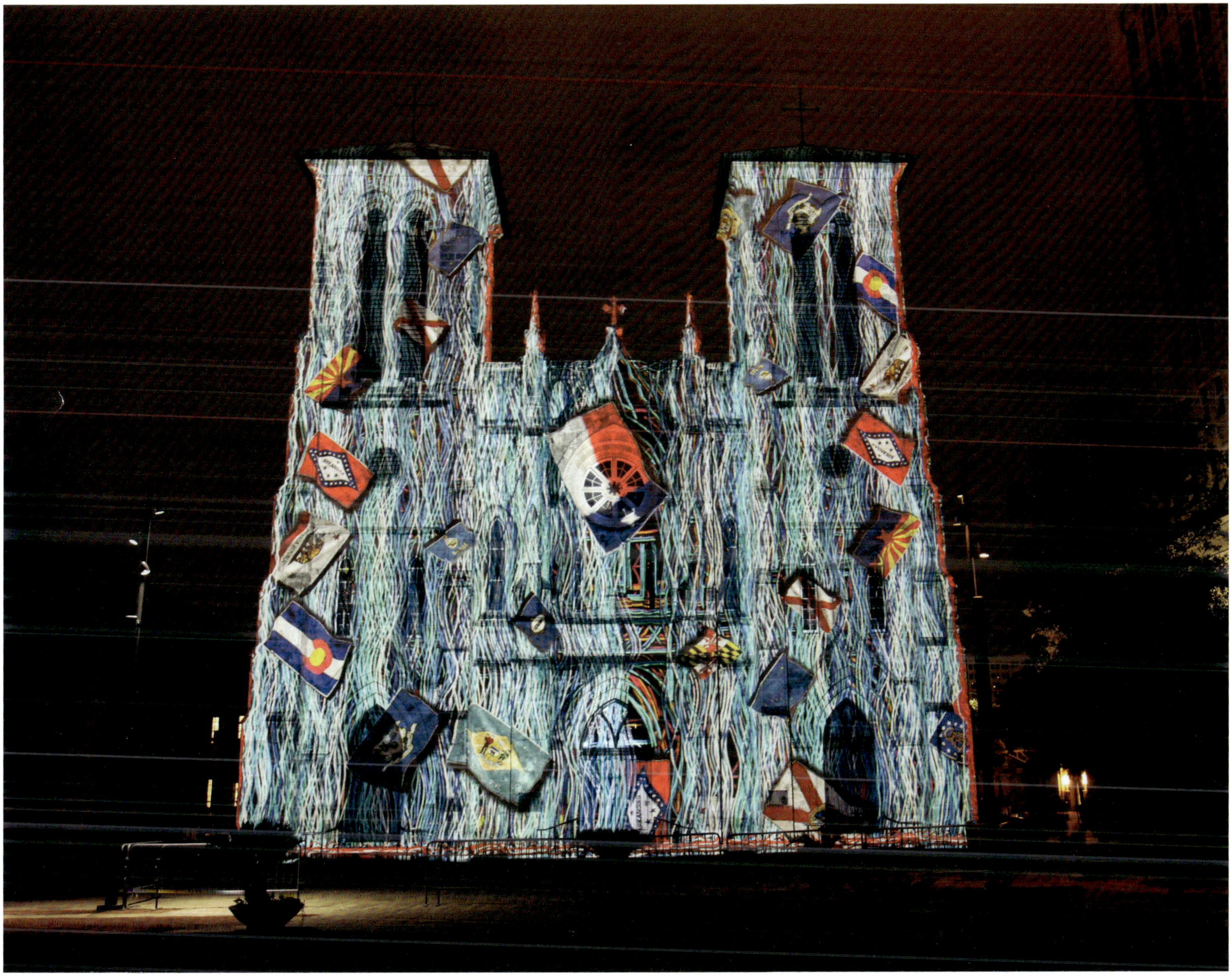

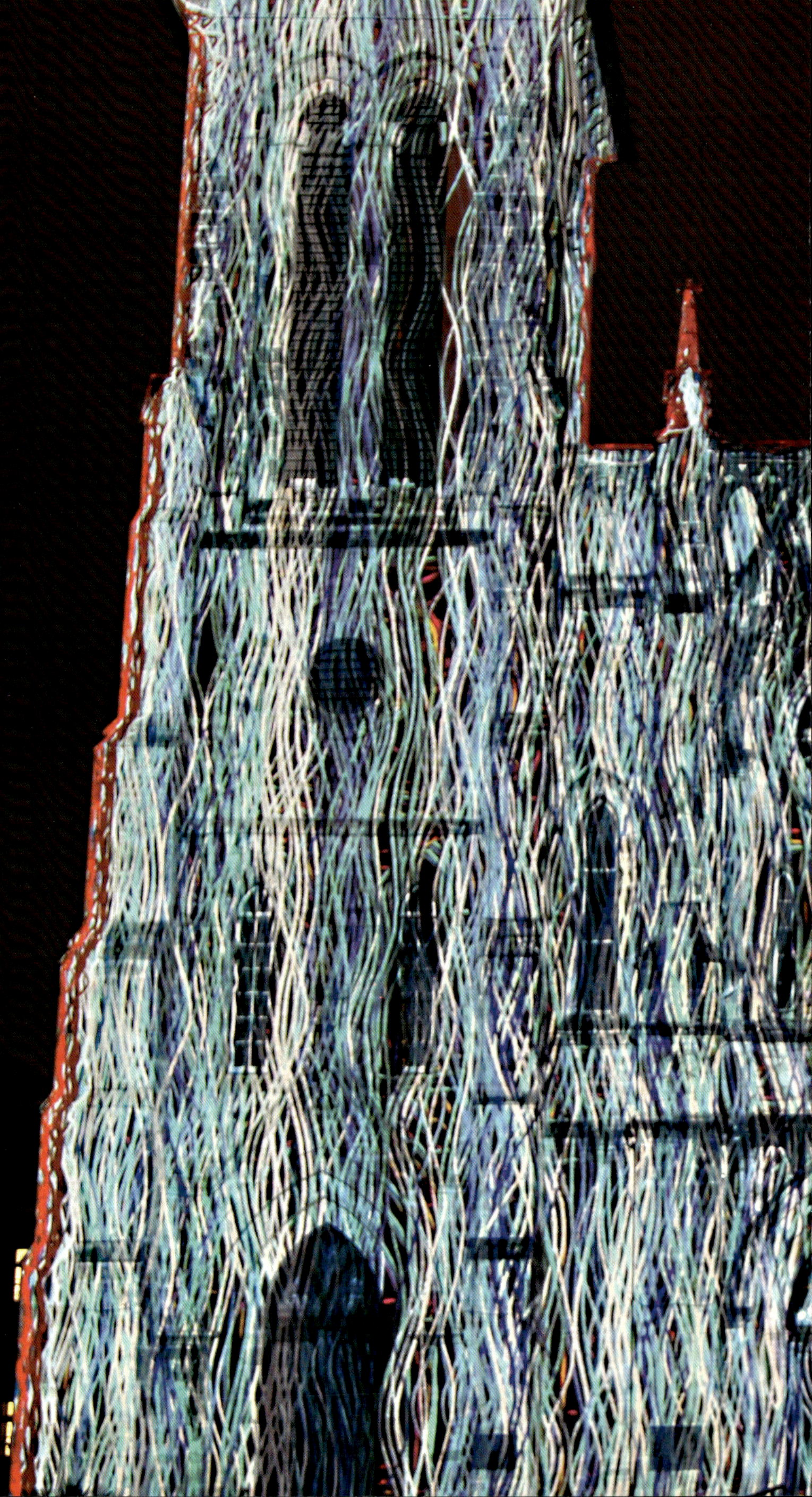

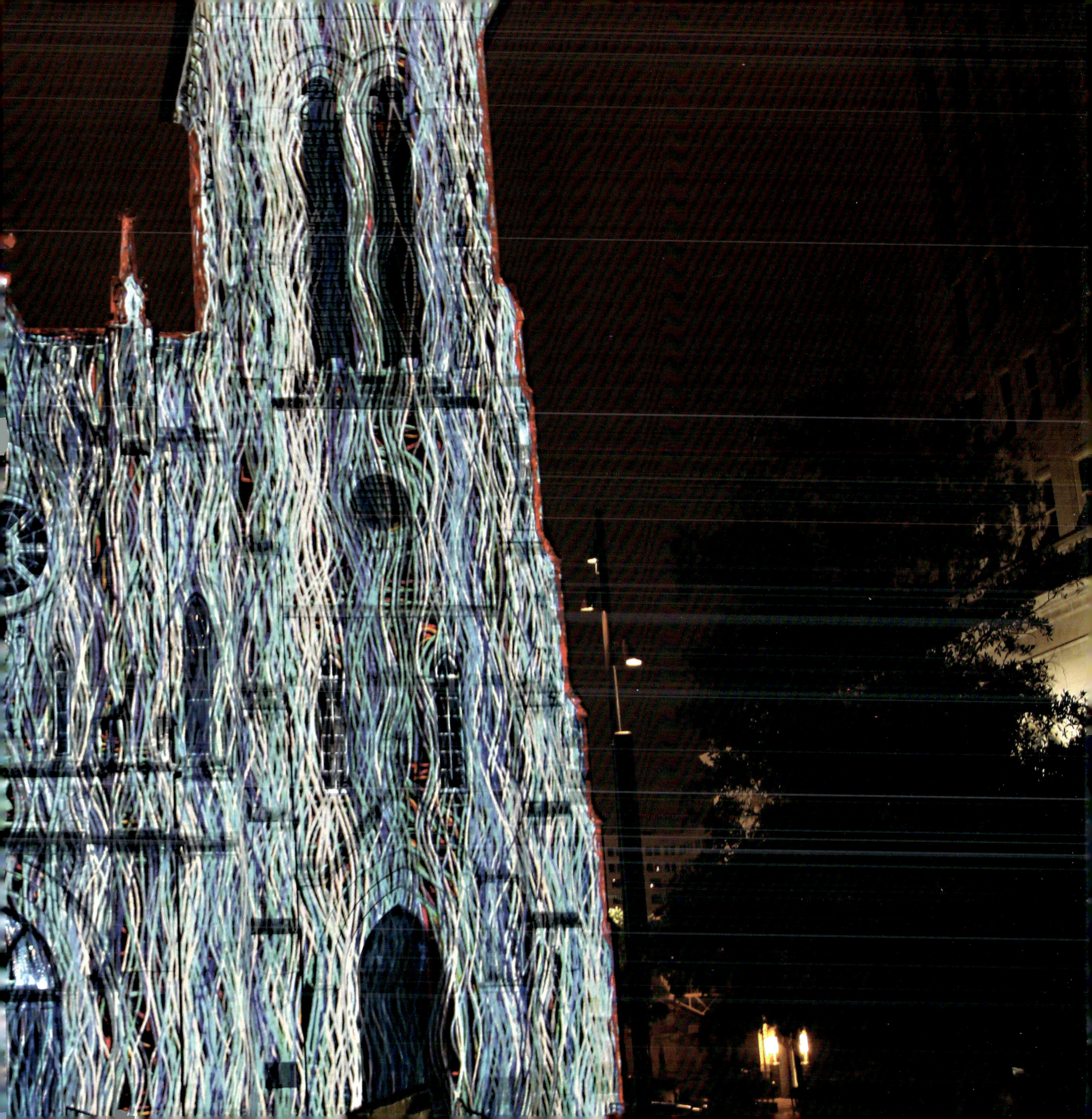

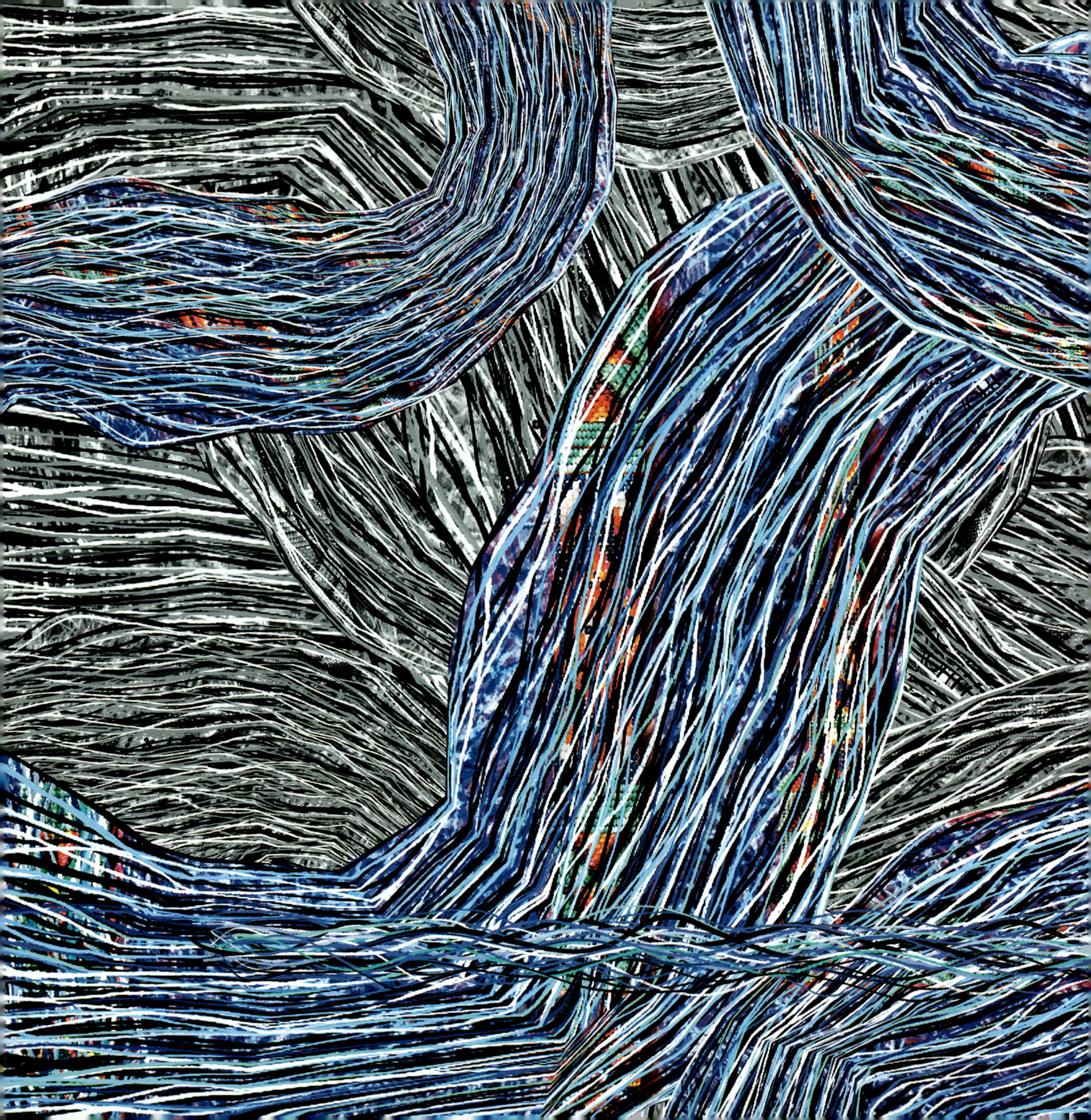

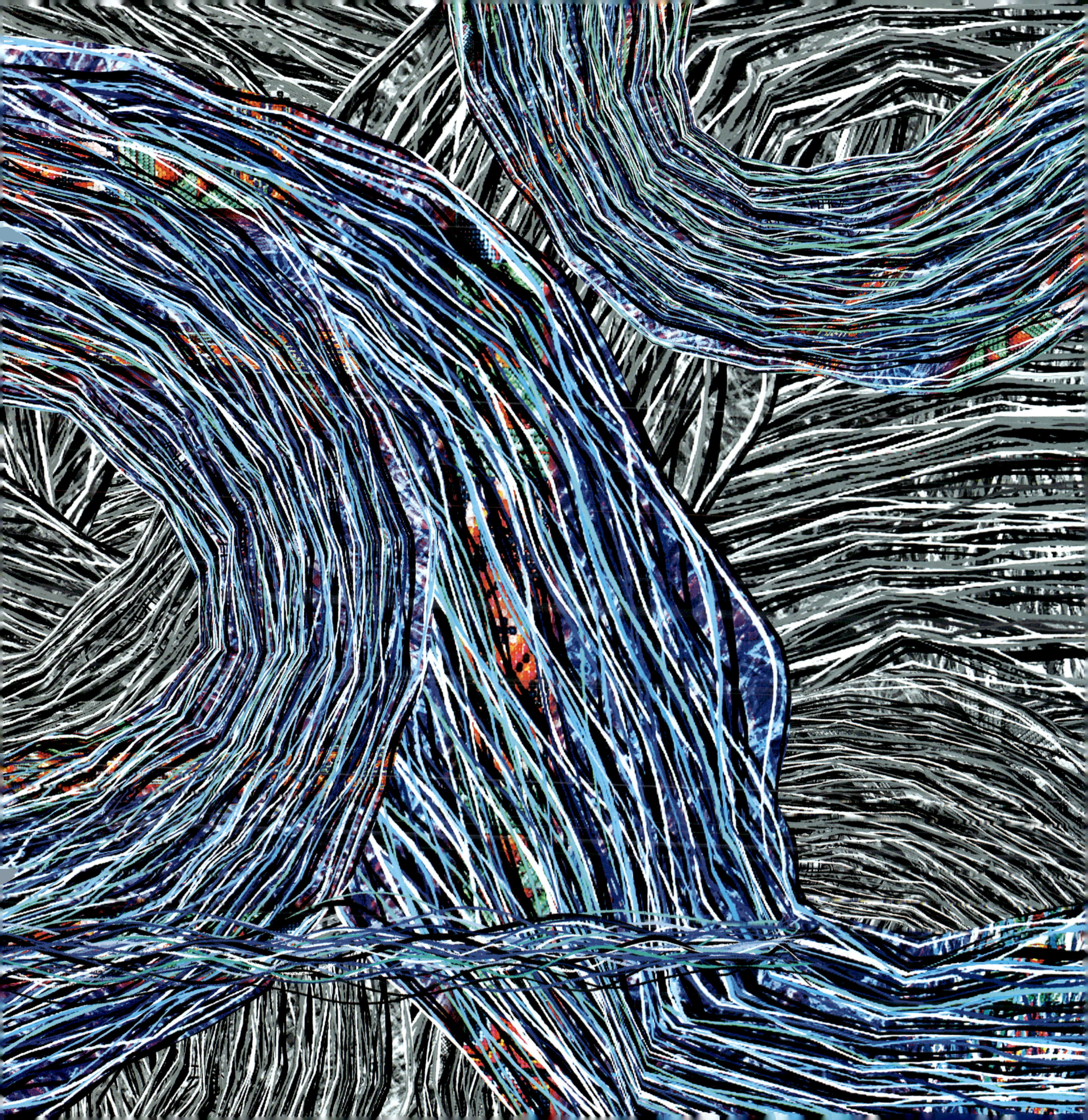

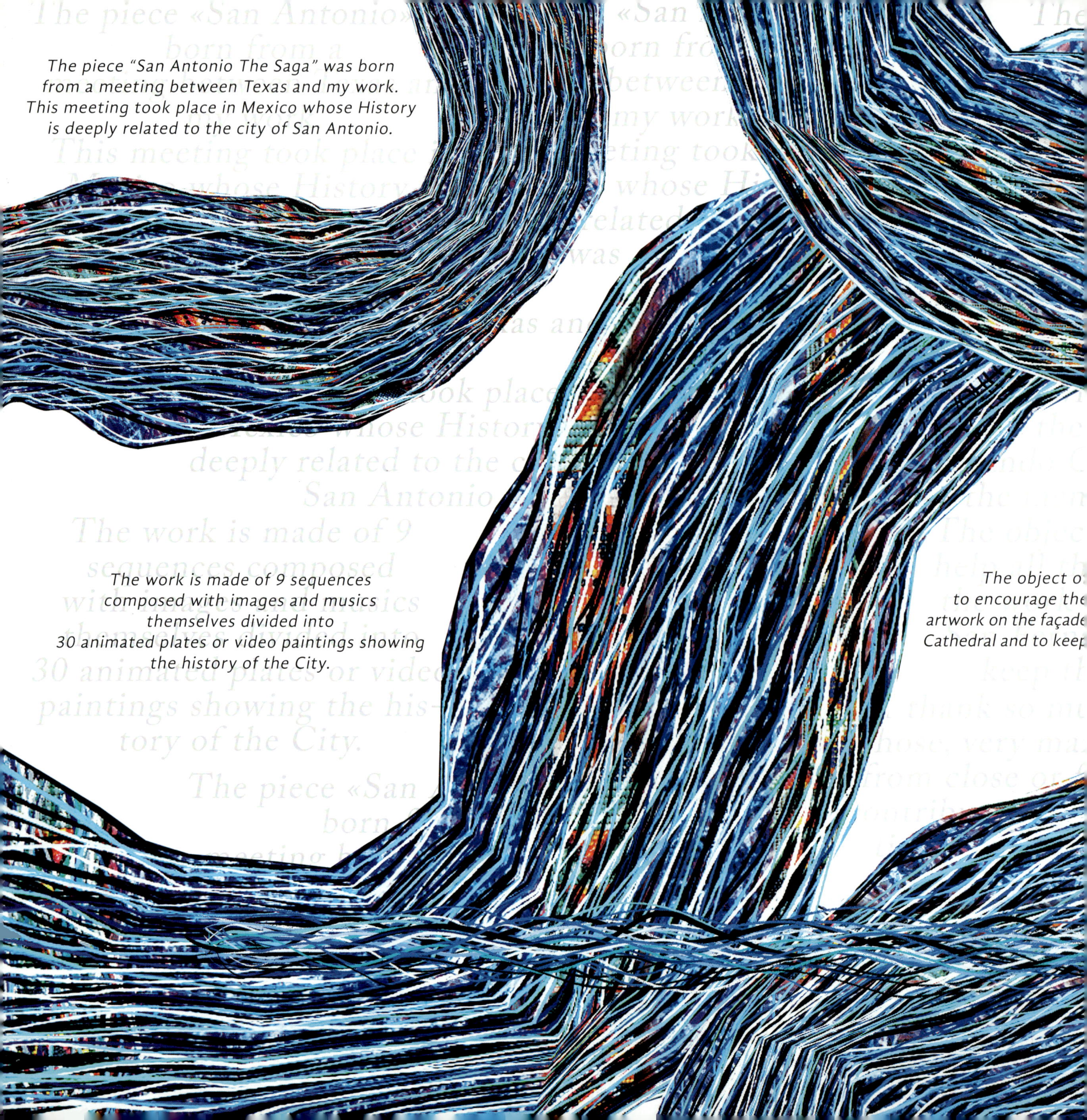

The piece "San Antonio The Saga" was born from a meeting between Texas and my work. This meeting took place in Mexico whose History is deeply related to the city of San Antonio.

The work is made of 9 sequences composed with images and musics themselves divided into 30 animated plates or video paintings showing the history of the City.

The object o
to encourage the
artwork on the façade
Cathedral and to keep

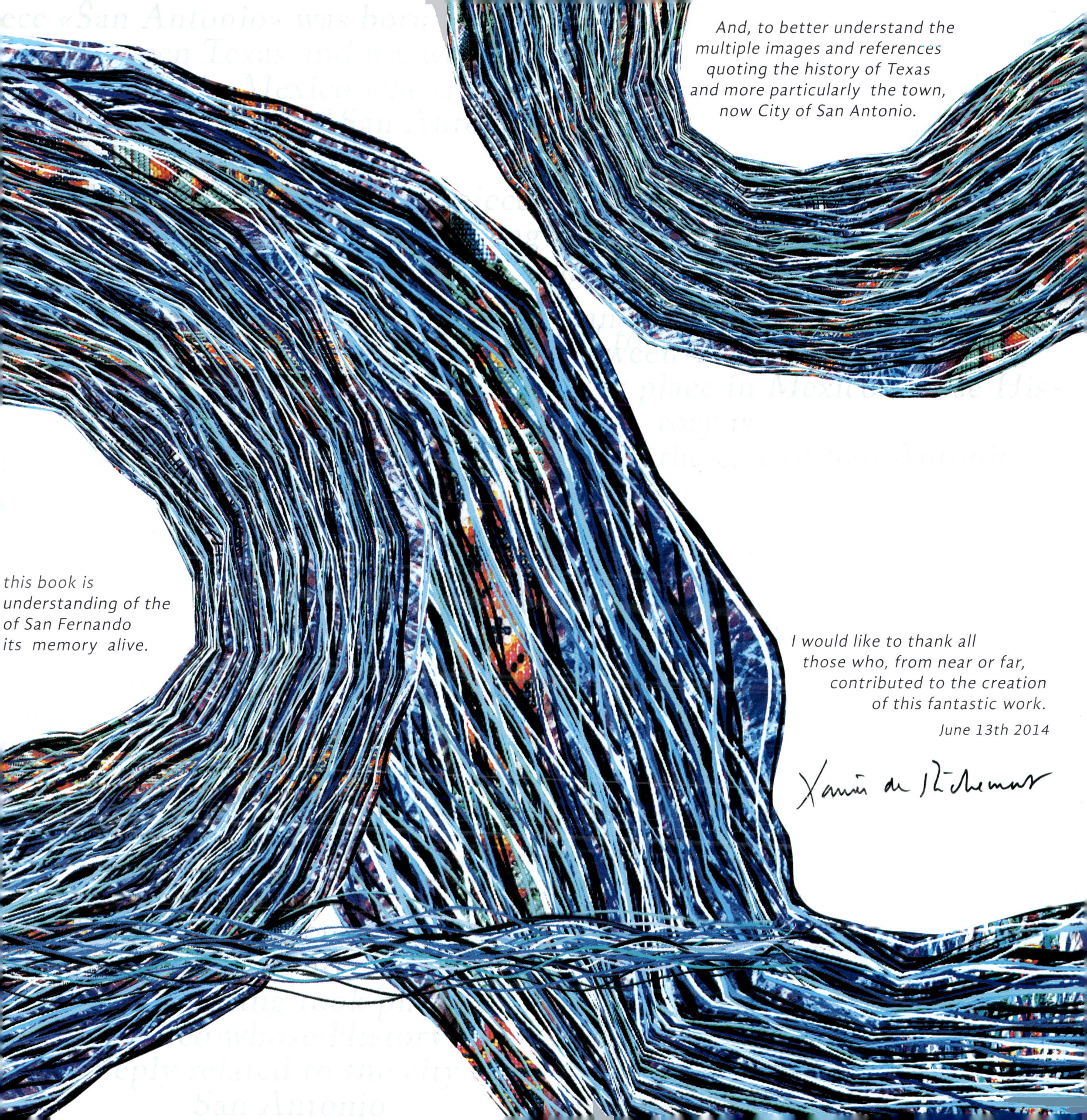

And, to better understand the
multiple images and references
quoting the history of Texas
and more particularly the town,
now City of San Antonio.

this book is
understanding of the
of San Fernando
its memory alive.

I would like to thank all
those who, from near or far,
contributed to the creation
of this fantastic work.

June 13th 2014

BIOGRAPHY

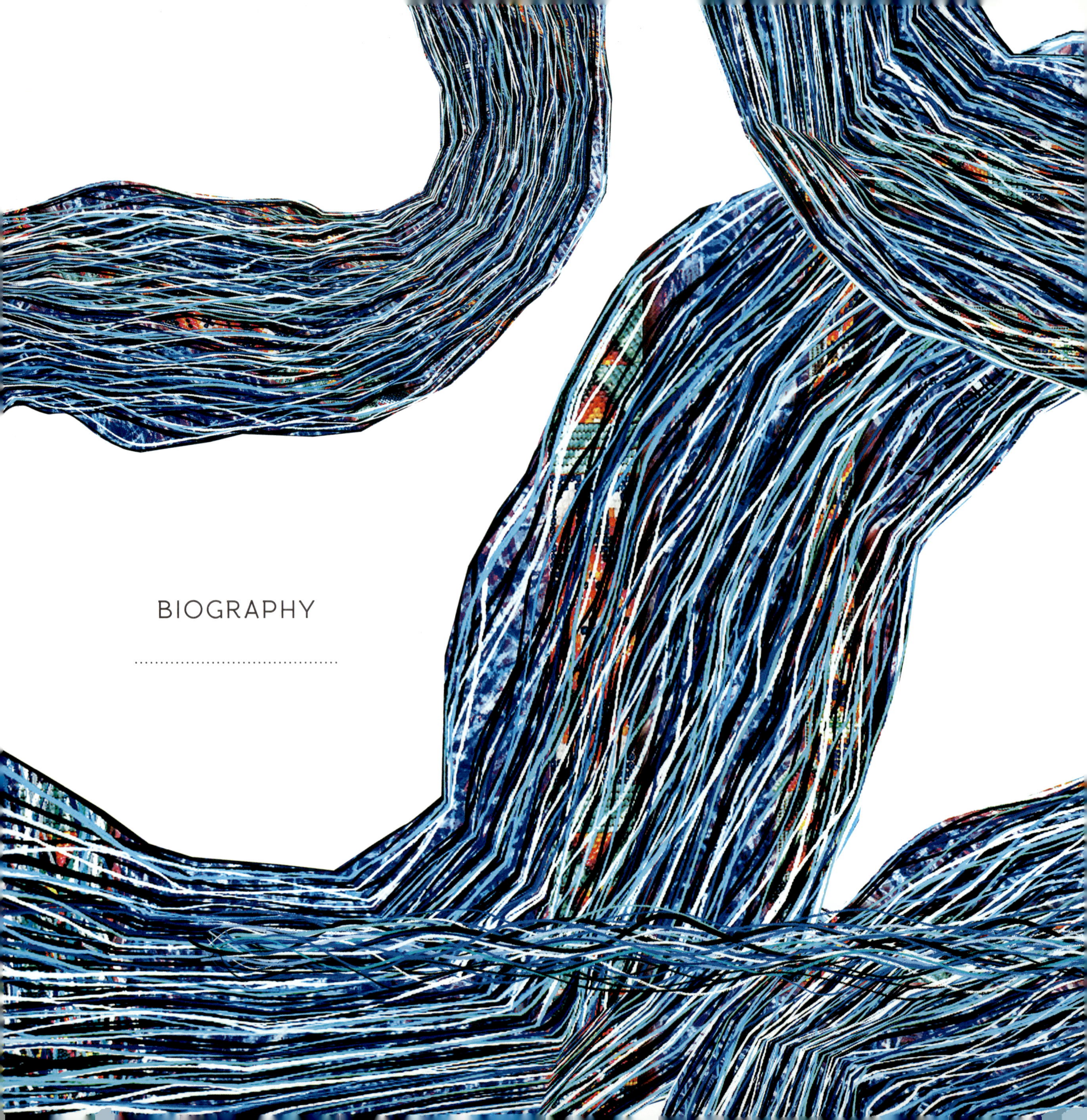

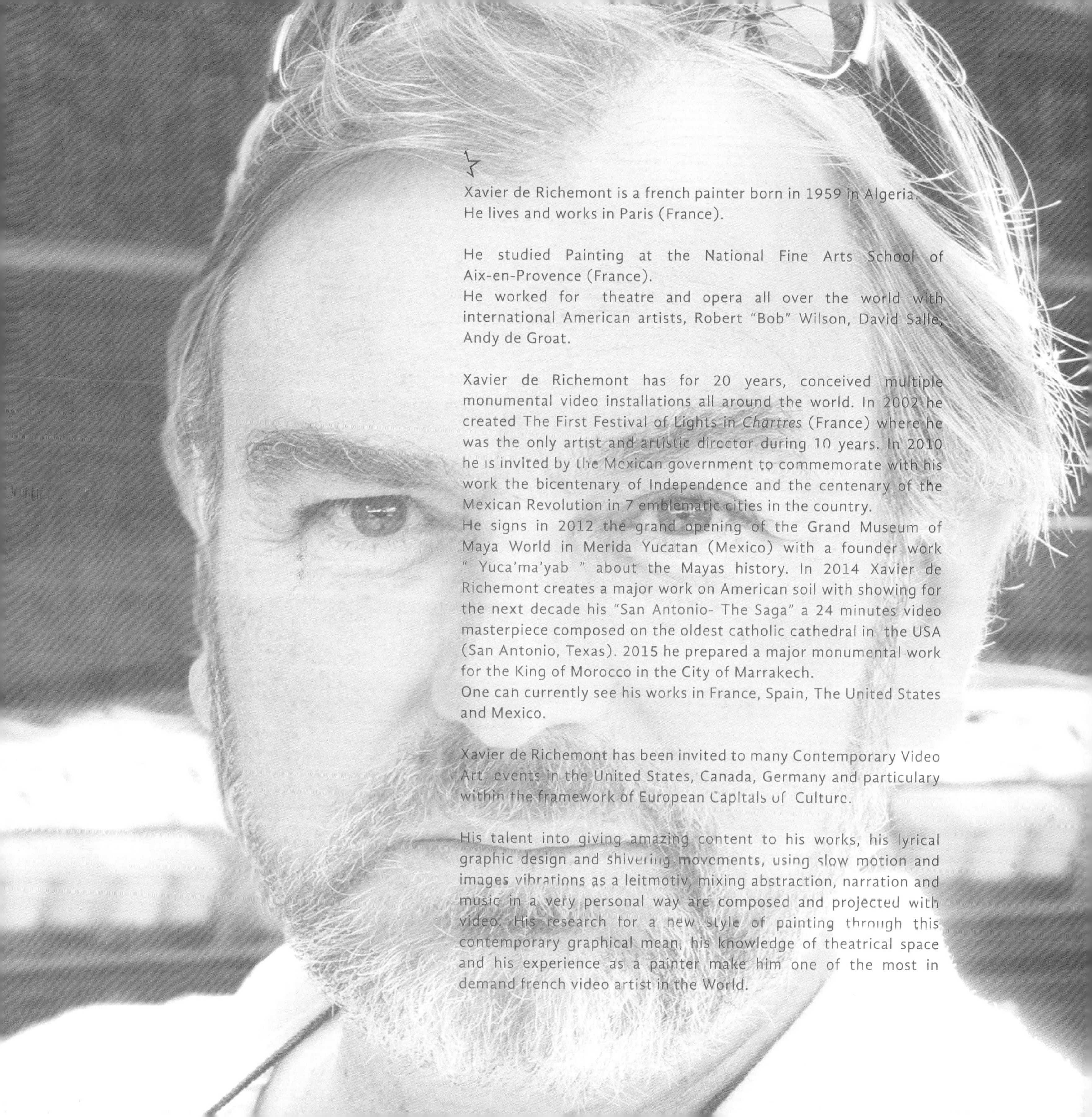

Xavier de Richemont is a french painter born in 1959 in Algeria.
He lives and works in Paris (France).

He studied Painting at the National Fine Arts School of Aix-en-Provence (France).
He worked for theatre and opera all over the world with international American artists, Robert "Bob" Wilson, David Salle, Andy de Groat.

Xavier de Richemont has for 20 years, conceived multiple monumental video installations all around the world. In 2002 he created The First Festival of Lights in *Chartres* (France) where he was the only artist and artistic director during 10 years. In 2010 he is invited by the Mexican government to commemorate with his work the bicentenary of Independence and the centenary of the Mexican Revolution in 7 emblematic cities in the country.
He signs in 2012 the grand opening of the Grand Museum of Maya World in Merida Yucatan (Mexico) with a founder work " Yuca'ma'yab " about the Mayas history. In 2014 Xavier de Richemont creates a major work on American soil with showing for the next decade his "San Antonio- The Saga" a 24 minutes video masterpiece composed on the oldest catholic cathedral in the USA (San Antonio, Texas). 2015 he prepared a major monumental work for the King of Morocco in the City of Marrakech.
One can currently see his works in France, Spain, The United States and Mexico.

Xavier de Richemont has been invited to many Contemporary Video Art events in the United States, Canada, Germany and particulary within the framework of European Capitals of Culture.

His talent into giving amazing content to his works, his lyrical graphic design and shivering movements, using slow motion and images vibrations as a leitmotiv, mixing abstraction, narration and music in a very personal way are composed and projected with video. His research for a new style of painting through this contemporary graphical mean, his knowledge of theatrical space and his experience as a painter make him one of the most in demand french video artist in the World.

MAIN PLAZA CONSERVANCY
WOULD LIKE TO THANK
ALL THOSE INDIVIDUALS AND
INSTITUTIONS WHO PARTICIPATED
IN THIS MONUMENTAL PROJECT.

SAN ANTONIO | THE SAGA
MAIN PLAZA CONSERVANCY

Art Video Monument History Inc.

MAIN PLAZA
The Heart of the City

XAVIERDERICHEMONT-USA.COM
WWW.XAVIER-DE-RICHEMONT.COM
FACEBOOK.COM/XAVIERDERICHEMONT
WWW.MAINPLAZA.ORG

Original images designed and texts written by Xavier de Richemont.

CONCEPT AND REALIZATION
Xavier de Richemont

PHOTO CREDIT
Xavier de Richemont

GRAPHISM AND BOOK DESIGN
Xavier de Richemont studio
45 Avenue de Suffren, 75007 Paris FRANCE
Leslie Epsztein, Virginie Martin

PRINTED June 2015
PUBLISHED BY Art Video Monument History Inc.
PRODUCED BY Main Plaza Conservancy
PRINTED BY Brenner Printing, Texas, USA

ISBN: 978-0-692-45917-1